THIS TRANSFORMING
CYCLE C WORD

Commentary on the Readings for Sundays and Feast Days
of Cycle C of the Lectionary through 2025,
including full Scripture passages from
The Message: Catholic/Ecumenical Edition
by Eugene Peterson and William Griffin

ALICE CAMILLE

THIS TRANSFORMING WORD, Cycle C
Commentary on the Readings for Sundays and Feast Days of Cycle C of the Lectionary through
2025, including full Scripture passages from _The Message: Catholic/Ecumenical Edition_
by Eugene Peterson and William Griffin

Copyright © 2015 by Alice Camille

Edited by Gregory F. Augustine Pierce
Designed and typeset by Patricia Lynch, Harvest Graphics
Cover art © "A Gleam of Glory," by Fr. Bob Gilroy, S.J. Courtesy of Trinity Stores,
www.trinitystores.com, (800) 699-4482

Published in association with the literary agency of Alive Communications, Inc., 7680 Goddard
Street, Suite 200, Colorado Springs, CO 80920, www.alivecom.com.

Library of Congress Control Number: 2015948507
ISBN: 978-0-87946-547-6
Printed in the United States of America by Total Printing Systems
Year: 25 24 23 22 21 20 19 18
Printing: 15 14 13 12 11 10 9 8 7 6 5 4 3

♻ Text printed on 30% post-consumer recycled paper

CONTENTS

DEDICATION

In memory of some lovely hidden souls who whispered the word incarnate to me: John Paskevich, Robert Koslosky, Mrs. Luce, Mireille Reiffel Gale, Dwight Leeray, Robert McKinley, Teresa Carpenter. They'd each be very surprised to find their names inside a book.

ACKNOWLEDGMENTS

Most of this commentary breathed its first life in the series *Exploring the Sunday Readings* (Twenty-Third Publications) through the assistance of my long-time editors, Mary Carol Kendzia and Daniel Connors. This book achieved its present form with a lot of help from my friends. Erin J. Boulton assembled the liturgical calendar projections and spotted any future missing weeks; when you find the stray moveable feast you're looking for, you can thank Erin for troubleshooting it first! Paul Boudreau inserted the complete Scripture passages from *The Message: Catholic/Ecumenical Edition* (ACTA Publications), considerably livening up the readings with a fresh Scriptural voice, as well as a thousand other excruciating editorial tasks. I thank God every day for friends like these, and please consider them your friends too as you reap the benefits of their labor on these pages.

A NOTE FROM THE PUBLISHER

Alice Camille is a true treasure of the Catholic Church in the United States: a woman who can make the Scriptures come alive in new and exciting ways; a serious student of the Bible who understands how to use it effectively in catechesis and religious education; a lay person who tries to live out the kingdom of God in her daily life. Camille has been reflecting on the meaning of the Bible for committed Catholics for many years and was instrumental in reviewing the translation of the additional writings for *The Message: Catholic/Ecumenical Edition*. So, when ACTA Publications wanted to produce a new series of three books containing reflections on the readings for each of the Sundays and Feast Days of Cycles A, B, and C and include the translation of those readings from *The Message*, Alice Camille was our first (and only) choice.

First, a word about *The Message* by Eugene Peterson. Many Catholics and others have never heard of it, even though it has sold over 16 million copies in various editions. It is a compelling, fresh, challenging, and faith-filled translation of the Bible from the original languages into contemporary, idiomatic American English. Eugene Peterson is a Presbyterian minister, pastor, writer, speaker, poet, Bible scholar, and translator. He specializes in what is called "paraphrasal" translation, which tries to reproduce the spirit of the original text rather than provide a literal translation of the words. Rev. Peterson did not include the additional writings of what some Jews and Protestants call the Apocrypha, and Catholics and others call the Deuterocanonical books in the original version of *The Message*. Instead he recruited his friend and colleague, William Griffin, to translate these works in his same style. Griffin, a Catholic layman, writer, and translator, took his text from the *Nova Vulgata*, the revised and expanded version of the original Latin Vulgate that was approved for use by Catholics by Pope John Paul II in 1998. These additions were added to *The Message* in the biblical order expected by Catholics and published in 2013 as *The Message: Catholic/Ecumenical Edition*.

You may find the Scripture passages in this book jarring at first. Certainly, you will not hear this translation read at Mass. But they might provide new insights into overly familiar texts and help you think again about what they might have to say to people today—especially when accompanied by Camille's accessible yet erudite reflections.

We encourage you to try *This Transforming Word* for your own prayer and spiritual discernment as you prepare to preach (if you are the homilist) or listen (if you are a congregant) or discuss (if you belong to a small intentional group or community). Included in this book for Cycle C are the Sunday and Feast Day readings for the years 2016, 2019, 2022, and 2025. Separate books are available for Cycle A in 2017, 2020, and 2023, and for Cycle B in 2015, 2018, 2021, and 2024. If you would like to receive the complete readings for each Sunday from *The Message* at no charge, simply go to www.TheMessageCatholic.com and sign up to receive them by email.

To purchase a copy of *The Message: Catholic/Ecumenical Edition* by Eugene Peterson and William Griffin or books by Alice Camille, including *Invitation to Catholicism, Invitation to the Old and New Testament, Isaiah and the Kingdom of God, The Forgiveness Book, The Rosary,* and *Seven Last Words,* go to any seller of books or visit www.actapublications.com. If you have any questions or comments, please contact me at gpierce@actapublications.com.

Gregory F. Augustine Pierce
President and Publisher
ACTA Publications
Chicago, Illinois

Note on translating the name of God. In the original Hebrew text of the Old Testament, the generic name for divinity used by both Israel and its neighbors is translated God (or god). But the unique and distinctively personal name for God that was revealed to Moses at the burning bush (Exodus 3:13-14) Rev. Peterson has translated as "God" in *The Message.*

INTRODUCTION

"Use words truly and well. Don't stoop to cheap whining.
    Then, but only then, you'll speak for me.
Let your words change them.
    Don't change your words to suit them."
Jeremiah 15:19

Words, words, words. The world is choked with them, as Hamlet wearily lamented. But most of them don't amount to much. Thomas Merton agreed. After a short trip beyond the silence of his cloister at Gethsemani Abbey, Merton observed: "There is so much talking that goes on that is utterly useless."

We talk, text, and email. Media shouts from every corner of the room and each bend in the road. Yet in the barrage of advertising and so-called reporting, little is actually communicated. "The world will little note, nor long remember what we say here." That sentence, from Abraham Lincoln, is a rare exception in a sea of forgettable phrases. What you and I say today will not only quickly disappear. It's a wonder if anyone hears us in the first place.

There is a cure for the endless, mindless, meaningless rant. Out of the silence, up from the deep, down from the heavens comes a transforming word that changes hearts—and *that* changes everything. This word transfigures because of its own remarkable metamorphosis: from cosmic eternal word to earthbound mortal flesh. This word shatters the barriers of time and needed to be spoken only once. Now it lives and moves and has being in those who hear it and reply.

This book is for those who are listening and hope to respond. Each Sunday and feast of the church year, the transforming word echoes its challenge. We hear it through stories of patriarchs and matriarchs who dare to embark in new directions trailing an untested divinity. It shouts in the oracles of wild prophets madly in love with an unlikely future. It sings in psalms and canticles. It beckons in Lady Wisdom. It invites us to come and see in the gospels, and to repent and believe in letters of instruction. Creation testifies to it. Apocalypse mystically reveals it. And all the while this longing word is calling through the centuries, eternity waits in hushed silence for the freely rendered human response. Yours. Mine. Everybody's.

ADVENT

FIRST SUNDAY OF ADVENT

.... Promises, Promises

FIRST READING » JEREMIAH 33:14-16

"'Watch for this: The time is coming'—GOD's Decree—'when I will keep the promise I made to the families of Israel and Judah. When that time comes, I will make a fresh and true shoot sprout from the David-Tree. He will run this country honestly and fairly. He will set things right. That's when Judah will be secure and Jerusalem live in safety. The motto for the city will be, 'GOD Has Set Things Right for Us.'"

Promises are made to be broken, as the saying goes. That may be true of the promises we make, but it has never been true for God. All too many of the commitments we make end up in splinters along the way of our good intentions. The heartbreak of divorce, the awkward relationships with our parents or children, the cheating that goes on in the workplace and in government—all remind us how far our ideals fall from our reality. But when God makes a covenant, nothing stands in the way of its fulfillment. Neither sin nor death itself bar the way of God's bringing into being all that the Divine Will intends.

The people Israel knew many generations when God's promise seemed distant and unlikely. At times their own failures kept them in hiding, like Adam and Eve discovering their nakedness. Seasons of slavery and exile made the hope of rescue fade away. But love goes in search of the beloved relentlessly, and God will not abandon a people so dearly formed and nurtured. In the seasons of our greatest failures, when we hide from God (and think God hides from us), we might surrender into the arms of love instead. Forgiveness is waiting there, and the joy of the old embrace.

Which of your promises is in need of mending this season?

SECOND READING » 1 THESSALONIANS 3:12 – 4:2

May the Master pour on the love so it fills your lives and splashes over on everyone around you, just as it does from us to you. May you be infused with strength and purity, filled with confidence in the presence of God our Father when our Master Jesus arrives with all his followers.

One final word, friends. We ask you—urge is more like it—that you keep on doing what we told you to do to please God, not in a dogged religious plod, but in a living, spirited dance. You know the guidelines we laid out for you from the Master Jesus.

Purity. Most of us know what that is: it's the first five minutes after we've come from the confessional, before we encounter the first live person! Purity is a rather inhuman state, if you take the concept of original sin to heart. Our world is marked by sin, weakened to the breaking point with opportunities to punt our integrity. If the cashier is rude, we snap back while knowing it's better to be charitable. It's hard to go through a single day without regretting some exchange that could have been more loving, more gracious, more holy.

Are we ever pure, or what used to be known as "in a state of grace"? A rich understanding of the term leads to a surprising conclusion: we are always in a state of grace—a country of grace—a kingdom of unsurpassing grace! Whether or not we partake of it is up to us, free will ever being operative. But we're never without the companionship of grace and the possibility of truly holy living. It's our baptismal birthright. Though we are ever sinners in need of God's mercy, we are likewise "splashed" with the love that God pours on lavishly. Sometimes religious language gets it just right.

> Imagine yourself standing in the kingdom of grace.
> What's perceptible to you here that you don't always see?

GOSPEL » LUKE 21:25-28, 34-36

"It will seem like all hell has broken loose—sun, moon, stars, earth, sea, in an uproar and everyone all over the world in a panic, the wind knocked out of them by the threat of doom, the powers-that-be quaking.

"And then—then!—they'll see the Son of Man welcomed in grand style—a glorious welcome! When all this starts to happen, up on your feet. Stand tall with your heads high. Help is on the way!

"But be on your guard. Don't let the sharp edge of your expectation get dulled by parties and drinking and shopping. Otherwise, that Day is going to take you by complete surprise, spring on you suddenly like a trap, for it's going to come on everyone, everywhere, at once. So, whatever you do, don't go to sleep at the switch. Pray constantly that you will have the strength and wits to make it through everything that's coming and end up on your feet before the Son of Man."

When we read end-of-the-world passages in Scripture, we usually focus on the destruction unleashed on the unsuspecting world. "Apocalypse now" sounds really scary—and it's supposed to. But not to believers. *Be not afraid* is one of the most oft-repeated pieces of advice in the New Testament. If you're with Jesus, there's nothing to fear, even when the boat is rocking in a violent storm.

Some may die of fright when disaster strikes, whether it's apocalyptic or a mere crisis of modern living. We all know folks who die a thousand deaths when their checking accounts are overdrawn. Fearful living is not faithful living. For believers there's no disaster large enough to be bigger than God's sovereignty. And though at first glance it seems strange to begin Advent and the new church year on such a note, on further examination it is the perfect place to start. We know we're not really awaiting the coming of the Christ child but rather the coming of Christ the King (remember, last Sunday?) Redemption is at hand. We have nothing to fear.

WE RESPOND

Revive an old promise that's been broken. Make peace with a friend or family member. Treat yourself as a holy vessel. Renew your promises to God in prayer and faithfulness.

"Whatever you do, don't go to sleep at the switch. Pray constantly that you will have the strength and wits to make it through everything that's coming and end up on your feet before the Son of Man."

SECOND SUNDAY OF ADVENT

FIRST READING » BARUCH 5:1-9

Jerusalem, get rid of the dull clothes of grief and put on your best dress, the clothes of glory meant for you from all eternity.

Wrap yourself in a lovely layered cloak; pick one from the justice collection. On your head put a crown in honor of the Eternal One.

God wants to show off how splendid you can look.

As of now, your name will be on the permanent divine invitation list; look under the headings of Peace and Justice and the Glory of God's Worship.

Arise, Jerusalem, and take your stand on high; look to the east, and you'll see your children gathering, rejoicing in the memory of God.

They were abducted a long time ago by their enemies and led away, made to walk the many miles on foot. God, however, will lead them back to you, carried with glory as though on a royal throne.

God has decided to level the mountains, turning the hard rock into gravel; the gorges and valleys he has ordered filled and leveled. He will do this so that the house of Israel may make the return trip to you in the security of the glory of the Most High.

At the command of God, forests and fragrant woods will spring up to provide shade for the returning pilgrims.

God will lead Israel home with joy, lighting the way with the majesty, mercy, and justice only he can command.

My parents exemplify the courage and innocence of an earlier generation, having raised heaps of children. Those children grew up and promptly moved away. It was understood that we would. Half of us, in fact, moved out of state. It must have been tough on my folks to have a house lined with children one moment, and empty the next.

But at least once a year thereafter, a swarm of us would descend on them from all directions; and more often, someone would drop in for a visit, complete with spouse and grandchildren. When such a visit was expected, Mom or Dad would be glancing out the windows periodically to catch the first sight of us. Dad would sometimes wait in the street and flag down the approaching car from five blocks away. It might have been embarrassing, if it weren't so wonderful to be loved like this.

The image of Jerusalem waiting for the return of her exiled children is like this. Expectant, excited, and all gussied up, the city of David awaits the children of the promise, led home by the Lord in joy. Wherever we roam we can expect to be greeted like this, when we return at last to the One who is our one true home.

Where are you received with joy?
What does this reception teach you of the power of welcome?

SECOND READING » PHILIPPIANS 1:4-6, 8-11

Each exclamation is a trigger to prayer. I find myself praying for you with a glad heart. I am so pleased that you have continued on in this with us, believing and proclaiming God's Message, from the day you heard it right up to the present. There has never been the slightest doubt in my mind that the God who started this great work in you would keep at it and bring it to a flourishing finish on the very day Christ Jesus appears.

He knows how much I love and miss you these days. Sometimes I think I feel as strongly about you as Christ does!

So this is my prayer: that your love will flourish and that you will not only love much but well. Learn to love appropriately. You need to use your head and test your feelings so that your love is sincere and intelligent, not sentimental gush. Live a lover's life, circumspect and exemplary, a life Jesus will be proud of: bountiful in fruits from the soul, making Jesus Christ attractive to all, getting everyone involved in the glory and praise of God.

Parents, teachers, and mentors know the satisfaction of watching those in their protection come to full flower. Having walked the distance between first inquiry to Easter with dozens of incoming Catholics, I've shared the joy of people falling in love with the gospel, little by little. When Paul expresses his enthusiasm for the blossoming community at Philippi, he reveals this same parental pride. A new generation of believers means new life for the whole church!

What we offer our children, or students, or catechumens, is the gift of our hope. We hope they will find God's love in their lives, lasting and strong. We hope they will increase in knowledge and understanding, make good choices for themselves and for the world. As my father would say as I returned to college each September: "Be good and stay out of trouble." A simple hope, but it encompassed his wish for my happiness.

Advent is the season of hope. We await the coming of a new heaven and a new earth. We await a birth and a fresh start, a brand new calendar. Even if we didn't "stay out of trouble" last year, we have a chance to try again. Hope teaches us that it's possible.

Whom do you teach? Who teaches you?
Where do lessons of hope come from in your experience?

GOSPEL » LUKE 3:1-6

In the fifteenth year of the rule of Caesar Tiberius—it was while Pontius Pilate was governor of Judea; Herod, ruler of Galilee; his brother Philip, ruler of Iturea and Trachonitis; Lysanias, ruler of Abilene; during the Chief-Priesthood of Annas and Caiaphas—John, Zachariah's son, out in the desert at the time, received a message from God. He went all through the country around the Jordan River preaching a baptism of life-change leading to forgiveness of sins, as described in the words of Isaiah the prophet:

Thunder in the desert!
"Prepare God's arrival!
Make the road smooth and straight!
Every ditch will be filled in,
Every bump smoothed out,
The detours straightened out,
All the ruts paved over.
Everyone will be there to see
The parade of God's salvation."

Imagine the valleys of your life. Those times when yawning need was met by silence. When the desire for companionship found only absence. When there were bills to pay and only holes in your pockets.

Now reflect on the mountains. The tasks that seemed insurmountable. The illnesses that dragged on and on. The hurt that seemed to grow rather than diminish with time. The challenges that seemed to have been designed with someone bigger and stronger than you in mind.

The way of the Lord is the smooth way. No valleys, no mountains, just a journey through pleasant country. Never been there? Neither had Jesus on this earth. He sums up his experience with a sad evaluation: "My kingdom is not of this world." This world has a rough topography, complete with sin, death, and crucifixion. Yet we trust the word of Jesus because he's traveled these same valleys and mountains on the road to salvation. We're never so lost that we can't be found on these wild roads.

> **Map out the prominent valleys and mountains of the past year.**
> **Where do you see hope in the smooth way?**

WE RESPOND

"Nothing should ever trouble or haunt thee," Teresa of Avila wrote in her prayer book. Hold a burial ceremony for the ghosts of the past year and put them to rest at last.

THIRD SUNDAY OF ADVENT

FIRST READING » ZEPHANIAH 3:14-18a

So sing, Daughter Zion!
    Raise the rafters, Israel!
Daughter Jerusalem,
    be happy! celebrate!
GOD has reversed his judgments against you
    and sent your enemies off chasing their tails.
From now on, GOD is Israel's king,
    in charge at the center.
There's nothing to fear from evil
    ever again!

Jerusalem will be told:
    "Don't be afraid.
Dear Zion,
    don't despair.
Your GOD is present among you,
    a strong Warrior there to save you.
Happy to have you back, he'll calm you with his love
    and delight you with his songs."

God sings for you. For YOU. The image is overwhelming. While the heavenly hosts sing their praise to God, and church choirs everywhere join their voices to the angels', the divine Lord of all raises the harmonic Triune Voice for your sake. Like a lover standing under the balcony of the beloved, God sings of love and desire for you.

Talk about Christmas carols! What does the song of God sound like? The ancients believed that angel-song held the stars and planets in alignment and kept the heavenly spheres from colliding into each other. Harmony is the sophisticated name for holding disparate sounds at a sufficient distance from one another so as not to cause a train wreck in the ear. We can imagine that the song of God was heard first at creation, bringing every creature into perfect alignment, from the largest galaxy to the smallest blade of grass. The harmony God installed in the universe has two notes, justice and peace. You don't have to wonder long how the discordance of sin interfered with our ability to hear it. But God's song is heard again wherever we regain the duet of justice and peace. Peace on earth, good will toward all!

Where do you hear the notes of justice and peace sounded most clearly?
How do you contribute to this song?

SECOND READING » PHILIPPIANS 4:4-7

Celebrate God all day, every day. I mean, revel in him! Make it as clear as you can to all you meet that you're on their side, working with them and not against them. Help them see that the Master is about to arrive. He could show up any minute!

Don't fret or worry. Instead of worrying, pray. Let petitions and praises shape your worries into prayers, letting God know your concerns. Before you know it, a sense of God's wholeness, everything coming together for good, will come and settle you down. It's wonderful what happens when Christ displaces worry at the center of your life.

How near is the Lord to your heart? If you had to make a list of your passions, would God be first? In the top five? Would God figure in your priorities at all?

However you answer, don't be ashamed. Be proactive. An examination of conscience isn't intended to inspire guilt but rather conversion. Now is the time to change. The Lord is near. So the good news is, we don't have to go very far to encounter God, no matter where our lives have taken us. As the prophets repeated over and over, all we have to do is turn. God is right here, with arms outstretched to receive us on the spot.

This is cause for celebration! The name of the Third Sunday of Advent, *Gaudete*, means "rejoice," celebrate. Even those for whom holidays bring no cheer—who experience the holiday season as the most desperate time of the year—are offered consolation this week. God is near. Though family may live faraway (or just behave that way), we are not abandoned. Though money is short and need is great, we are seen, known, and protected in Christ. Those who believe this are free to give their joy away.

How have you demonstrated today our faith in the nearness of the Lord?

GOSPEL » LUKE 3:10-18

The crowd asked John the Baptist, "Then what are we supposed to do?"

"If you have two coats, give one away," he said. "Do the same with your food."

Tax men also came to be baptized and said, "Teacher, what should we do?"

He told them, "No more extortion—collect only what is required by law."

Soldiers asked him, "And what should we do?"

He told them, "No shakedowns, no blackmail—and be content with your rations."

The interest of the people by now was building. They were all beginning to wonder, "Could this John be the Messiah?"

But John intervened: "I'm baptizing you here in the river. The main character in this drama, to whom I'm a mere stagehand, will ignite the kingdom life, a fire, the Holy Spirit within you, changing you from the inside out. He's going to clean house—make a clean sweep of your lives. He'll place everything true in its proper place before God; everything false he'll put out with the trash to be burned."

There was a lot more of this—words that gave strength to the people, words that put heart in them. The Message!

No doubt about it: John the Baptist was an amazing, impressive, charismatic figure in his generation. Yet he did everything in his power to direct the attention away from himself and toward the One yet to come. His teaching, even his baptizing, was mere preparation for the Christ. John knew he was a bit player in a cosmic story.

Being human, we often fail to look past the messenger to the message. How many of us have become unglued when our favorite pastor is transferred, when an admired spiritual teacher falls from grace, when a hero we've followed across the years dies or disappears from view. We may find we've pinned our faith to the wrong source, settling for the herald instead of the heralded. Human beings will always disappoint, but God never does.

If our joy is to be complete, we can't fasten it to anything material. Rust sets in and moths destroy, but Jesus Christ is the same yesterday, today, and forever. If lasting joy is what we want, we have to find it in the One whose life and love endures.

Who or what is the source of your joy?

WE RESPOND

People of *Gaudete* share their joy in acts of kindness. Recall a kindness you may have withheld. There's still time to offer it.

Let petitions and praises
shape your worries into prayers,
letting God know your concerns.

FOURTH SUNDAY OF ADVENT

FIRST READING » MICAH 5:1-4a

But you, Bethlehem, David's country,
*   the runt of the litter—*
From you will come the leader
*   who will shepherd-rule Israel.*
He'll be no upstart, no pretender.
*   His family tree is ancient and distinguished.*
Meanwhile, Israel will be in foster homes
*   until the birth pangs are over and the child is born,*
And the scattered brothers come back
*   home to the family of Israel.*
He will stand tall in his shepherd-rule by GOD's strength,
*   centered in the majesty of GOD-Revealed.*
And the people will have a good and safe home,
*   for the whole world will hold him in respect—*
Peacemaker of the world!

In parochial school one year, the Sister decided to seat us according to size. There was a logic to it, of course. She wanted to be sure we could all see the blackboard. But woe to the person who wound up in the first row, first seat. That meant you were a real pipsqueak! It was as humiliating as being dressed in a sailor suit! It led to unflattering names and endless teasing! As you might expect, I hated sitting there.

Kids don't like to have their littleness pointed out. Nor do nations, minority groups, or the poor. Small things get trampled in a world that values size and power. In too many ways and too many places, small is defined as unimportant.

God loves small. Nothing is bigger, more potent, more important than the Source of all that is, and yet the Maker of all chooses small over large, every time. God chooses the poor over the rich, widows over kings, the barren woman over the mother, children over adults, Israel over the whole Roman Empire. Only in the eyes of human beings does big count. How blest is little Bethlehem to bring forth the hope of ages.

Who is "small" in your family? Neighborhood? Workplace?
How are they treated?

SECOND READING » HEBREWS 10:5-10

That is what is meant by this prophecy, put in the mouth of Christ:

*   You don't want sacrifices and offerings year after year;*
*   you've prepared a body for me for a sacrifice.*

It's not fragrance and smoke from the altar
*   that whet your appetite.*
So I said, "I'm here to do it your way, O God,
*   the way it's described in your Book."*

When he said, "You don't want sacrifices and offerings," he was referring to practices according to the old plan. When he added, "I'm here to do it your way," he set aside the first in order to enact the new plan—God's way—by which we are made fit for God by the once-for-all sacrifice of Jesus.

When we hear the word sacrifice, we're liable to cringe. *Sacrifice* generally means we're obliged to give something up and get nothing in return. But the word has its roots in a similar word: *sacred*. Sacrifice literally means to make something or someone holy.

The routine holocausts at the Jerusalem Temple were intended for the consecration of God's holy people. In the word *consecration* we again hear that root meaning: to make sacred. The people offered the best they had: crops or livestock from the unblemished portion of their wealth. By offering the best, they didn't seek to lose but to gain or regain the holiness of the rest. In sin-offerings, they literally surrendered a portion in order to save the whole. The point was not to lose but to restore what had been lost by sin.

When we speak of the sacrifice of Jesus, we acknowledge what was lost. But we emphasize what is restored to us: reconciliation with God, access to unending life. The cross is about victory, the consecration of God's people once for all. Next time you're asked to make a sacrifice, try thinking of it as an invitation to holiness and wholeness.

How do you make a sacrifice from what you've been given?

GOSPEL » LUKE 1:39-45

Mary didn't waste a minute. She got up and traveled to a town in Judah in the hill country, straight to Zachariah's house, and greeted Elizabeth. When Elizabeth heard Mary's greeting, the baby in her womb leaped. She was filled with the Holy Spirit, and sang out exuberantly,

You're so blessed among women,
*   and the babe in your womb, also blessed!*
And why am I so blessed that
*   the mother of my Lord visits me?*
The moment the sound of your
*   greeting entered my ears,*
The babe in my womb
*   skipped like a lamb for sheer joy.*
Blessed woman, who believed what God said,
*   believed every word would come true!*

At our parish we call them L.O.L.s: Little Old Ladies. They're the backbone of the community. They come to meetings, bake for bake sales, crochet for fundraisers, pray up a storm, drop their money in the baskets, bring communion to the sick, volunteer for everything. They go about their work almost invisibly, but what they accomplish is enormous. Without L.O.L.s, a pastor once observed, you could close the doors of most parishes.

Elizabeth was a Little Old Lady. To look at her, one might not expect much more to come from a person of her advanced years. Certainly, the contribution of new life was biologically beyond her. Yet God's grace proved that assumption wrong, as it often explodes our careful theories and plans. God's grace can overshadow us and bring new life from the "too old," the "too young," and every other place where we've closed a door in our minds. God may be opening a door for you right now, in the place you least expect.

What aspect of your life have you already determined is fruitless or barren?
Do you believe God can act there?

WE RESPOND

'Tis the season to be generous. As we wrap those last presents and send those last cards, remember those who will receive no gift and no friendly greeting. Give a gift that won't be returned in kind, just as God gave Jesus to us. Merry Christmas.

He will stand tall in his shepherd-rule
by GOD's strength,
centered in the majesty of GOD-Revealed.
And the people will have a good and safe home.

CHRISTMAS SEASON

THE NATIVITY OF THE LORD

.... Merry Is the Word

FIRST READING » ISAIAH 52:7-10

How beautiful on the mountains
*   are the feet of the messenger bringing good news,*
Breaking the news that all's well,
*   proclaiming good times, announcing salvation,*
*   telling Zion, "Your God reigns!"*
Voices! Listen! Your scouts are shouting, thunderclap shouts,
*   shouting in joyful unison.*
They see with their own eyes
*   GOD coming back to Zion.*
Break into song! Boom it out, ruins of Jerusalem:
*   "GOD has comforted his people!*
*   He's redeemed Jerusalem!"*
GOD has rolled up his sleeves.
*   All the nations can see his holy, muscled arm.*
Everyone, from one end of the earth to the other,
*   sees him at work, doing his salvation work.*

Maybe there was a time when "merry" was a part of every person's working vocabulary. But now we mothball this word from about December 26 until the following December. Nothing else gets to be merry anymore except Christmastime. And that may be as it should be.

Perhaps we need a singular word to describe the spirit of this season. God does something in the nativity of Jesus that happens once in history and is never repeated. And while we speak of "good news" in situations as wide-ranging as an unexpected snow day or a clean bill of health from the doctor, the news of this one special birth in eons of babies makes all other good news seem remarkably situational. God not only rolls up the divine sleeves, but dives into a straw-covered bassinet to share our predicament. And from there to redeem it.

"Beautiful" is Isaiah's word for the bearer of such news. "Merry" is the effusive spirit that believes it and the one whose path is transformed by such a reality.

What are the elements that make the season of Christmas beautiful?
How can you carry them forward throughout the year?

SECOND READING » HEBREWS 1:1-6

Going through a long line of prophets, God has been addressing our ancestors in different ways for centuries. Recently he spoke to us directly through his Son. By his Son, God created the world in the beginning, and it will all belong to the Son at the end. This Son perfectly mirrors God, and is stamped with God's nature. He holds everything together by what he says—powerful words!

After he finished the sacrifice for sins, the Son took his honored place high in the heavens right alongside God, far higher than any angel in rank and rule. Did God ever say to an angel, "You're my Son; today I celebrate you"? Or, "I'm his Father, he's my Son"? When he presents his honored Son to the world, he says, "All angels must worship him."

God made the world in the beginning. It will be delivered to Christ in the end. In the meantime, the world is in our hands. What an awesome responsibility, an incredible privilege, and a tremendous opportunity!

The world is ours. What are we doing with it? Liberating or exploiting? Grabbing or sharing? Celebrating or criticizing? Investing our talents or burying them in the ground? Blessing or cursing? On Christmas day we're often on our best behavior, giving freely and forgiving lavishly. After all, "'tis the season." But when we take down the tinsel, will we revert to our normal Scrooge selves? Is God-with-us just an octave of days that interrupts our otherwise narrow lives and shuttered hearts?

The Christmas spirit isn't meant to be abnormal. It shouldn't be put away with the last ornament or discarded with the shedding pine tree. Time remains in our custody from Creation till Kingdom Coming. What will you do with yours?

What will you take with you from this Christmas season into the new year?

GOSPEL » JOHN 1:1-18

The Word was first,
*   the Word present to God,*
God present to the Word.
The Word was God,
*   in readiness for God from day one.*

Everything was created through him;
*   nothing—not one thing!—*
*   came into being without him.*
What came into existence was Life,
*   and the Life was Light to live by.*
The Life-Light blazed out of the darkness;
*   the darkness couldn't put it out.*

There once was a man, his name John, sent by God to point out the way to the Life-Light. He came to show everyone where to look, who to believe in. John was not himself the Light; he was there to show the way to the Light.

The Life-Light was the real thing:
    Every person entering Life
    he brings into Light.
He was in the world,
    the world was there through him,
    and yet the world didn't even notice.
He came to his own people,
    but they didn't want him.
But whoever did want him,
    who believed he was who he claimed
    and would do what he said,
He made to be their true selves,
    their child-of-God selves.
These are the God-begotten,
    not blood-begotten,
    not flesh-begotten,
    not sex-begotten.

The Word became flesh and blood,
    and moved into the neighborhood.
We saw the glory with our own eyes,
    the one-of-a-kind glory,
    like Father, like Son,
Generous inside and out,
    true from start to finish.

John pointed him out and called, "This is the One! The One I told you was coming after me but in fact was ahead of me. He has always been ahead of me, has always had the first word."

We all live off his generous bounty,
    gift after gift after gift.
We got the basics from Moses,
    and then this exuberant giving and receiving,
This endless knowing and understanding—
    all this came through Jesus, the Messiah.
No one has ever seen God,
    not so much as a glimpse.
This one-of-a-kind God-Expression,
    who exists at the very heart of the Father,
    has made him plain as day.

Of all four gospels, John's is easily the most mystical. The first community of faith gave way to a second or a third before John's story was written down. These later disciples had something the original ones never had: time to process what they were learning about living the faith of Jesus. Reflecting on their experience, they saw that most of human history was a dark place into which God's hope shone like the noon-day sun.

And when you try to talk about the light that Jesus brings into the life of a true believer, you start to sound like the passage quoted above. It's breathless and curious and enthusiastic and sort of weird all at once. If Christ lives in you already, then you totally get it. And if your "child-of-God" self hasn't yet encountered the "Life-Light" and experienced "one-of-a-kind glory" in the "God-expression" of Jesus—well, frankly, it's all going to sound rather mad. And it is mad, weird, wonderful that God chooses to emerge from within the swamp of our history to meet us. Only love behaves so inscrutably.

> What have you done for love's sake
> that seemed utterly mad to the people around you?

WE RESPOND

Love is crazy, not rational, impossible to reason with. Love follows love-logic and responds accordingly. Do something for love's sake today that you would do for no other reason. And have a Merry Christmas!

No one has ever seen God,
*   not so much as a glimpse.*
This one-of-a-kind God-Expression,
*   who exists at the very heart of the Father,*
*   has made him plain as day.*

THE HOLY FAMILY OF JESUS, MARY, AND JOSEPH

....Family Is a Risky Business

FIRST READING » SIRACH 3:2-7, 12-14

Yes, you children, listen to the advice of your parents. Follow it and you'll be saved. Parents should be honored and respected by their children. Honor your mother and father and God will wipe out your past sins; he'll help you deal with the occasions of present sins; he'll hear your daily prayer. Honor your mother and it's like putting money in the bank. Honor your father and your own children will honor you. Your prayers will be answered. You'll live a longer life. Obey your father and your mother will rest well.

Child, support your father in his old age; don't do something that will make him sad. If he shows signs of senility, give him a pass. Don't turn from him in his last days. Caring for a father won't go unnoticed. Your reputation will increase. In the day of trial you'll be remembered and your sins will melt like ice in the sun.

I've gone on record as an adult who gets along with her parents. For the sake of today's feast, I'll tell the rest of the story. I didn't grow up in an Ozzie-and-Harriet home. The problems we faced as a family were not resolved in a half hour, generally speaking. My parents quarreled, and since there were ten of us in a handful of rooms, they argued "in front of the children" as a matter of course. I'd say we broke a lot of the rules that family guidebooks advocate. By the time I got to college, I identified with the majority of my peers who complained that their parents drove them up the wall.

The flip side of the story is that we kids drove our FOLKS up the wall. Our music, our attitudes, our choices were maddening to them. For some years there was a direct correlation between the times my father and I argued, and the number of times we were speaking to each other at all. Once in my twenties, I remember shouting angrily across a room at him, "No matter what you say, I believe you LOVE me!" And he shouted back just as aggressively, "And I believe YOU love ME!" Then we collapsed tearfully in each other's arms. It was the bottom line of every argument, spoken or not.

> How do you honor a parent and still disagree?
> Is it possible to honor a parent who is,
> by any objective measure, a bad parent?

SECOND READING » COLOSSIANS 3:12-21

So, chosen by God for this new life of love, dress in the wardrobe God picked out for you: compassion, kindness, humility, quiet strength, discipline. Be even-tempered, content with second place, quick to forgive an offense. Forgive as quickly and completely as the Master forgave you. And regardless of what else you put on, wear love. It's your basic, all-purpose garment. Never be without it.

Let the peace of Christ keep you in tune with each other, in step with each other. None of this going off and doing your own thing. And cultivate thankfulness. Let the Word of Christ—the Message—have the run of the house. Give it plenty of room in your lives. Instruct and direct one another using good common sense. And sing, sing your hearts out to God! Let every detail in your lives—words, actions, whatever—be done in the name of the Master, Jesus, thanking God the Father every step of the way.

Wives, understand and support your husbands by submitting to them in ways that honor the Master.

Husbands, go all out in love for your wives. Don't take advantage of them.

Children, do what your parents tell you. This delights the Master no end.

Parents, don't come down too hard on your children or you'll crush their spirits.

The ancient world used household codes to spell out appropriate behaviors between members of a household, from the patriarch down to the lowest servant. The codes listed here did not belong to Christians only, but were taken for granted by Jews, Romans, and Greeks alike. The hierarchy itself—men over women, parents over children, masters over servants—was not in question. People were naturally situated in the household based on gender, age, and station. The codes that worked their way into Christian correspondence are softened by mutual responsibilities of the dominant person to his (generally his) subordinates. Husbands are instructed to treat their wives affectionately. Parents must nurture the self-esteem of their children, and masters should not treat slaves harshly (see Colossians 4:1). Introducing the dignity of the subordinate was a liberal idea back then.

Our country was founded on the radical principle that the old-world system of class and hierarchy no longer apply. Since the start of the American experiment, we've wrestled with putting equality into practice. Race, gender, and the economic divide continue to assert tangible barriers. The tyranny of the old has been replaced in some ways with the tyranny of the youth culture. We may be on the way, but the dignity of each individual remains a liberal idea.

> **We live with hierarchies in politics, religion,**
> **the school system, the workplace, and family life.**
> **where do you see the dignity of the subordinate championed,**
> **and where is it challenged?**

GOSPEL » LUKE 2:41-52

Every year Jesus' parents traveled to Jerusalem for the Feast of Passover. When he was twelve years old, they went up as they always did for the Feast. When it was over and they left for home, the child Jesus stayed behind in Jerusalem, but his parents didn't know it. Thinking he was somewhere in the company of pilgrims, they journeyed for a whole day and then began looking for him among relatives and neighbors. When they didn't find him, they went back to Jerusalem looking for him.

The next day they found him in the Temple seated among the teachers, listening to them and asking questions. The teachers were all quite taken with him, impressed with the sharpness of his answers. But his parents were not impressed; they were upset and hurt.

His mother said, "Young man, why have you done this to us? Your father and I have been half out of our minds looking for you."

He said, "Why were you looking for me? Didn't you know that I had to be here, dealing with the things of my Father?" But they had no idea what he was talking about.

So he went back to Nazareth with them, and lived obediently with them. His mother held these things dearly, deep within herself. And Jesus matured, growing up in both body and spirit, blessed by both God and people.

We're offered only one glimpse of the childhood of Jesus. Curiously, it isn't a tale of the remarkable serenity of Joseph's household, or how famously they all got along. The story of the holy family as we know it centers on an event familiar to every parent: the day the child got lost. Or we could retell it in more accurate terms: the day the child was found.

Jesus is found where we recognize, even before Mary and Joseph do, he rightly belongs. Just because his parents didn't know where he was doesn't mean that he's lost. He's been in God's house all along. This is an encouraging word to every parent who has "lost" a child through divorce, disagreement, or some incomprehensible life choice. We may not know how to "regain" our children, but they are never out of God's hands. God knows where they are, even when we don't, and God is not about to let one of the little ones be lost. God loves our children even more than we do. Though our anxiety for them is great when they disappear from view, our trust in God assures us that they're not out of God's sight.

> **Have you ever been lost, literally or otherwise?**
> **Have you ever "lost" anyone? How did you find them again?**

WE RESPOND

Take a risk with your family, living and deceased. Forgive the wrongs that have been done, ask forgiveness for the wrongs you've committed. Find each other again within the household of love.

MARY, MOTHER OF GOD

FIRST READING » NUMBERS 6:22-27

GOD spoke to Moses: "Tell Aaron and his sons, This is how you are to bless the People of Israel. Say to them,

> *GOD bless you and keep you,*
> *GOD smile on you and gift you,*
> *GOD look you full in the face*
>   *and make you prosper.*

In so doing, they will place my name on the People of Israel—
I will confirm it by blessing them."

Happy new year! What shall we call it? This isn't a question we normally ask of a year in our culture. When I lived in Chinatown in San Francisco years ago, I found it intriguing that my Chinese neighbors name and celebrate each year according to the animal spirit associated with that year: rooster or horse, snake or dog or dragon or rat. While this makes for a fabulous annual parade, I rarely found that the following twelve months lived up to its advance press, animal-wise.

While I don't advocate the Chinese zodiac, or the one in the daily papers either, I do acknowledge the power of names to endow a certain sense of purpose. If we name a child after a saint, that patron's intercession is always accessible. If we look upon an event as a blessing or a curse, it tends to deliver what we expect. God claims a people with the divine Name, just as in Baptism we're each claimed for Christ. So call the new year Rita or Jose if you like, but be sure to consecrate it to holy purposes.

Name three things you hope for this year.
How will you invest yourself in those hopes: in prayer, action, resources, time?

SECOND READING » GALATIANS 4:4-7

But when the time arrived that was set by God the Father, God sent his Son, born among us of a woman, born under the conditions of the law so that he might redeem those of us who have been kidnapped by the law. Thus we have been set free to experience our rightful heritage. You can tell for sure that you are now fully adopted as his own children because God sent the Spirit of his Son into our lives crying out, "Papa! Father!" Doesn't that privilege of intimate conversation with God make it plain that you are not a slave, but a child? And if you are a child, you're also an heir, with complete access to the inheritance.

It would deeply pain Saint Paul today to be called anti-Semitic. Not only was he Jewish and proudly so, he was a Pharisee: one of the estimated 6,000 or so of his generation who chose to live out an exacting obedience to the law of Moses. Though he was corralled into the camp of Jesus by a personal experience of the Risen Lord, Paul never stopped being a devout Jewish believer, nor did he see this loyalty as a conflict of interest with his all-out devotion to Christ Jesus.

So when Paul is quoted above as saying Jesus redeems us from being "kidnapped by the law," he's not saying the law of Moses is an evil hijacker from which we need to be rescued. What we all need redemption from is the truly misguided notion that our own moral exactness can ever be the means of our rescue. Paul was a perfect Pharisee in his own words, flawless and without blame. Yet when he encountered Jesus he understood how brittle and little moral perfection is compared with being a child of God.

> **Have we been having an "intimate conversation with God,"**
> **or an imperative relationship with religious law?**

GOSPEL » LUKE 2:16-21

They left, running, and found Mary and Joseph, and the baby lying in the manger. Seeing was believing. They told everyone they met what the angels had said about this child. All who heard the sheepherders were impressed.

Mary kept all these things to herself, holding them dear, deep within herself. The sheepherders returned and let loose, glorifying and praising God for everything they had heard and seen. It turned out exactly the way they'd been told!

When the eighth day arrived, the day of circumcision, the child was named Jesus, the name given by the angel before he was conceived.

Mary and Joseph name their child Jesus, which means "God saves." Later he'll be called Messiah or Christ, which means (in Hebrew and in Greek), "the anointed one." John's gospel also calls him "the Word" that existed with God before time began. And Saint Paul will call him the wisdom of God.

But eight centuries before Jesus was born, the prophet Isaiah had predicted a child by the name of Immanuel, "God with us." It's a grand and ambitious name. Could God possibly come so close to us that Divinity could actually reside inside our humanity? Did the humble shepherds who witnessed the revelation of the angels that night fully appreciate what was being communicated in this birth announcement? It seems that Mary, full of the "feminine genius" that Pope Francis talks about, understood how one life can hide inside another and didn't question the mystery she embodied and delivered. Once God is with us, can that reality ever be taken back?

> **Do you name God as near or far, adversary**
> **or friend, saving help or source of condemnation?**

WE RESPOND

The gift of time is placed in your hands. God is as near as you allow. Say a prayer, inviting the Lord of the Universe to be your guest this coming year.

THE EPIPHANY OF THE LORD

FIRST READING » ISAIAH 60:1-6

"Get out of bed, Jerusalem!
Wake up. Put your face in the sunlight.
GOD's bright glory has risen for you.
The whole earth is wrapped in darkness,
all people sunk in deep darkness,
But GOD rises on you,
his sunrise glory breaks over you.
Nations will come to your light,
kings to your sunburst brightness.
Look up! Look around!
Watch as they gather, watch as they approach you:
Your sons coming from great distances,
your daughters carried by their nannies.
When you see them coming you'll smile—big smiles!
Your heart will swell and, yes, burst!
All those people returning by sea for the reunion,
a rich harvest of exiles gathered in from the nations!
And then streams of camel caravans as far as the eye can see,
young camels of nomads in Midian and Ephah,
Pouring in from the south from Sheba,
loaded with gold and frankincense,
preaching the praises of GOD."

God's favorite. That was the name we used for a friend of ours who always seemed to move in the fast lane of good fortune. If he lost a job, another was offered to him before sundown. He had a knack for finding live/work situations in which he was exempt from paying rent. And that isn't to say he lived in garrets; most of these situations involved living in the finest homes with spectacular views. He never owed a dime and never made an enemy. He seemed to lead a charmed existence, and every fresh example of it caused us great wonder.

Our friend lived like a king, but he owned nearly nothing. Everything he possessed could be put into his car. When he died, we cleaned out his rooms in a day. This apparently poor man had traveled to all the great capitals of the world, and we found pictures of him standing in front of cathedrals and landscapes we had only heard about. With nothing but a smile to pay for it all, he hadn't left one dream unfulfilled.

Was he really God's favorite, or did he know something the rest of us haven't learned yet? Upon this simple man, God's glory shone, and what we once called luck, we now call grace.

SECOND READING » EPHESIANS 3:2-3a, 5-6

I take it that you're familiar with the part I was given in God's plan for including everybody. I got the inside story on this from God himself.

You'll be able to see for yourselves into the mystery of Christ. None of our ancestors understood this. Only in our time has it been made clear by God's Spirit through his holy apostles and prophets of this new order. The mystery is that people who have never heard of God and those who have heard of him all their lives (what I've been calling outsiders and insiders) stand on the same ground before God. They get the same offer, same help, same promises in Christ Jesus. The Message is accessible and welcoming to everyone, across the board.

Can a fresh word come from God? Or is revelation a door that swung closed after the time of the Bible? Many believe "there is nothing new under the sun," as the writer of Ecclesiastes concluded. God has spoken; it is written. If you want to know the truth of a thing, look to the past.

Those who hold a fundamentalist approach to revealed truth sit tight on the cover of the Bible and refuse to admit a new word. But our Catholic faith maintains there are two prongs to the truth: Scripture and Tradition. The ongoing experience of the community contributes to Tradition like the mouth of a river collects minerals deposited there across generations. We believe in the Holy Spirit, as we profess in the Creed. That is, we believe God's Spirit lives among us and guides us ever deeper into the heart of the mystery. We're citizens of the New Testament every bit as much as Paul and Barnabas, Mary Magdalene, and the Twelve. If you want to know the truth of a thing, look to the community that gathers at each Eucharist.

What truth might be made known in our generation
that was not known before now?

GOSPEL » MATTHEW 2:1-12

After Jesus was born in Bethlehem village, Judah territory—this was during Herod's kingship—a band of scholars arrived in Jerusalem from the East. They asked around, "Where can we find and pay homage to the newborn King of the Jews? We observed a star in the eastern sky that signaled his birth. We're on pilgrimage to worship him."

When word of their inquiry got to Herod, he was terrified—and not Herod alone, but most of Jerusalem as well. Herod lost no time. He gathered all the high priests and religion scholars in the city together and asked, "Where is the Messiah supposed to be born?"

They told him, "Bethlehem, Judah territory. The prophet Micah wrote it plainly:

It's you, Bethlehem, in Judah's land,
*   no longer bringing up the rear.*
From you will come the leader
*   who will shepherd-rule my people, my Israel."*

Herod then arranged a secret meeting with the scholars from the East. Pretending to be as devout as they were, he got them to tell him exactly when the birth-announcement star appeared. Then he told them the prophecy about Bethlehem, and said, "Go find this child. Leave no stone unturned. As soon as you find him, send word and I'll join you at once in your worship."

Instructed by the king, they set off. Then the star appeared again, the same star they had seen in the eastern skies. It led them on until it hovered over the place of the child. They could hardly contain themselves: They were in the right place! They had arrived at the right time!

They entered the house and saw the child in the arms of Mary, his mother. Overcome, they kneeled and worshiped him. Then they opened their luggage and presented gifts: gold, frankincense, myrrh.

In a dream, they were warned not to report back to Herod. So they worked out another route, left the territory without being seen, and returned to their own country.

The magi from the east had been on the road a long time. They had invested many seasons journeying after this foreign star. They invested more than time, but also money and a certain amount of professional esteem. If it should turn out that they'd followed this star for nothing, they would seem like utter fools.

Herod invested nothing in his quest to find the child they were ardently looking for. Herod was above such a diligent search. He wasn't going to stir one foot from his throne to locate this alleged new king. And so he never found him. Never found him to destroy him nor to recognize him and offer his gift.

How much have we invested in our search for the Christ child? Do we send others to do the job for us—priests, religious, missionaries, lay leaders—or have we made a personal commitment to follow the light wherever it leads and whatever it costs? How much time and wealth are we willing to spend? Or will we never take the journey at all?

> **Examine your commitment to seek and follow Christ.**
> **What are you willing to give, and what do you withhold?**

WE RESPOND

Epiphany means "the manifestation," or literally to be "hit by the hand" of truth. Consider how you have been hit by the reality of God's presence in your experience, and what it teaches you.

BAPTISM OF THE LORD

FIRST READING » ISAIAH 40:1-5, 9-11

"Comfort, oh comfort my people,"
says your God.
"Speak softly and tenderly to Jerusalem,
but also make it very clear
That she has served her sentence,
that her sin is taken care of—forgiven!
She's been punished enough and more than enough,
and now it's over and done with."

Thunder in the desert!
"Prepare for GOD's arrival!
Make the road straight and smooth,
a highway fit for our God.
Fill in the valleys,
level off the hills,
Smooth out the ruts,
clear out the rocks.
Then GOD's bright glory will shine
and everyone will see it.
Yes. Just as GOD has said."

Climb a high mountain, Zion.
You're the preacher of good news.
Raise your voice. Make it good and loud, Jerusalem.
You're the preacher of good news.
Speak loud and clear. Don't be timid!
Tell the cities of Judah,
"Look! Your God!"
Look at him! GOD, the Master, comes in power,
ready to go into action.
He is going to pay back his enemies
and reward those who have loved him.
Like a shepherd, he will care for his flock,
gathering the lambs in his arms,
Hugging them as he carries them,
leading the nursing ewes to good pasture.

Would you know God by sight? Isaiah presents the Holy One in vivid and versatile ways. God is the source of comfort as well as correction for the wayward soul. The Lord is the celestial bulldozer that straightens out roads, raises valleys, and levels mountains. The Almighty comes with all the force of an army, yet behaves like a shepherd caring for his flock. God is glorious, and yet tender and gentle. How would you know such a God if the Holy One stood before you?

One of the reasons God may prefer no graven images is to keep us from imagining the Alpha and Omega in a single revelation and kidding ourselves that we've captured the whole picture of divinity. God has no race or gender, no age or shoe size. God is a protective father, a mother hen, a monarch, and a shepherd. God is a creator at one end of the spectrum of life and a savior at the other. God is One, and God is Triune. God "is, was, and ever shall be." God also dives into history, living and suffering and dying among us. God has too many faces for us to settle for one.

> How does a religion with no set image of God
> differ from one with a clear and visibly formed deity?
> Which images of God have most meaning for you?

SECOND READING » TITUS 2:11-14; 3:4-7

God's readiness to give and forgive is now public. Salvation's available for everyone! We're being shown how to turn our backs on a godless, indulgent life, and how to take on a God-filled, God-honoring life. This new life is starting right now, and is whetting our appetites for the glorious day when our great God and Savior, Jesus Christ, appears. He offered himself as a sacrifice to free us from a dark, rebellious life into this good, pure life, making us a people he can be proud of, energetic in goodness.

But when God, our kind and loving Savior God, stepped in, he saved us from all that. It was all his doing; we had nothing to do with it. He gave us a good bath, and we came out of it new people, washed inside and out by the Holy Spirit. Our Savior Jesus poured out new life so generously. God's gift has restored our relationship with him and given us back our lives. And there's more life to come—an eternity of life!

Even as we acknowledge God's infinity, as Christians we also embrace the particular revelation of God in Jesus Christ. God is ageless and endless, but in Jesus we get to see God's power and mercy in action in history at close range. If God's variety makes the divine seem unknowable, then Jesus' humanity makes the Holy One remarkably familiar.

And we need God close, because salvation that's far away can be hard to believe in. You and I suffer the ache of the particular, being born with this nose, these parents, this ethnicity and address, and no other. We've got to make do with certain talents and limitations. We're stuck with the present generation, and can never return to the past nor fast-forward to an age to come. Hunkered down in time and place can be a terrible poverty when it comes to opportunity. If you're born after the dodo bird and before the cure for cancer, there are some things you just can't have. Jesus reveals to us that God is willing to share our poverty in order to save us from it. No other proof will do but for Jesus to be here as he says it.

Which particulars of your life are especially difficult?
How does Jesus being with us speak to those?

GOSPEL » LUKE 3:15-16, 21-22

The interest of the people by now was building. They were all beginning to wonder, "Could this John be the Messiah?"

But John intervened: "I'm baptizing you here in the river. The main character in this drama, to whom I'm a mere stagehand, will ignite the kingdom life, a fire, the Holy Spirit within you, changing you from the inside out."

After all the people were baptized, Jesus was baptized. As he was praying, the sky opened up and the Holy Spirit, like a dove descending, came down on him. And along with the Spirit, a voice: "You are my Son, chosen and marked by my love, pride of my life."

John the Baptist speaks so powerfully and seems so extraordinary that people wonder if he might be the Christ they're expecting. John puts that idea to rest immediately and completely. Compared with the star of this show, John knows he's hardly fit to share the same stage.

It's rare that a charismatic individual points away from himself or herself. It's strange when any of us, no matter how humble, does less than call attention to ourselves! We all want to be important to somebody, to be needed and valued and not overlooked. The Baptizer understood that the baptism he offered would pass away, and something much greater was on the horizon. John was content that his work was only the preface to a bigger story.

When people meet us, are they aware that we're ambassadors of a greater Coming? Do they know our story is a prelude to the great story God is telling through us? Do they sense that the love in us has its roots in the Source of love itself?

How do you reveal, not simply yourself, but the presence of God to others?
Do your words stand in the way of others hearing God's word through you?

WE RESPOND

Look for God in new places: in strangers, in humble neighborhoods, in suffering, in the face of an enemy. Bring God's love to new places, especially to those in need of reconciliation, kindness, generosity, and peace.

LENT

ASH WEDNESDAY

FIRST READING » JOEL 2:12-18

But there's also this, it's not too late—
  GOD's personal Message!—
"Come back to me and really mean it!
  Come fasting and weeping, sorry for your sins!"
Change your life, not just your clothes.
  Come back to GOD, your God.
And here's why: God is kind and merciful.
  He takes a deep breath, puts up with a lot,
This most patient God, extravagant in love,
  always ready to cancel catastrophe.
Who knows? Maybe he'll do it now,
  maybe he'll turn around and show pity.
Maybe, when all's said and done,
  there'll be blessings full and robust for your GOD!

Blow the ram's horn trumpet in Zion!
  Declare a day of repentance, a holy fast day.
Call a public meeting.
  Get everyone there. Consecrate the congregation.
Make sure the elders come,
  but bring in the children, too, even the nursing babies,
Even men and women on their honeymoon—
  interrupt them and get them there.
Between Sanctuary entrance and altar,
  let the priests, GOD's servants, weep tears of repentance.
Let them intercede: "Have mercy, GOD, on your people!
  Don't abandon your heritage to contempt.
Don't let the pagans take over and rule them
  and sneer, 'And so where is this God of theirs?'"

At that, GOD went into action to get his land back.
  He took pity on his people.

How many times have you approached the season of Lent before? Is this the first time, or the twentieth, or the fiftieth? Cradle Catholics know the drill: fasting, prayer, almsgiving. This three-fold program has been ushering believers from Ash Wednesday to Easter for thousands of years.

So today we stop to consider what our fast will entail, according to what's appropriate for our age, health, and circumstance in life. What needs to be lessened, limited, or disciplined in order to bring us wisdom in the next forty days? Next, we consider adopting a special prayer practice to heighten our intimacy with God. It could be communal, familial, or solitary; sung, read, or time spent in silence. Finally, no lenten practice is complete without our sacrificial giving to those in need. You might share money, but also time, attention, kind words, or a skill you have that others might benefit from. Fidelity to these three simple practices has turned many ordinary people into saints.

> **Which practices have led to fruitful lenten experiences in the past?**
> **How will you commit to the deepened conversion of your heart this season?**

SECOND READING » 2 CORINTHIANS 5:20 – 6:2

We're Christ's representatives. God uses us to persuade men and women to drop their differences and enter into God's work of making things right between them. We're speaking for Christ himself now: Become friends with God; he's already a friend with you.

How? you ask. In Christ. God put the wrong on him who never did anything wrong, so we could be put right with God.

Companions as we are in this work with you, we beg you, please don't squander one bit of this marvelous life God has given us. God reminds us,

> *I heard your call in the nick of time;*
> *The day you needed me, I was there to help.*

Well, now is the right time to listen, the day to be helped.

If you hang around church enough, you hear a lot about God. Cultivating a relationship with God is what the religion business is all about, right? Yet try asking your fellow Catholics who or what God is. It seems we know a lot of Catholic answers to Catholic questions about God. But apart from a few doctrines we recite in every profession of faith, the Divine mystery remains veiled in significant ways. We know a lot of things ABOUT God. But do we know God—as more than a character in an old story? Is God a real Presence or just a story we've heard?

I asked the kids in my junior high catechism class this question. A smart girl raised her hand and asked me: "Well, do YOU know God?" I marveled at how shy I felt to answer that I do. How can we pray, take Eucharist, seek the Spirit's guidance, celebrate the beauty of creation, participate in the daily bread of God's saving activity in our lives and those of others around us and not know God in perceptible ways? Lent is the season to deepen our friendship with God so that the relationship can grow stronger.

> **God may be stranger, acquaintance, dear friend, or hearsay.**
> **What is God to you at this season of life,**
> **and where do you hope this relationship will go?**

GOSPEL » MATTHEW 6:1-6, 16-18

"Be especially careful when you are trying to be good so that you don't make a performance out of it. It might be good theater, but the God who made you won't be applauding.

"When you do something for someone else, don't call attention to yourself. You've seen them in action, I'm sure—'playactors' I call them—treating prayer meeting and street corner alike as a stage, acting compassionate as long as someone is watching, playing to the crowds. They get applause, true, but that's all they get. When you help someone out, don't think about how it looks. Just do it— quietly and unobtrusively. That is the way your God, who conceived you in love, working behind the scenes, helps you out.

"And when you come before God, don't turn that into a theatrical production either. All these people making a regular show out of their prayers, hoping for stardom! Do you think God sits in a box seat?

"Here's what I want you to do: Find a quiet, secluded place so you won't be tempted to role-play before God. Just be there as simply and honestly as you can manage. The focus will shift from you to God, and you will begin to sense his grace.

"When you practice some appetite-denying discipline to better concentrate on God, don't make a production out of it. It might turn you into a small-time celebrity but it won't make you a saint. If you 'go into training' inwardly, act normal outwardly. Shampoo and comb your hair, brush your teeth, wash your face. God doesn't require attention-getting devices. He won't overlook what you are doing: he'll reward you well.

It's time to shift the focus of our spiritual life from us to God. It's not about tidying up our habits, being a better person, shining up our halo, or perfecting our spiritual act. We come to the life of the church to engage a relationship that, like all relationships, only succeeds when it's not all about us. The practice of our faith isn't about what we personally stand to gain, whether it's eternal life or personal perfection. We seek the source of all Truth, Goodness, and Beauty, as the theologians tell us. To get from where we are to that Ultimate Other requires a little stretching out of our arms, hearts, and minds. The One we seek will never fit in the box we've already designed for our God quest. Higher, wider, and deeper is always required.

Whatever else we "do" in relationship to God, just being there "as simply and honestly as you can manage" is the most important element to bring along. No relationship grows without being really present to it and to the other. From there, love becomes possible.

> How does being present to those you love
> create new spaces for understanding and intimacy?
> When was the last time you learned
> something new about someone you love?

WE RESPOND

Make a pledge this Lent not simply to talk to God, but also to listen. Find or create a place where you can enter the silence regularly to hear what God has to say.

"Find a quiet, secluded place so you won't be tempted to role-play before God. Just be there as simply and honestly as you can manage. The focus will shift from you to God, and you will begin to sense his grace."

FIRST SUNDAY OF LENT

FIRST READING » DEUTERONOMY 26:4-10

Moses said to the people:
"The priest will take the basket from you and place it on the Altar of GOD,
your God. And there in the Presence of GOD, your God, you will recite:

A wandering Aramean was my father,
he went down to Egypt and sojourned there,
he and just a handful of his brothers at first, but soon
they became a great nation, mighty and many.
The Egyptians abused and battered us,
in a cruel and savage slavery.
We cried out to GOD, the God-of-Our-Fathers:
He listened to our voice, he saw
our destitution, our trouble, our cruel plight.
And GOD took us out of Egypt
with his strong hand and long arm, terrible and great,
with signs and miracle-wonders.
And he brought us to this place,
gave us this land flowing with milk and honey.
So here I am. I've brought the firstfruits
of what I've grown on this ground you gave me, O God.

Then place it in the Presence of GOD, your God. Prostrate yourselves in the
Presence of GOD, your God."

What makes the past live again? One sure way to do it is to tell the story. When we tell nostalgic tales from our childhood, the spirit of joy and wonder comes alive in us again, and we feel younger. When we speak of old wounds, they ache as if freshly made. How we choose to tell the story is as important as whether or not to tell it at all. We frame our history as its victors or its victims. We can remember the past with pride, or with shame.

Moses wants to make sure that the people tell the right story in the right way, in order to remember who they are and what their identity means. It is, of course, not strictly accurate for the Israelites to say, "My father was a wandering Aramean," a reference to ancestors long dead. But for each Israelite throughout history to claim those ancestors as immediate predecessors is to embrace the story of Israel as one's own family history. No longer a distant and irrelevant tale, the story of enslavement in Egypt and salvation by God becomes something personally suffered and redeemed. Every Eucharist tells the Christian story in the same way.

*Just as Jews tell the story of Exodus as an immediate part of their story,
we Christians say, "Jesus died on the cross for me."
What meaning does the crucifixion and resurrection have for you?*

SECOND READING » ROMANS 10:8-13

So what exactly was Moses saying?

> *The word that saves is right here,
> as near as the tongue in your mouth,
> as close as the heart in your chest.*

It's the word of faith that welcomes God to go to work and set things right for us. This is the core of our preaching. Say the welcoming word to God—"Jesus is my Master"—embracing, body and soul, God's work of doing in us what he did in raising Jesus from the dead. That's it. You're not "doing" anything; you're simply calling out to God, trusting him to do it for you. That's salvation. With your whole being you embrace God setting things right, and then you say it, right out loud: "God has set everything right between him and me!"

Scripture reassures us, "No one who trusts God like this—heart and soul— will ever regret it." It's exactly the same no matter what a person's religious background may be: the same God for all of us, acting the same incredibly generous way to everyone who calls out for help. "Everyone who calls, 'Help, God!' gets help."

When Moses describes the ritual the people are to follow in the First Reading today, he breaks it into three parts: Tell the story. Make your offering. Bow down. It's a good formula for worship in any age. Saint Paul picks up the theme again in urging his audience to confess "Jesus is Lord." First, tell the story of Jesus being raised from the dead. Next, offer your confession of faith. Third, accept his authority over your life. It's this last step, frankly, that causes us the most trouble.

Accepting Jesus as Lord isn't as easy as saying the right creed. When we bow our heads we must also humble our hearts—and humility is no one's favorite virtue. Humility is admitting that we're not God, not even on a good day, and that we're not in control of the powers of life and death, nor much in between. Humility means accepting that all we have is gift, and all we can count on is grace. Humility involves surrender and trust in God. When Jesus truly is our Lord, the course of life changes dramatically.

*How do you make your offering before God?
How do you bow down and acknowledge Jesus as Lord in your life?*

GOSPEL » LUKE 4:1-13

Now Jesus, full of the Holy Spirit, left the Jordan and was led by the Spirit into the wild. For forty wilderness days and nights he was tested by the Devil. He ate nothing during those days, and when the time was up he was hungry.

The Devil, playing on his hunger, gave the first test: "Since you're God's Son, command this stone to turn into a loaf of bread."

Jesus answered by quoting Deuteronomy: "It takes more than bread to really live."

For the second test he led him up and spread out all the kingdoms of the earth on display at once. Then the Devil said, "They're yours in all their splendor to serve your pleasure. I'm in charge of them all and can turn them over to whomever I wish. Worship me and they're yours, the whole works."

Jesus refused, again backing his refusal with Deuteronomy: "Worship the Lord your God and only the Lord your God. Serve him with absolute single-heartedness."

For the third test the Devil took him to Jerusalem and put him on top of the Temple. He said, "If you are God's Son, jump. It's written, isn't it, that 'he has placed you in the care of angels to protect you; they will catch you; you won't so much as stub your toe on a stone'?"

"Yes," said Jesus, "and it's also written, 'Don't you dare tempt the Lord your God.'"

That completed the testing. The Devil retreated temporarily, lying in wait for another opportunity.

The devil had a few bargains he was peddling that day in the desert: all the bread you can eat, power and glory fit for a king, a legion of angels for protection. But Jesus wasn't buying. He knew those bargains had a supreme price tag that no one should pay. As Son of God, all of those things were already available to him. And as heirs of God's kingdom, those things will be ours as well. The only currency the devil was really peddling was the word *Now*. Immediate gratification is the definition of most of our temptations.

Do we want to eat and drink and be merry now, regardless of the hunger of the world around us, not to mention the danger to our own over-indulged bodies? Do we want to live in our dream house now, while our sisters and brothers live on the street? Do we want our children to go to the best schools today, while much of the world cannot read and write? Do we want to sit in front of the TV tonight, when a lonely person is starving for our company not far away? If we bow to God alone, then the devil's bargain won't sound like such a deal. "Now or never" is not the choice. It's now or forever.

> Which of the devil's three temptations—self-satisfaction, power, or security—has the strongest allure for you?
> What helps you to resist the temptation?

WE RESPOND

Examine the greatest temptation to worldly advantage that you struggle against. Make a pledge this Lent to challenge the authority of this "demon."

SECOND SUNDAY OF LENT

....The Darkness and the Light

FIRST READING » GENESIS 15:5-12, 17-18

GOD took Abram outside and said, "Look at the sky. Count the stars. Can you do it? Count your descendants! You're going to have a big family, Abram!"

And he believed! Believed GOD! God declared him "Set-Right-with-God."

GOD continued, "I'm the same GOD who brought you from Ur of the Chaldees and gave you this land to own."

Abram said, "Master GOD, how am I to know this, that it will all be mine?"

GOD said, "Bring me a heifer, a goat, and a ram, each three years old, and a dove and a young pigeon."

He brought all these animals to him, split them down the middle, and laid the halves opposite each other. But he didn't split the birds. Vultures swooped down on the carcasses, but Abram scared them off. As the sun went down a deep sleep overcame Abram and then a sense of dread, dark and heavy.

When the sun was down and it was dark, a smoking firepot and a flaming torch moved between the split carcasses. That's when GOD made a covenant with Abram: "I'm giving this land to your children, from the Nile River in Egypt to the River Euphrates in Assyria."

Many saints have reported that when they went looking for God, they found darkness instead. Saint John of the Cross called it "the dark night of the soul." Just when you thought it was safe to be God's friend, all communication seems lost. Having gotten used to having God as advisor, protector, and traveling companion, it must have seemed terrifying indeed to Abram when the deep darkness rolled between them. For just a moment, he might have wondered if he was following the right God.

The covenant may have begun in darkness, but it was soon illuminated by a blazing fire. This ritual of blood sacrifice reminds us that more blood will seal this covenant: the rite of circumcision, the blood of the Passover lamb in Egypt, the generations of animal sacrifices at the Temple in Jerusalem and, finally and completely, the blood of Jesus. What begins in darkness and doubt will lead to the light of Easter and renewed faith. When we find ourselves having a dark night of doubt, feeling the sacrifice all too keenly, we might remember righteous Abram crouched in the darkness.

When and how have you experienced doubt on the road of faith?

SECOND READING » PHILIPPIANS 3:17 – 4:1

Stick with me, friends. Keep track of those you see running this same course, headed for this same goal. There are many out there taking other paths, choosing other goals, and trying to get you to go along with them. I've warned you of them many times; sadly, I'm having to do it again. All they want is easy street. They hate Christ's Cross. But easy street is a dead-end street. Those who live there *make their bellies their gods; belches are their praise; all they can think of is their appetites.*

But there's far more to life for us. We're citizens of high heaven! We're waiting the arrival of the Savior, the Master, Jesus Christ, who will transform our earthy bodies into glorious bodies like his own. He'll make us beautiful and whole with the same powerful skill by which he is putting everything as it should be, under and around him.

My dear, dear friends! I love you so much. I do want the very best for you. You make me feel such joy, fill me with such pride. Don't waver. Stay on track, steady in God.

It would be easy for most of us to compose a mental list of the "haters of Christ's Cross." Who would be on yours? Murderers, tyrants, racists, people of physical and moral violence all the way down the line? Leaders who persecute and purge believers from their midst? People who turn from their religious upbringing and choose the secular way?

These aren't the folks Paul has in mind when he warns his flock tearfully of those who will take their faith away. He means religious leaders more interested in enforcing the Sabbath than observing it, or in whipping people into shape rather than leading them to God. These are the keepers of the dietary laws (serving the belly gods) and exterior criteria like circumcision. Caught up in the letter of the law, they squander its spirit. As Jesus said, the laws of religion are made to assist us; we were not created to uphold them. Any leader who destroys faith is not a leader we're obliged to follow.

> **When have you encountered a law which seemed to destroy the people it was intended to support? How does your parish respond pastorally to those who live outside of its laws?**

GOSPEL » LUKE 9:28b-36

Jesus climbed the mountain to pray, taking Peter, John, and James along. While he was in prayer, the appearance of his face changed and his clothes became blinding white. At once two men were there talking with him. They turned out to be Moses and Elijah—and what a glorious appearance they made! They talked over his exodus, the one Jesus was about to complete in Jerusalem.

Meanwhile, Peter and those with him were slumped over in sleep. When they came to, rubbing their eyes, they saw Jesus in his glory and the two men standing with him. When Moses and Elijah had left, Peter said to Jesus, "Master, this is a great moment! Let's build three memorials: one for you, one for Moses, and one for Elijah." He blurted this out without thinking.

While he was babbling on like this, a light-radiant cloud enveloped them. As they found themselves buried in the cloud, they became deeply aware of God.

Then there was a voice out of the cloud: "This is my Son, the Chosen! Listen to him."

When the sound of the voice died away, they saw Jesus there alone. They were speechless. And they continued speechless, said not one thing to anyone during those days of what they had seen.

Jesus and his three best friends climbed the mountain to pray, but Jesus did all the praying. The others napped, exhausted by the climb or bored by the task of praying. And because they slept, they very nearly missed the radiance of the Transfiguration. When they awoke, the glory still lingered around Jesus, not to mention his two unmistakable guests.

But they hardly saw the radiance before being overshadowed by a cloud. Where would you expect God to be found: in the brilliance or the shadow? Actually, God is revealed in both. God's glory is seen in the light, but God's voice is heard clearly in the darkness. How often has this been true in our experience as well? We celebrate God's nearness and blessing in the happy times, at the birth of a child or the marvel of a new snowfall. But we can hear God's voice ring out on a bleak city backstreet, and in the season of illness. When we insist on seeing God only in good times, we find ourselves apparently abandoned when we need God's comforting presence the most. God is with us, in the light and in the darkness.

> Where do you find it easy to experience
> God's presence in your world?
> How might God be present in the "absence,"
> while you've been looking elsewhere?

WE RESPOND

Seek God's in the light: at sunrise and sunset, in candle's glow, in the radiance of the faces you love. Listen for God's word in darkness: in sickness and worry, when the path before you seems obscure or lonely.

THIRD SUNDAY OF LENT

FIRST READING » EXODUS 3:1-8a, 13-15

Moses was shepherding the flock of Jethro, his father-in-law, the priest of Midian. He led the flock to the west end of the wilderness and came to the mountain of God, Horeb. The angel of GOD appeared to him in flames of fire blazing out of the middle of a bush. He looked. The bush was blazing away but it didn't burn up.

Moses said, "What's going on here? I can't believe this! Amazing! Why doesn't the bush burn up?"

GOD saw that he had stopped to look. God called to him from out of the bush, "Moses! Moses!"

He said, "Yes? I'm right here!"

God said, "Don't come any closer. Remove your sandals from your feet. You're standing on holy ground."

Then he said, "I am the God of your father: The God of Abraham, the God of Isaac, the God of Jacob."

Moses hid his face, afraid to look at God.

GOD said, "I've taken a good, long look at the affliction of my people in Egypt. I've heard their cries for deliverance from their slave masters; I know all about their pain. And now I have come down to help them, pry them loose from the grip of Egypt, get them out of that country and bring them to a good land with wide-open spaces, a land lush with milk and honey."

Then Moses said to God, "Suppose I go to the People of Israel and I tell them, 'The God of your fathers sent me to you'; and they ask me, 'What is his name?' What do I tell them?"

God said to Moses, "I-AM-WHO-I-AM. Tell the People of Israel, 'I-AM sent me to you.'"

God continued with Moses: "This is what you're to say to the Israelites: 'GOD, the God of your fathers, the God of Abraham, the God of Isaac, and the God of Jacob sent me to you.' This has always been my name, and this is how I always will be known."

Moses had left Egypt far behind. Back there he had a Hebrew family and an Egyptian one; the two identities made him doubt who he was and what his responsibilities should be. Out here in the desert of Midian, he had a wife and a home and a simple livelihood. He wasn't looking for trouble. Nor was he looking for God. Moses was just trying to forget the past and concentrate on the here and now.

Guess who showed up in the here and now. That's God all over: being present in the present and turning reality topsy-turvy, the way Jesus loved to tell stories where the last get to be first. All of a sudden, Moses had a God and a mission and a place in posterity. He might have preferred a flock of sheep to call his own and a couple of kids down the line. The burning bush, like the tabernacle in our churches, is an icon of the ever-powerful reality of God at all times and in all places. We expect to find God in church, but don't count out the Holy in the most desolate places.

How is God available to you "in church?"
In which unlikely places have you also encountered God's presence?

SECOND READING » 1 CORINTHIANS 10:1-6, 10-12

Remember our history, friends, and be warned. All our ancestors were led by the providential Cloud and taken miraculously through the Sea. They went through the waters, in a baptism like ours, as Moses led them from enslaving death to salvation life. They all ate and drank identical food and drink, meals provided daily by God. They drank from the Rock, God's fountain for them that stayed with them wherever they were. And the Rock was Christ. But just experiencing God's wonder and grace didn't seem to mean much—most of them were defeated by temptation during the hard times in the desert, and God was not pleased.

These are all warning markers—DANGER!—in our history books, written down so that we don't repeat their mistakes. Our positions in the story are parallel—they at the beginning, we at the end—and we are just as capable of messing it up as they were. Don't be so naive and self-confident. You're not exempt. You could fall flat on your face as easily as anyone else. Forget about self-confidence; it's useless. Cultivate God-confidence.

What does it mean to be baptized into something? When the Israelites were "baptized into Moses" at the crossing of the Red Sea, they cast their lot with him, uniting their lives and destiny with his. If Moses dared to walk into the sea, so would they. If he followed the power of God conveyed by a cloud, they would follow too. If he led them to suffer and face hardship and possible death in the desert...well, then they would grumble and complain and threaten a revolt. Their baptism into Moses wasn't perfect. The Israelites wanted freedom and the land of milk and honey, but within reason.

You and I are baptized into Christ. This means we're baptized into his death for the sake of eternal life. Some of us accept Baptism without reading the fine print: We overlook Good Friday for the sake of Easter. But Baptism is a comprehensive package. It's as absurd to be a Resurrection Christian who refuses to suffer as it is to be a Crucifixion Christian who will not celebrate.

How have you been willing to suffer for the sake of Christ?
When and how do you celebrate in the name of Christ?

GOSPEL » LUKE 13:1-9

About that time some people came up and told him about the Galileans Pilate had killed while they were at worship, mixing their blood with the blood of the sacrifices on the altar. Jesus responded, "Do you think those murdered Galileans were worse sinners than all other Galileans? Not at all. Unless you turn to God, you too will die. And those eighteen in Jerusalem the other day, the ones crushed and killed when the Tower of Siloam collapsed and fell on them, do you think they were worse citizens than all other Jerusalemites? Not at all. Unless you turn to God, you too will die."

Then he told them a story: "A man had an apple tree planted in his front yard. He came to it expecting to find apples, but there weren't any. He said to his gardener, 'What's going on here? For three years now I've come to this tree expecting apples and not one apple have I found. Chop it down! Why waste good ground with it any longer?'

"The gardener said, 'Let's give it another year. I'll dig around it and fertilize, and maybe it will produce next year; if it doesn't, then chop it down.'"

I'm a sucker for the strays of the plant world. I cultivate a small, shade-loving garden on my balcony, and there's not a plant out there that wasn't rescued from someone else's garbage. I wouldn't call it an attractive collection of life forms, but I have the satisfaction of knowing that every single stick out there owes me one. Some of them recover from original rejection and flourish, even blooming to the astonishment of my friends. Others waver between life and death for a season or longer. I'm very patient with my orphans. But even I have a limit to the amount of time I can allow my confined space to be taken up by a plant that refuses to give back even a little life for my efforts.

I have great sympathy for the gardener who defends the life of the tree for a fourth and final year. But if the tree continues to exhaust the soil with no return, it will be cut down, and even the gardener will agree it's time to give the spot to a tree with more promise. Those of us currently exhausting the soil to no purpose should wonder what time it is, and where we stand in the gardener's forbearance.

> **Which aspects of your life—career, relationships, activities—are bearing fruit right now? How can you fertilize the parts that aren't?**

WE RESPOND

Choose an area of your life that's least productive now—prayer life, marriage, job, or recreational time—and recommit that territory to God's will.

FOURTH SUNDAY OF LENT

FIRST READING » JOSHUA 5:9a, 10-12

God said to Joshua, "Today I have rolled away the reproach of Egypt."

The People of Israel continued to camp at The Gilgal. They celebrated the Passover on the evening of the fourteenth day of the month on the plains of Jericho.

Right away, the day after the Passover, they started eating the produce of that country, unraised bread and roasted grain. And then no more manna; the manna stopped. As soon as they started eating food grown in the land, there was no more manna for the People of Israel. That year they ate from the crops of Canaan.

Consider it God's welfare-to-work program. After forty years of free lunches in the desert, a manna diet interrupted by the occasional quail sandwich, there came a time when manna was off the menu. The manna quit when Israel, finally arrived in the land beyond the Jordan, were able to provide for themselves. Did they miss the manna? Did they long for the good old days of gathering up the flakes of bread at dawn? Did some hunger for the security of knowing God was looking out for them in this intimate way? That seems reasonable. Does a new college student wish Mom was still doing the laundry and Dad was handing out the allowance?

But as each of us learns, there's one thing nicer than being provided for: the satisfaction of providing for yourself and the dignity of being entrusted with the task. Does it mean God will never, ever hand out manna again? Twenty years later, when I visit my folks, my Mom still does my laundry, and Dad slips me a few bills.

> **In what circumstance of your life have you known the security of "manna from heaven?"**
> **How can you offer the "manna effect" to someone else?**

SECOND READING » 2 CORINTHIANS 5:17-21

Now we look inside, and what we see is that anyone united with the Messiah gets a fresh start, is created new. The old life is gone; a new life burgeons! Look at it! All this comes from the God who settled the relationship between us and him, and then called us to settle our relationships with each other. God put the world square with himself through the Messiah, giving the world a fresh start by offering forgiveness of sins. God has given us the task of telling everyone what he is doing. We're Christ's representatives. God uses us to persuade men and women to drop their differences and enter into God's work of making things right between them. We're speaking for Christ himself now: Become friends with God; he's already a friend with you.

How? you say. In Christ. God put the wrong on him who never did anything wrong, so we could be put right with God.

Confession. Penance. These words have a forbidding and medieval sound to them. Although there are things for which I must admit guilt and accept responsibility, confession has a rather criminal ring to it. And though at times I have to restore right where I have done wrong, the idea of penance conjures up those monastics of old, beating the pride out of themselves. Still, most of us use these terms freely when talking about our celebration of God's great mercy and love. The irony is certainly not lost on outsiders.

When the Church introduced the term Reconciliation for this sacrament, God's forgiveness came to the forefront, and brooding shame made a retreat. We celebrate that God restores what was lost, heals whatever is broken in our choices against the holy will. This is not the "dark sacrament" meant to provoke shudders as we stand in line contemplating our badness. Reconciliation reunites our hearts to God and challenges us to forgive as we've been forgiven. Far from a fearful hour, it's the pathway to peace.

> **Are there ways in which you're unreconciled
> with the will of God as you understand it?**

GOSPEL » LUKE 15:1-3, 11-32

By this time a lot of men and women of doubtful reputation were hanging around Jesus, listening intently. The Pharisees and religion scholars were not pleased, not at all pleased. They growled, "He takes in sinners and eats meals with them, treating them like old friends." Their grumbling triggered this story.

"There was once a man who had two sons. The younger said to his father, 'Father, I want right now what's coming to me.'

"So the father divided the property between them. It wasn't long before the younger son packed his bags and left for a distant country. There, undisciplined and dissipated, he wasted everything he had. After he had gone through all his money, there was a bad famine all through that country and he began to hurt. He signed on with a citizen there who assigned him to his fields to slop the pigs. He was so hungry he would have eaten the corncobs in the pig slop, but no one would give him any.

"That brought him to his senses. He said, 'All those farmhands working for my father sit down to three meals a day, and here I am starving to death. I'm going back to my father. I'll say to him, Father, I've sinned against God, I've sinned before you; I don't deserve to be called your son. Take me on as a hired hand.' He got right up and went home to his father.

"When he was still a long way off, his father saw him. His heart pounding, he ran out, embraced him, and kissed him. The son started his speech: 'Father, I've sinned against God, I've sinned before you; I don't deserve to be called your son ever again.'

"But the father wasn't listening. He was calling to the servants, 'Quick. Bring a clean set of clothes and dress him. Put the family ring on his finger and sandals

on his feet. Then get a grain-fed heifer and roast it. We're going to feast! We're going to have a wonderful time! My son is here—given up for dead and now alive! Given up for lost and now found!' And they began to have a wonderful time.

"All this time his older son was out in the field. When the day's work was done he came in. As he approached the house, he heard the music and dancing. Calling over one of the houseboys, he asked what was going on. He told him, 'Your brother came home. Your father has ordered a feast—barbecued beef! — because he has him home safe and sound.'

"The older brother stalked off in an angry sulk and refused to join in. His father came out and tried to talk to him, but he wouldn't listen. The son said, 'Look how many years I've stayed here serving you, never giving you one moment of grief, but have you ever thrown a party for me and my friends? Then this son of yours who has thrown away your money on whores shows up and you go all out with a feast!'

"His father said, 'Son, you don't understand. You're with me all the time, and everything that is mine is yours—but this is a wonderful time, and we had to celebrate. This brother of yours was dead, and he's alive! He was lost, and he's found!'"

Think of a time when you've been unexpectedly, generously, undeservedly forgiven. I remember a dreadful day in college when I hurt my closest friend. Nadine was from a Pentecostal Christian tradition, and I, in a ham-fisted attempt to "defend the faith," told her all about her theological errors as they were abundantly clear to me after twelve years of parochial schooling. (Lucky for me, no one was in the room at the time to point out mine!) This "correction" caused my friend a great deal of pain, since I patently rejected her sincere walk with Jesus. I retired to my dorm room feeling curiously awful about being so very "right" about God. Thank God one of us understood something about the nature of Christianity. Later that evening, Nadine sought me out and put her arm around me. We both cried together about the spirit of self-righteousness that had made me willing to forsake our friendship. You don't make that mistake twice in a lifetime. When you understand the love that's yours in the arms of God, you don't leave home again.

> When have you felt like the prodigal son, undeserving of his father's love?
> When have you been the self-righteous brother,
> unwilling to welcome the wayfarer home?

WE RESPOND

Lent is the season to get right with God and others. Only you know the places where your heart is broken. Sometimes we need to reconcile with people who have died. It's never too late to forgive.

FIFTH SUNDAY OF LENT

FIRST READING » ISAIAH 43:16-21

This is what GOD says,
the God who builds a road right through the ocean,
who carves a path through pounding waves,
The God who summons horses and chariots and armies—
they lie down and then can't get up;
they're snuffed out like so many candles:
"Forget about what's happened;
don't keep going over old history.
Be alert, be present. I'm about to do something brand-new.
It's bursting out! Don't you see it?
There it is! I'm making a road through the desert,
rivers in the badlands.
Wild animals will say 'Thank you!'
—the coyotes and the buzzards—
Because I provided water in the desert,
rivers through the sun-baked earth,
Drinking water for the people I chose,
the people I made especially for myself,
a people custom-made to praise me."

A friend from Germany emails several times a week, asking me to correct her English. Her vocabulary is very broad; her use of American slang is excellent. But when she gets excited about an idea, all sense of "time" drops out of her letters. She reports everything in the present tense, whether it happened in the past or is expected in the future. Sometimes the results are so charming, I can scarcely bring myself to change a word of it.

In communication, distinctions in time are helpful. But in God's relationship to us, the present tense is all you need. Too often, we read the Bible as "the history of God's involvement with humanity," as if it were a closed book. The miracles, the saving acts, the rich intimacy of God's relationship with Moses or Mary sound as faraway as a fairy tale. Yet the story of salvation history is really about salvation present. The Spirit is springing forth joyous new life right now.

Forget yesterday and the day before.
Where is God at work in your life right now?

SECOND READING » PHILIPPIANS 3:8-14

All the things I once thought were so important are gone from my life. Compared to the high privilege of knowing Christ Jesus as my Master, firsthand, everything I once thought I had going for me is insignificant—dog dung. I've dumped it all in the trash so that I could embrace Christ and be embraced by him. I didn't want some petty, inferior brand of righteousness that comes from keeping a list of rules when I could get the robust kind that comes from trusting Christ—God's righteousness.

I gave up all that inferior stuff so I could know Christ personally, experience his resurrection power, be a partner in his suffering, and go all the way with him to death itself. If there was any way to get in on the resurrection from the dead, I wanted to do it.

I'm not saying that I have this all together, that I have it made. But I am well on my way, reaching out for Christ, who has so wondrously reached out for me. Friends, don't get me wrong: By no means do I count myself an expert in all of this, but I've got my eye on the goal, where God is beckoning us onward—to Jesus. I'm off and running, and I'm not turning back.

Have you ever heard the football homily-opener in your parish? It's the one where the preacher talks about the recent game ("How 'bout them Raiders?") before talking about the gospel, in order to grab the fragile attention of the assembly. Sports metaphors also abound in the preaching event itself. Sometimes if you go the whole nine yards with it, you can drop-kick your people just where you want them.

Evidently this is an ancient tradition, because Saint Paul does it more than a few times in his letters. Here he talks about the "high privilege," which sports fans in the Empire would have recognized as a reference to the way a winner was called by name to ascend the steps to receive his crown of victory. During the race, the athlete focuses ahead to the sweet dream of being called by name to the roar of the crowds. To be distracted by past mistakes would be to risk momentum and slow down. Meanwhile Jesus is waiting, calling us by name.

> **In what ways do past failures discourage you?**
> **How is Jesus calling you beyond the past and into the future?**

GOSPEL » JOHN 8:1-11

Jesus went across to Mount Olives, but he was soon back in the Temple again. Swarms of people came to him. He sat down and taught them.

The religion scholars and Pharisees led in a woman who had been caught in an act of adultery. They stood her in plain sight of everyone and said, "Teacher, this woman was caught red-handed in the act of adultery. Moses, in the Law, gives orders to stone such persons. What do you say?" They were trying to trap him into saying something incriminating so they could bring charges against him.

Jesus bent down and wrote with his finger in the dirt. They kept at him, badgering him. He straightened up and said, "The sinless one among you, go first: Throw the stone." Bending down again, he wrote some more in the dirt.

Hearing that, they walked away, one after another, beginning with the oldest. The woman was left alone. Jesus stood up and spoke to her. "Woman, where are they? Does no one condemn you?"

"No one, Master."

"Neither do I," said Jesus. "Go on your way. From now on, don't sin."

Wherever we may be, Jesus is always calling us higher. It's not enough for us to know right from wrong, as the scribes and the Pharisees certainly do in the story of the adulterous woman. We also need to know the correct response to right and wrong, which the self-righteous ones in this story failed to consider. The elders know the commandments; they know the law of Moses. But they seem to know only one thing about "this woman," and even less about their own sinfulness.

Jesus sets them straight by pointing the finger away from the woman and back at her accusers. Her sin is never contested, proven or disproven. It's simply put in perspective. Whenever we're tempted to judge another person, it's a clear sign that it's time to look into our own hearts. And to hope no one starts throwing stones in our direction!

> **Think of a person in your acquaintance or in the media whom you've judged harshly. What does your condemnation of that person teach you about the state of your own heart?**

WE RESPOND

Take some time to do a thorough examination of conscience. Make a list of things you want to change about yourself. Spend time in prayer, thanking God for call to go higher.

I didn't want some petty, inferior brand of righteousness that comes from keeping a list of rules when I could get the robust kind that comes from trusting Christ—God's righteousness.

THIS TRANSFORMING WORD

HOLY WEEK AND THE TRIDUUM

PALM SUNDAY OF THE LORD'S PASSION

....The Hour of Darkness

FIRST READING » ISAIAH 50:4-7

The Master, GOD, has given me
a well-taught tongue,
So I know how to encourage tired people.
He wakes me up in the morning,
Wakes me up, opens my ears
to listen as one ready to take orders.
The Master, GOD, opened my ears,
and I didn't go back to sleep,
didn't pull the covers back over my head.
I followed orders,
stood there and took it while they beat me,
held steady while they pulled out my beard,
Didn't dodge their insults,
faced them as they spit in my face.
And the Master, GOD, stays right there and helps me,
so I'm not disgraced.
Therefore I set my face like flint,
confident that I'll never regret this.

Sometimes it may appear as if we're living a charmed life. Our families are close, our friendships warm, our careers stimulating, our finances secure. Everyone is healthy, and we seem to move from delight to delight. I remember thinking once, during one of these gracious seasons, that life was almost too good, and maybe I should look around for a new challenge. Then, needless to say, the bottom dropped out of the situation, and challenge found me instead.

When the hour of darkness arrives, it can seem as if God won't return your calls. Popular superstition claims bad things happen in threes. That may be a conservative estimate. "Deep calls upon deep," the Scripture says, and often a single death seems to lead to a season of funerals, or one tragedy to a field of them. The rhythm of life goes offbeat for a long season. As the darkness descends, Isaiah's servant remains faithful, remembering the beauty of the light.

> **When have you encountered an hour of darkness?**
> **Who or what helped you hold on to the promise of the light?**

SECOND READING » PHILIPPIANS 2:6-11

Jesus had equal status with God but didn't think so much of himself that he had to cling to the advantages of that status no matter what. Not at all. When the time came, he set aside the privileges of deity and took on the status of a slave, became human! *Having become human, he stayed human. It was an incredibly humbling process. He didn't claim special privileges. Instead, he lived a selfless, obedient life and then died a selfless, obedient death—and the worst kind of death at that: a crucifixion.*

Because of that obedience, God lifted him high and honored him far beyond anyone or anything, ever, so that all created beings in heaven and on earth— even those long ago dead and buried—will bow in worship before this Jesus Christ, and call out in praise that he is the Master of all, to the glorious honor of God the Father.

Palm Sunday generates such mixed emotions in the believer's heart. On the one hand, Jesus is honored with great procession and song. We wave palm branches and celebrate with glad hosannas. His arrival into Jerusalem is a huge success, and the tide seems to be moving in his favor. This is, of course, five days before they kill him. Our reading of the Passion account conveys this mixture of triumph and tragedy all at once, the confusion of humanity's response to the one before whom every knee should bend. Do we follow him? Honor him? Betray him? Eradicate him? Our mood and commitment waver. Jesus never could count on his followers for the long haul. Yet God allows it all, allows Jesus to be brought low for a time, while exaltation is waiting in the wings. Our response may be in doubt, but the divine movement is always toward glory.

> On this Palm Sunday, where do you find yourself in the crowd:
> a follower, a worshipper, a schemer, or a deserter?
> What will you say to Jesus when he passes
> the place where you stand?

GOSPEL » LUKE 22:14 – 23:56

When it was time, he sat down, all the apostles with him, and said, "You've no idea how much I have looked forward to eating this Passover meal with you before I enter my time of suffering. It's the last one I'll eat until we all eat it together in the kingdom of God."

Taking the cup, he blessed it, then said, "Take this and pass it among you. As for me, I'll not drink wine again until the kingdom of God arrives."

Taking bread, he blessed it, broke it, and gave it to them, saying, "This is my body, given for you. Eat it in my memory."

He did the same with the cup after supper, saying, "This cup is the new covenant written in my blood, blood poured out for you.

"Do you realize that the hand of the one who is betraying me is at this

moment on this table? It's true that the Son of Man is going down a path already marked out—no surprises there. But for the one who turns him in, turns traitor to the Son of Man, this is doomsday."

They immediately became suspicious of each other and began quizzing one another, wondering who might be about to do this.

Within minutes they were bickering over who of them would end up the greatest. But Jesus intervened: "Kings like to throw their weight around and people in authority like to give themselves fancy titles. It's not going to be that way with you. Let the senior among you become like the junior; let the leader act the part of the servant.

"Who would you rather be: the one who eats the dinner or the one who serves the dinner? You'd rather eat and be served, right? But I've taken my place among you as the one who serves. And you've stuck with me through thick and thin. Now I confer on you the royal authority my Father conferred on me so you can eat and drink at my table in my kingdom and be strengthened as you take up responsibilities among the congregations of God's people.

"Simon, stay on your toes. Satan has tried his best to separate all of you from me, like chaff from wheat. Simon, I've prayed for you in particular that you not give in or give out. When you have come through the time of testing, turn to your companions and give them a fresh start."

Peter said, "Master, I'm ready for anything with you. I'd go to jail for you. I'd die for you!"

Jesus said, "I'm sorry to have to tell you this, Peter, but before the rooster crows you will have three times denied that you know me."

Then Jesus said, "When I sent you out and told you to travel light, to take only the bare necessities, did you get along all right?"

"Certainly," they said, "we got along just fine."

He said, "This is different. Get ready for trouble. Look to what you'll need; there are difficult times ahead. Pawn your coat and get a sword. What was written in Scripture, 'He was lumped in with the criminals,' gets its final meaning in me. Everything written about me is now coming to a conclusion."

They said, "Look, Master, two swords!"

But he said, "Enough of that; no more sword talk!"

Leaving there, he went, as he so often did, to Mount Olives. The disciples followed him. When they arrived at the place, he said, "Pray that you don't give in to temptation."

He pulled away from them about a stone's throw, knelt down, and prayed, "Father, remove this cup from me. But please, not what I want. What do you want?" At once an angel from heaven was at his side, strengthening him. He prayed on all the harder. Sweat, wrung from him like drops of blood, poured off his face.

He got up from prayer, went back to the disciples and found them asleep, drugged by grief. He said, "What business do you have sleeping? Get up. Pray so you won't give in to temptation."

No sooner were the words out of his mouth than a crowd showed up, Judas, the one from the Twelve, in the lead. He came right up to Jesus to kiss him. Jesus said, "Judas, you would betray the Son of Man with a kiss?"

When those with him saw what was happening, they said, "Master, shall we fight?" One of them took a swing at the Chief Priest's servant and cut off his right ear.

Jesus said, "Let them be. Even in this." Then, touching the servant's ear, he healed him.

Jesus spoke to those who had come—high priests, Temple police, religion leaders: "What is this, jumping me with swords and clubs as if I were a dangerous criminal? Day after day I've been with you in the Temple and you've not so much as lifted a hand against me. But do it your way—it's a dark night, a dark hour."

Arresting Jesus, they marched him off and took him into the house of the Chief Priest. Peter followed, but at a safe distance. In the middle of the courtyard some people had started a fire and were sitting around it, trying to keep warm. One of the serving maids sitting at the fire noticed him, then took a second look and said, "This man was with him!"

He denied it, "Woman, I don't even know him."

A short time later, someone else noticed him and said, "You're one of them." But Peter denied it: "Man, I am not."

About an hour later, someone else spoke up, really adamant: "He's got to have been with him! He's got 'Galilean' written all over him."

Peter said, "Man, I don't know what you're talking about." At that very moment, the last word hardly off his lips, a rooster crowed. Just then, the Master turned and looked at Peter. Peter remembered what the Master had said to him: "Before the rooster crows, you will deny me three times." He went out and cried and cried and cried.

The men in charge of Jesus began poking fun at him, slapping him around. They put a blindfold on him and taunted, "Who hit you that time?" They were having a grand time with him.

When it was morning, the religious leaders of the people and the high priests and scholars all got together and brought him before their High Council. They said, "Are you the Messiah?"

He answered, "If I said yes, you wouldn't believe me. If I asked what you meant by your question, you wouldn't answer me. So here's what I have to say: From here on the Son of Man takes his place at God's right hand, the place of power."

They all said, "So you admit your claim to be the Son of God?"

"You're the ones who keep saying it," he said.

But they had made up their minds, "Why do we need any more evidence? We've all heard him as good as say it himself."

Then they all took Jesus to Pilate and began to bring up charges against him. They said, "We found this man undermining our law and order, forbidding taxes to be paid to Caesar, setting himself up as Messiah-King."

Pilate asked him, "Is this true that you're 'King of the Jews'?"

"Those are your words, not mine," Jesus replied.

Pilate told the high priests and the accompanying crowd, "I find nothing wrong here. He seems harmless enough to me."

But they were vehement. "He's stirring up unrest among the people with his teaching, disturbing the peace everywhere, starting in Galilee and now all through Judea. He's a dangerous man, endangering the peace."

When Pilate heard that, he asked, "So, he's a Galilean?" Realizing that he properly came under Herod's jurisdiction, he passed the buck to Herod, who just happened to be in Jerusalem for a few days.

Herod was delighted when Jesus showed up. He had wanted for a long time to see him, he'd heard so much about him. He hoped to see him do something spectacular. He peppered him with questions. Jesus didn't answer—not one word. But the high priests and religion scholars were right there, saying their piece, strident and shrill in their accusations.

Mightily offended, Herod turned on Jesus. His soldiers joined in, taunting and jeering. Then they dressed him up in an elaborate king costume and sent him back to Pilate. That day Herod and Pilate became thick as thieves. Always before they had kept their distance.

Then Pilate called in the high priests, rulers, and the others and said, "You brought this man to me as a disturber of the peace. I examined him in front of all of you and found there was nothing to your charge. And neither did Herod, for he has sent him back here with a clean bill of health. It's clear that he's done nothing wrong, let alone anything deserving death. I'm going to warn him to watch his step and let him go."

At that, the crowd went wild: "Kill him! Give us Barabbas!" (Barabbas had been thrown in prison for starting a riot in the city and for murder.) Pilate still wanted to let Jesus go, and so spoke out again.

But they kept shouting back, "Crucify! Crucify him!"

He tried a third time. "But for what crime? I've found nothing in him deserving death. I'm going to warn him to watch his step and let him go."

But they kept at it, a shouting mob, demanding that he be crucified. And finally they shouted him down. Pilate caved in and gave them what they wanted. He released the man thrown in prison for rioting and murder, and gave them Jesus to do whatever they wanted.

As they led him off, they made Simon, a man from Cyrene who happened to be coming in from the countryside, carry the cross behind Jesus. A huge crowd of *people followed, along with women weeping and carrying on. At one point Jesus turned to the women and said, "Daughters of Jerusalem, don't cry for me. Cry for yourselves and for your children. The time is coming when they'll say, 'Lucky the women who never conceived! Lucky the wombs that never gave birth! Lucky the breasts that never gave milk!' Then they'll start calling to the mountains, 'Fall down on us!' calling to the hills, 'Cover us up!' If people do these things to a live, green tree, can you imagine what they'll do with deadwood?"*

Two others, both criminals, were taken along with him for execution.

When they got to the place called Skull Hill, they crucified him, along with the criminals, one on his right, the other on his left.

Jesus prayed, "Father, forgive them; they don't know what they're doing."

Dividing up his clothes, they threw dice for them. The people stood there staring at Jesus, and the ringleaders made faces, taunting, "He saved others. Let's see him save himself! The Messiah of God—ha! The Chosen—ha!"

The soldiers also came up and poked fun at him, making a game of it. They toasted him with sour wine: "So you're King of the Jews! Save yourself!"

Printed over him was a sign: THIS IS THE KING OF THE JEWS.

One of the criminals hanging alongside cursed him: "Some Messiah you are! Save yourself! Save us!"

But the other one made him shut up: "Have you no fear of God? You're getting the same as him. We deserve this, but not him—he did nothing to deserve this."

Then he said, "Jesus, remember me when you enter your kingdom."

He said, "Don't worry, I will. Today you will join me in paradise."

By now it was noon. The whole earth became dark, the darkness lasting three hours—a total blackout. The Temple curtain split right down the middle. Jesus called loudly, "Father, I place my life in your hands!" Then he breathed his last.

When the captain there saw what happened, he honored God: "This man was innocent! A good man, and innocent!"

All who had come around as spectators to watch the show, when they saw what actually happened, were overcome with grief and headed home. Those who knew Jesus well, along with the women who had followed him from Galilee, stood at a respectful distance and kept vigil.

There was a man by the name of Joseph, a member of the Jewish High Council, a man of good heart and good character. He had not gone along with the plans and actions of the council. His hometown was the Jewish village of Arimathea. He lived in alert expectation of the kingdom of God. He went to Pilate and asked for the body of Jesus. Taking him down, he wrapped him in a linen shroud and placed him in a tomb chiseled into the rock, a tomb never yet used. It was the day before Sabbath, the Sabbath just about to begin.

The women who had been companions of Jesus from Galilee followed along. They saw the tomb where Jesus' body was placed. Then they went back to prepare burial spices and perfumes. They rested quietly on the Sabbath, as commanded.

Darkness descends on Jesus in the garden, not the tranquil dark of night but the starless gloom of sin. He spoke of it often as he healed those who were physically blind, or saw the impenetrable blindness of those who were morally shuttered. Jesus came to bring light, and called his followers to be that light for the world. But there are always those who would dash out the light to keep it from illuminating their own moral failures.

Darkness is a comfortable place for sin to dwell, far from exposure to self-examination and reflection. We can't repent the sin we don't see in ourselves. Those aspects of our personalities that are closed and "off limits" for inspection are the very places upon which we most need to shine the light of our faith. The monsters in the dark are the scariest ones. The only thing they fear is the coming of the day.

> **About which negative aspect of your personality or behavior are you most likely to say, "That's just how I am"? How might an encounter with Jesus challenge that assumption?**

WE RESPOND

Prepare your heart for Holy Week. Take a few minutes each day to sit in silence before the cross. Invite Jesus to illuminate the corners of your life where you're most afraid to go. Ask him to heal your blindness, and to bring you to the light of Easter.

The whole earth became dark,
the darkness lasting three hours—a total blackout.
The Temple curtain split right down the middle.
Jesus called loudly, "Father, I place my life in your
hands!" Then he breathed his last.

HOLY THURSDAY

FIRST READING » EXODUS 12:1-8, 11-14

God said to Moses and Aaron while still in Egypt, "This month is to be the first month of the year for you. Address the whole community of Israel; tell them that on the tenth of this month each man is to take a lamb for his family, one lamb to a house. If the family is too small for a lamb, then share it with a close neighbor, depending on the number of persons involved. Be mindful of how much each person will eat. Your lamb must be a healthy male, one year old; you can select it from either the sheep or the goats. Keep it penned until the fourteenth day of this month and then slaughter it—the entire community of Israel will do this—at dusk. Then take some of the blood and smear it on the two doorposts and the lintel of the houses in which you will eat it. You are to eat the meat, roasted in the fire, that night, along with bread, made without yeast, and bitter herbs.

"And here is how you are to eat it: Be fully dressed with your sandals on and your stick in your hand. Eat in a hurry; it's the Passover to God.

"I will go through the land of Egypt on this night and strike down every firstborn in the land of Egypt, whether human or animal, and bring judgment on all the gods of Egypt. I am God. The blood will serve as a sign on the houses where you live. When I see the blood I will pass over you—no disaster will touch you when I strike the land of Egypt.

"This will be a memorial day for you; you will celebrate it as a festival to God down through the generations, a fixed festival celebration to be observed always."

Meals celebrate life. And some, like the original Passover and the Last Supper, keep death in view as well. This may seem contradictory: the very act of eating nourishes our bodies and ensures that we will continue. At the same time, most funerals are followed by a reception where survivors gather to share a meal at which stories are told, memories relived, and hope renewed. The house of mourning continues to be a place where neighbors and friends bring food. Loved ones often gather on the anniversary of a death to remember the one who's gone at a restaurant he or she once favored.

Today it's impossible for me to eat polenta without remembering my father: it was his favorite food. Or to make herb spaghetti without recalling my friend Dale who taught me how to prepare it. A naval orange brings my grandmother's face to mind: she handed them around like candy. Food helps us to remember the past as much as it restores and sustains us for the future.

> **Which food traditions help you to recall the past,**
> **even as they sustain you for the future?**

SECOND READING » 1 CORINTHIANS 11:23-26

Let me go over with you again exactly what goes on in the Lord's Supper and why it is so centrally important. I received my instructions from the Master himself and passed them on to you. The Master, Jesus, on the night of his betrayal, took bread. Having given thanks, he broke it and said,

> *This is my body, broken for you.*
> *Do this to remember me.*

After supper, he did the same thing with the cup:

> *This cup is my blood, my new covenant with you.*
> *Each time you drink this cup, remember me.*

What you must solemnly realize is that every time you eat this bread and every time you drink this cup, you reenact in your words and actions the death of the Master.

I have a fifty-seven-year-old friend who has learned to cook just this year. Hard as it is to believe, she's spent her entire adult life eating out. Quite a few of those meals have been at my house. Living alone in apartments with marginal kitchens, my friend never found the incentive to invest time and money into pots and pans, cookbooks and meal design.

Until now. Her sister's become ill and my friend is now a caregiver. After ordering out for several seasons, the two of them decided a change in diet was in order. My friend took the plunge into a cooking class, and is now creating meals worth inviting people over to share. When she talks about preparing food these days, it's as if she invented the idea. Her enthusiasm knows no bounds when she exclaims: "I feed people!"—a role in every family that often goes uncelebrated. But how wonderful it is, really, to feed people.

Every meal is a celebration of life. This concept may be harder to grasp while reaching for a cheeseburger served in a greasy bag. Eating affirms the life we're living right now.

> **How often do you eat alone, and how many meals do you share?**
> **Who eats with you? What does a shared meal imply?**

GOSPEL » JOHN 13:1-15

Just before the Passover Feast, Jesus knew that the time had come to leave this world to go to the Father. Having loved his dear companions, he continued to love them right to the end. It was suppertime. The Devil by now had Judas, son of Simon the Iscariot, firmly in his grip, all set for the betrayal.

Jesus knew that the Father had put him in complete charge of everything, that he came from God and was on his way back to God. So he got up from the supper table, set aside his robe, and put on an apron. Then he poured water into a basin and began to wash the feet of the disciples, drying them with his apron.

When he got to Simon Peter, Peter said, "Master, you wash my feet?"

Jesus answered, "You don't understand now what I'm doing, but it will be clear enough to you later."

Peter persisted, "You're not going to wash my feet—ever!"

Jesus said, "If I don't wash you, you can't be part of what I'm doing."

"Master!" said Peter. "Not only my feet, then. Wash my hands! Wash my head!"

Jesus said, "If you've had a bath in the morning, you only need your feet washed now and you're clean from head to toe. My concern, you understand, is holiness, not hygiene. So now you're clean. But not every one of you." (He knew who was betraying him. That's why he said, "Not every one of you.") After he had finished washing their feet, he took his robe, put it back on, and went back to his place at the table.

Then he said, "Do you understand what I have done to you? You address me as 'Teacher' and 'Master,' and rightly so. That is what I am. So if I, the Master and Teacher, washed your feet, you must now wash each other's feet. I've laid down a pattern for you. What I've done, you do."

Where there is food, there can be food fights. This one between Jesus and Peter started before the meal was on the table. Some people need to be in charge, even if it means being in charge of *serving*. One can be a control freak on both sides of the equation. Peter always had an agenda and found it tough to surrender his perspective on how things should be when the game shifted before his eyes. Remember how upset he was when Jesus started talking about passion and death? Jesus had to call him "Satan" to get Peter to calm down.

Consider what happens when parishes try to drum up twelve people to have their feet washed on Holy Thursday. Suddenly everyone invited to participate becomes Peter, convinced this is an honor they don't deserve. Jesus demonstrates that genuine humility means not identifying with a prescribed role. He assumes leadership as a teacher and healer, and is equally content to lay it down and be servant of all. Leaders who serve, servants unafraid of asserting leadership: that's the formula for church.

It's usually easy to sniff out false humility in other people.
Do you recognize it in yourself?
Are you fluid in moving among the roles you're asked to perform?

WE RESPOND

Celebrate life by feeding people: in your kitchen, from your wallet, or at a local food pantry. Allow room for death: in embracing service roles that may be uncomfortable or foreign or a bit scary.

GOOD FRIDAY

FIRST READING » ISAIAH 52:13 – 53:12

"Just watch my servant blossom!
    Exalted, tall, head and shoulders above the crowd!
But he didn't begin that way.
    At first everyone was appalled.
He didn't even look human—
    a ruined face, disfigured past recognition.
Nations all over the world will be in awe, taken aback,
    kings shocked into silence when they see him.
For what was unheard of they'll see with their own eyes,
    what was unthinkable they'll have right before them."

Who believes what we've heard and seen?
    Who would have thought GOD's saving power would look like this?

The servant grew up before God—a scrawny seedling,
    a scrubby plant in a parched field.
There was nothing attractive about him,
    nothing to cause us to take a second look.
He was looked down on and passed over,
    a man who suffered, who knew pain firsthand.
One look at him and people turned away.
    We looked down on him, thought he was scum.
But the fact is, it was our *pains he carried—*
    our disfigurements, all the things wrong with us.
We thought he brought it on himself,
    that God was punishing him for his own failures.
But it was our sins that did that to him,
    that ripped and tore and crushed him—our sins!
He took the punishment, and that made us whole.
    Through his bruises we get healed.
We're all like sheep who've wandered off and gotten lost.
    We've all done our own thing, gone our own way.
And GOD has piled all our sins, everything we've done wrong,
    on him, on him.

He was beaten, he was tortured,
    but he didn't say a word.
Like a lamb taken to be slaughtered
    and like a sheep being sheared,

he took it all in silence.
Justice miscarried, and he was led off—
  and did anyone really know what was happening?
He died without a thought for his own welfare,
  beaten bloody for the sins of my people.
They buried him with the wicked,
  threw him in a grave with a rich man,
Even though he'd never hurt a soul
  or said one word that wasn't true.

Still, it's what GOD had in mind all along,
  to crush him with pain.
The plan was that he give himself as an offering for sin
  so that he'd see life come from it—life, life, and more life.
  And GOD's plan will deeply prosper through him.

Out of that terrible travail of soul,
  he'll see that it's worth it and be glad he did it.
Through what he experienced, my righteous one, my servant,
  will make many "righteous ones,"
  as he himself carries the burden of their sins.
Therefore I'll reward him extravagantly—
  the best of everything, the highest honors—
Because he looked death in the face and didn't flinch,
  because he embraced the company of the lowest.
He took on his own shoulders the sin of the many,
  he took up the cause of all the black sheep.

Of all the times you want to pray for a great lector at the ambo, Good Friday is among those days. This passage about the Suffering Servant in Isaiah is part poetry, part enthralling drama, and all of it deeply moving. The lector must communicate the sound of a broken heart, a tortured body, a humiliated spirit. And that same reader has to be capable of restoring hope in the final lines, lifting up the assembly in tones that are strong and solemn and sure.

Because the plan is "life, life, and more life," as *The Message* nimbly puts it. The Servant's subjection is only for this mortal moment. Glory is the next and final and eternal stage of the plan. We get the sense that Isaiah isn't talking about some future mythical figure in abstract terms, one willing to go all the way for justice. The prophet himself was a suffering faithful servant of God, often humiliated and heartbroken while he carried God's word to people hostile to accepting it. Jesus, a keen reader of Isaiah's scroll, looked into this passage as into a mirror, and saw his own reflection.

Which images in this passage move you the most?
Does real-life injustice make you sad, angry, determined, or helpless?

SECOND READING » HEBREWS 4:14-16; 5:7-9

Now that we know what we have—Jesus, this great High Priest with ready access to God—let's not let it slip through our fingers. We don't have a priest who is out of touch with our reality. He's been through weakness and testing, experienced it all—all but the sin. So let's walk right up to him and get what he is so ready to give. Take the mercy, accept the help.

While he lived on earth, anticipating death, Jesus cried out in pain and wept in sorrow as he offered up priestly prayers to God. Because he honored God, God answered him. Though he was God's Son, he learned trusting-obedience by what he suffered, just as we do. Then, having arrived at the full stature of his maturity and having been announced by God as high priest in the order of Melchizedek, he became the source of eternal salvation to all who believingly obey him.

I want to know this Jesus. I hope you do too. The writer of the Letter to the Hebrews—who may be Paul's companion Barnabas, although no one knows for sure—understands Jesus as the greatest High Priest of all time. Jesus is a priest who "gets" it! He doesn't dispense advice from a sterile pulpit high about our concerns and dilemmas. Jesus is the kind of priest who "smells like the sheep," in Pope Francis' gritty phrase. He's sat at our table, and he's washed our feet. He had his own tired feet rubbed clean with a grateful woman's hair. He's not an untouchable fearless leader, but a man who cried and felt anguish at the thought of dying. And then dried his tears and did it.

No one needs a leader who floats above the very injustices he or she claims to be intent on correcting. Sin and suffering and death are the wounds of this world, and Jesus bears them all with us. There's nothing like a leader who not only knows where he's going, but also knows where we've been. Follow that guy!

> **Consider leaders you've had—in the family, on the job, in parish life, in government—whom you were glad to follow. What qualities made them inspiring?**

GOSPEL » JOHN 18:1 - 19:42

Jesus, having prayed this prayer, left with his disciples and crossed over the brook Kidron at a place where there was a garden. He and his disciples entered it.

Judas, his betrayer, knew the place because Jesus and his disciples went there often. So Judas led the way to the garden, and the Roman soldiers and police sent by the high priests and Pharisees followed. They arrived there with lanterns and torches and swords. Jesus, knowing by now everything that was coming down on him, went out and met them. He said, "Who are you after?"

They answered, "Jesus the Nazarene."

He said, "That's me." The soldiers recoiled, totally taken aback. Judas, his betrayer, stood out like a sore thumb.

Jesus asked again, "Who are you after?"

They answered, "Jesus the Nazarene."

"I told you," said Jesus, "that's me. I'm the one. So if it's me you're after, let these others go." (This validated the words in his prayer, "I didn't lose one of those you gave.")

Just then Simon Peter, who was carrying a sword, pulled it from its sheath and struck the Chief Priest's servant, cutting off his right ear. Malchus was the servant's name.

Jesus ordered Peter, "Put back your sword. Do you think for a minute I'm not going to drink this cup the Father gave me?"

Then the Roman soldiers under their commander, joined by the Jewish police, seized Jesus and tied him up. They took him first to Annas, father-in-law of Caiaphas. Caiaphas was the Chief Priest that year. It was Caiaphas who had advised the Jews that it was to their advantage that one man die for the people.

Simon Peter and another disciple followed Jesus. That other disciple was known to the Chief Priest, and so he went in with Jesus to the Chief Priest's courtyard. Peter had to stay outside. Then the other disciple went out, spoke to the doorkeeper, and got Peter in.

The young woman who was the doorkeeper said to Peter, "Aren't you one of this man's disciples?"

He said, "No, I'm not."

The servants and police had made a fire because of the cold and were huddled there warming themselves. Peter stood with them, trying to get warm.

Annas interrogated Jesus regarding his disciples and his teaching. Jesus answered, "I've spoken openly in public. I've taught regularly in meeting places and the Temple, where the Jews all come together. Everything has been out in the open. I've said nothing in secret. So why are you treating me like a conspirator? Question those who have been listening to me. They know well what I have said. My teachings have all been aboveboard."

When he said this, one of the policemen standing there slapped Jesus across the face, saying, "How dare you speak to the Chief Priest like that!"

Jesus replied, "If I've said something wrong, prove it. But if I've spoken the plain truth, why this slapping around?"

Then Annas sent him, still tied up, to the Chief Priest Caiaphas.

Meanwhile, Simon Peter was back at the fire, still trying to get warm. The others there said to him, "Aren't you one of his disciples?"

He denied it, "Not me."

One of the Chief Priest's servants, a relative of the man whose ear Peter had cut off, said, "Didn't I see you in the garden with him?"

Again, Peter denied it. Just then a rooster crowed.

They led Jesus then from Caiaphas to the Roman governor's palace. It was early morning. They themselves didn't enter the palace because they didn't want to be disqualified from eating the Passover. So Pilate came out to them and spoke. "What charge do you bring against this man?"

They said, "If he hadn't been doing something evil, do you think we'd be here bothering you?"

Pilate said, "You take him. Judge him by your law."

The Jews said, "We're not allowed to kill anyone." (This would confirm Jesus' word indicating the way he would die.)

Pilate went back into the palace and called for Jesus. He said, "Are you the 'King of the Jews'?"

Jesus answered, "Are you saying this on your own, or did others tell you this about me?"

Pilate said, "Do I look like a Jew? Your people and your high priests turned you over to me. What did you do?"

"My kingdom," said Jesus, "doesn't consist of what you see around you. If it did, my followers would fight so that I wouldn't be handed over to the Jews. But I'm not that kind of king, not the world's kind of king."

Then Pilate said, "So, are you a king or not?"

Jesus answered, "You tell me. Because I am King, I was born and entered the world so that I could witness to the truth. Everyone who cares for truth, who has any feeling for the truth, recognizes my voice."

Pilate said, "What is truth?"

Then he went back out to the Jews and told them, "I find nothing wrong in this man. It's your custom that I pardon one prisoner at Passover. Do you want me to pardon the 'King of the Jews'?"

They shouted back, "Not this one, but Barabbas!" Barabbas was a Jewish freedom fighter.

So Pilate took Jesus and had him whipped. The soldiers, having braided a crown from thorns, set it on his head, threw a purple robe over him, and approached him with, "Hail, King of the Jews!" Then they greeted him with slaps in the face.

Pilate went back out again and said to them, "I present him to you, but I want you to know that I do not find him guilty of any crime." Just then Jesus came out wearing the thorn crown and purple robe.

Pilate announced, "Here he is: the Man."

When the high priests and police saw him, they shouted in a frenzy, "Crucify! Crucify!"

Pilate told them, "You take him. You crucify him. I find nothing wrong with him."

The Jews answered, "We have a law, and by that law he must die because he claimed to be the Son of God."

When Pilate heard this, he became even more scared. He went back into the palace and said to Jesus, "Where did you come from?"

Jesus gave no answer.

Pilate said, "You won't talk? Don't you know that I have the authority to pardon you, and the authority to—crucify you?"

Jesus said, "You haven't a shred of authority over me except what has been given you from heaven. That's why the one who betrayed me to you has committed a far greater fault."

At this, Pilate tried his best to pardon him, but the Jews shouted him down: "If you pardon this man, you're no friend of Caesar's. Anyone setting himself up as 'king' defies Caesar."

When Pilate heard those words, he led Jesus outside. He sat down at the judgment seat in the area designated Stone Court (in Hebrew, Gabbatha). It was the preparation day for Passover. The hour was noon. Pilate said to the Jews, "Here is your king."

They shouted back, "Kill him! Kill him! Crucify him!"

Pilate said, "I am to crucify your king?"

The high priests answered, "We have no king except Caesar."

Pilate caved in to their demand. He turned him over to be crucified.

They took Jesus away. Carrying his cross, Jesus went out to the place called Skull Hill (the name in Hebrew is Golgotha), where they crucified him, and with him two others, one on each side, Jesus in the middle. Pilate wrote a sign and had it placed on the cross. It read:

JESUS THE NAZARENE
THE KING OF THE JEWS

Many of the Jews read the sign because the place where Jesus was crucified was right next to the city. It was written in Hebrew, Latin, and Greek. The Jewish high priests objected. "Don't write," they said to Pilate, "'The King of the Jews.' Make it, 'This man said, "I am the King of the Jews.""

Pilate said, "What I've written, I've written."

When they crucified him, the Roman soldiers took his clothes and divided them up four ways, to each soldier a fourth. But his robe was seamless, a single piece of weaving, so they said to each other, "Let's not tear it up. Let's throw dice to see who gets it." This confirmed the Scripture that said, "They divided up my clothes among them and threw dice for my coat." (The soldiers validated the Scriptures!)

While the soldiers were looking after themselves, Jesus' mother, his aunt, Mary the wife of Clopas, and Mary Magdalene stood at the foot of the cross. Jesus saw his mother and the disciple he loved standing near her. He said to his mother, "Woman, here is your son." Then to the disciple, "Here is your mother." From that moment the disciple accepted her as his own mother.

Jesus, seeing that everything had been completed so that the Scripture record might also be complete, then said, "I'm thirsty."

A jug of sour wine was standing by. Someone put a sponge soaked with the wine on a javelin and lifted it to his mouth. After he took the wine, Jesus said, "It's done…complete." Bowing his head, he offered up his spirit.

Then the Jews, since it was the day of Sabbath preparation, and so the bodies wouldn't stay on the crosses over the Sabbath (it was a high holy day that year), petitioned Pilate that their legs be broken to speed death, and the bodies taken down. So the soldiers came and broke the legs of the first man crucified with Jesus, and then the other. When they got to Jesus, they saw that he was already dead, so they didn't break his legs. One of the soldiers stabbed him in the side with his spear. Blood and water gushed out.

The eyewitness to these things has presented an accurate report. He saw it himself and is telling the truth so that you, also, will believe.

These things that happened confirmed the Scripture, "Not a bone in his body was broken," and the other Scripture that reads, "They will stare at the one they pierced."

After all this, Joseph of Arimathea (he was a disciple of Jesus, but secretly, because he was intimidated by the Jews) petitioned Pilate to take the body of Jesus. Pilate gave permission. So Joseph came and took the body.

Nicodemus, who had first come to Jesus at night, came now in broad daylight carrying a mixture of myrrh and aloes, about seventy-five pounds. They took Jesus' body and, following the Jewish burial custom, wrapped it in linen with the spices. There was a garden near the place he was crucified, and in the garden a new tomb in which no one had yet been placed. So, because it was Sabbath preparation for the Jews and the tomb was convenient, they placed Jesus in it.

Last year during Holy Week I was in a classroom reviewing the passion story with some junior high students. I pointed out to them that when we went into church for the service, we'd be participating in the gospel reading as the crowd. We'd play the part of those who preferred the release of Barabbas, a violent and dangerous man, to the pardon of Jesus. We'd be shouting "Kill him! Crucify him!" when asked what should be done with Jesus.

One dumbfounded boy raised his hand and asked, "Like, aren't we on the wrong side of this thing? Shouldn't we be screaming to save Jesus? He's our God after all." I was glad to assure this boy that our taking the part of the crowd did indeed put us on the wrong side of the argument, and the wrong side of salvation history. The tragic thing is we're already there. We're already the folks who seek violent solutions over just ones, and put the Savior to death every time we do so. Like this boy, I too am tired of shouting for the death of my own God. I'm working every day to get on the right side of history.

> **In how many small ways can you liberate Jesus,
> and keep Barabbas under lock and key?**

WE RESPOND

Venerate the crucifix. Kneel or bow or sit before it. Kiss or touch its surfaces, wood and flesh and blood and nails. Contemplate the world's suffering affixed to that wood with Jesus. Resolve to assist one suffering person today.

"Because I am King, I was born and entered the world so that I could witness to the truth. Everyone who cares for truth, who has any feeling for the truth, recognizes my voice."

EASTER VIGIL

FIRST READING » GENESIS 1:1 – 2:2

First this: God created the Heavens and Earth—all you see, all you don't see.
Earth was a soup of nothingness, a bottomless emptiness, an inky blackness.
God's Spirit brooded like a bird above the watery abyss.

> *God spoke: "Light!"*
> *And light appeared.*
> *God saw that light was good*
> *and separated light from dark.*
> *God named the light Day,*
> *he named the dark Night.*
> *It was evening, it was morning—*
> *Day One.*
>
> *God spoke: "Sky! In the middle of the waters;*
> *separate water from water!"*
> *God made sky.*
> *He separated the water under sky*
> *from the water above sky.*
> *And there it was:*
> *he named sky the Heavens;*
> *It was evening, it was morning—*
> *Day Two.*
>
> *God spoke: "Separate!*
> *Water-beneath-Heaven, gather into one place;*
> *Land, appear!"*
> *And there it was.*
> *God named the land Earth.*
> *He named the pooled water Ocean.*
> *God saw that it was good.*
>
> *God spoke: "Earth, green up! Grow all varieties*
> *of seed-bearing plants,*
> *Every sort of fruit-bearing tree."*
> *And there it was.*
> *Earth produced green seed-bearing plants,*
> *all varieties,*
> *And fruit-bearing trees of all sorts.*
> *God saw that it was good.*

It was evening, it was morning—
Day Three.

God spoke: "Lights! Come out!
 Shine in Heaven's sky!
Separate Day from Night.
 Mark seasons and days and years,
Lights in Heaven's sky to give light to Earth."
 And there it was.

God made two big lights, the larger
 to take charge of Day,
The smaller to be in charge of Night;
 and he made the stars.
God placed them in the heavenly sky
 to light up Earth
And oversee Day and Night,
 to separate light and dark.
God saw that it was good.
It was evening, it was morning—
Day Four.

God spoke: "Swarm, Ocean, with fish and all sea life!
 Birds, fly through the sky over Earth!"
God created the huge whales,
 all the swarm of life in the waters,
And every kind and species of flying birds.
 God saw that it was good.
God blessed them: "Prosper! Reproduce! Fill Ocean!
 Birds, reproduce on Earth!"
It was evening, it was morning—
Day Five.

God spoke: "Earth, generate life! Every sort and kind:
 cattle and reptiles and wild animals—all kinds."
And there it was:
 wild animals of every kind,
Cattle of all kinds, every sort of reptile and bug.
 God saw that it was good.

God spoke: "Let us make human beings in our image, make them
 reflecting our nature
So they can be responsible for the fish in the sea,
 the birds in the air, the cattle,
And, yes, Earth itself,

and every animal that moves on the face of Earth."
God created human beings;
he created them godlike,
Reflecting God's nature.
He created them male and female.
God blessed them:
"Prosper! Reproduce! Fill Earth! Take charge!
Be responsible for fish in the sea and birds in the air,
for every living thing that moves on the face of Earth."

Then God said, "I've given you
every sort of seed-bearing plant on Earth
And every kind of fruit-bearing tree,
given them to you for food.
To all animals and all birds,
everything that moves and breathes,
I give whatever grows out of the ground for food."
And there it was.

God looked over everything he had made;
it was so good, so very good!
It was evening, it was morning—
Day Six.

Heaven and Earth were finished,
down to the last detail.

By the seventh day
God had finished his work.
On the seventh day
he rested from all his work.
God blessed the seventh day.
He made it a Holy Day
Because on that day he rested from his work,
all the creating God had done.

**God's instructions in creation are one-word commands: "Light!" "Separate!"
"Swarm!" "Prosper!"** Nature is malleable to the divine will, meekly and instantly doing what God asks. The invention of the human changed all that. A creature with a will can always choose to say no. This isn't "good," in the Genesis catchword. Might we take a weekly one-word command from Scripture and follow it through as obediently as a cloud?

SECOND READING » GENESIS 22:1-18

After all this, God tested Abraham. God said, "Abraham!"

"Yes?" answered Abraham. "I'm listening."

He said, "Take your dear son Isaac whom you love and go to the land of Moriah. Sacrifice him there as a burnt offering on one of the mountains that I'll point out to you."

Abraham got up early in the morning and saddled his donkey. He took two of his young servants and his son Isaac. He had split wood for the burnt offering. He set out for the place God had directed him. On the third day he looked up and saw the place in the distance. Abraham told his two young servants, "Stay here with the donkey. The boy and I are going over there to worship; then we'll come back to you."

Abraham took the wood for the burnt offering and gave it to Isaac his son to carry. He carried the flint and the knife. The two of them went off together.

Isaac said to Abraham his father, "Father?"

"Yes, my son."

"We have flint and wood, but where's the sheep for the burnt offering?"

Abraham said, "Son, God will see to it that there's a sheep for the burnt offering." And they kept on walking together.

They arrived at the place to which God had directed him. Abraham built an altar. He laid out the wood. Then he tied up Isaac and laid him on the wood. Abraham reached out and took the knife to kill his son.

Just then an angel of God called to him out of Heaven, "Abraham! Abraham!"

"Yes, I'm listening."

"Don't lay a hand on that boy! Don't touch him! Now I know how fearlessly you fear God; you didn't hesitate to place your son, your dear son, on the altar for me."

Abraham looked up. He saw a ram caught by its horns in the thicket. Abraham took the ram and sacrificed it as a burnt offering instead of his son.

Abraham named that place GOD-Yireh (GOD-Sees-to-It). That's where we get the saying, "On the mountain of God, he sees to it."

The angel of God spoke from Heaven a second time to Abraham: "I swear— GOD's sure word!—because you have gone through with this, and have not refused to give me your son, your dear, dear son, I'll bless you—oh, how I'll bless you! And I'll make sure that your children flourish—like stars in the sky! like sand on the beaches! And your descendants will defeat their enemies. All nations on Earth will find themselves blessed through your descendants because you obeyed me."

Some blessings are harder to earn than others. Traditional religion says suffering is our most excellent, if demanding, teacher. By no means does that make suffering welcome, or even more bearable. But it is true: We learn as we go deeper into the realm of our humanity, and nothing is more human than to suffer. Take the blessing. And flee Moriah as fast as possible.

THIRD READING » EXODUS 14:15 – 15:1

God said to Moses: "Why cry out to me? Speak to the Israelites. Order them to get moving. Hold your staff high and stretch your hand out over the sea: Split the sea! The Israelites will walk through the sea on dry ground.

"Meanwhile I'll make sure the Egyptians keep up their stubborn chase—I'll use Pharaoh and his entire army, his chariots and horsemen, to put my Glory on display so that the Egyptians will realize that I am God."

The angel of God that had been leading the camp of Israel now shifted and got behind them. And the Pillar of Cloud that had been in front also shifted to the rear. The Cloud was now between the camp of Egypt and the camp of Israel. The Cloud enshrouded one camp in darkness and flooded the other with light. The two camps didn't come near each other all night.

Then Moses stretched out his hand over the sea and God, with a terrific east wind all night long, made the sea go back. He made the sea dry ground. The seawaters split.

The Israelites walked through the sea on dry ground with the waters a wall to the right and to the left. The Egyptians came after them in full pursuit, every horse and chariot and driver of Pharaoh racing into the middle of the sea. It was now the morning watch. God looked down from the Pillar of Fire and Cloud on the Egyptian army and threw them into a panic. He clogged the wheels of their chariots; they were stuck in the mud.

The Egyptians said, "Run from Israel! God is fighting on their side and against Egypt!"

God said to Moses, "Stretch out your hand over the sea and the waters will come back over the Egyptians, over their chariots, over their horsemen."

Moses stretched his hand out over the sea: As the day broke and the Egyptians were running, the sea returned to its place as before. God dumped the Egyptians in the middle of the sea. The waters returned, drowning the chariots and riders of Pharaoh's army that had chased after Israel into the sea. Not one of them survived.

But the Israelites walked right through the middle of the sea on dry ground, the waters forming a wall to the right and to the left. God delivered Israel that day from the oppression of the Egyptians. And Israel looked at the Egyptian dead, washed up on the shore of the sea, and realized the tremendous power that God brought against the Egyptians. The people were in reverent awe before God and trusted in God and his servant Moses.

*Then Moses and the Israelites sang this song to G*OD*, giving voice together,*

> *I'm singing my heart out to G*OD*—what a victory!*
> *He pitched horse and rider into the sea.*

Abraham was squeezed between the inscrutable sacrifice of his son and his long-practiced obedience to God. Moses faced an insurmountable sea ahead, an enemy army behind. God rescued both heroes and got them to the far side of catastrophe. But what about stories, some of which we've lived ourselves, in which the hero doesn't survive unscathed? Can we still sing out our hearts to God?

FOURTH READING » ISAIAH 54:5-14

> *"For your Maker is your bridegroom,*
> *his name, G*OD*-of-the-Angel-Armies!*
> *Your Redeemer is The Holy of Israel,*
> *known as God of the whole earth.*
> *You were like an abandoned wife, devastated with grief,*
> *and G*OD *welcomed you back,*
> *Like a woman married young*
> *and then left," says your God.*
> *Your Redeemer G*OD *says:*

> *"I left you, but only for a moment.*
> *Now, with enormous compassion, I'm bringing you back.*
> *In an outburst of anger I turned my back on you—*
> *but only for a moment.*
> *It's with lasting love*
> *that I'm tenderly caring for you.*

> *This exile is just like the days of Noah for me:*
> *I promised then that the waters of Noah*
> *would never again flood the earth.*
> *I'm promising now no more anger,*
> *no more dressing you down.*
> *For even if the mountains walk away*
> *and the hills fall to pieces,*
> *My love won't walk away from you,*
> *my covenant commitment of peace won't fall apart."*
> *The G*OD *who has compassion on you says so.*

> *"Afflicted city, storm-battered, unpitied:*
> *I'm about to rebuild you with stones of turquoise,*
> *Lay your foundations with sapphires,*
> *construct your towers with rubies,*
> *Your gates with jewels,*

and all your walls with precious stones.
All your children will have GOD for their teacher—
what a mentor for your children!
You'll be built solid, grounded in righteousness,
far from any trouble—nothing to fear!
far from terror—it won't even come close!"

Sapphires, rubies, jewels, and precious stones. Imagine constructing a city so lavish that its foundations, gates, and walls are stuffed with gems. This gleaming land has filled the religious imagination of centuries of believers. Call it Heaven, Paradise, the New Jerusalem, or Kingdom Come. But plan on calling it home!

FIFTH READING » ISAIAH 55:1-11

"Hey there! All who are thirsty,
come to the water!
Are you penniless?
Come anyway—buy and eat!
Come, buy your drinks, buy wine and milk.
Buy without money—everything's free!
Why do you spend your money on junk food
your hard-earned cash on cotton candy?
Listen to me, listen well: Eat only the best,
fill yourself with only the finest.
Pay attention, come close now,
listen carefully to my life-giving, life-nourishing words.
I'm making a lasting covenant commitment with you,
the same that I made with David: sure, solid, enduring love.
I set him up as a witness to the nations,
made him a prince and leader of the nations,
And now I'm doing it to you:
You'll summon nations you've never heard of,
and nations who've never heard of you
will come running to you
Because of me, your GOD,
because The Holy of Israel has honored you."

Seek GOD while he's here to be found,
pray to him while he's close at hand.
Let the wicked abandon their way of life
and the evil their way of thinking.
Let them come back to GOD, who is merciful,
come back to our God, who is lavish with forgiveness.

"I don't think the way you think.
  The way you work isn't the way I work."
    GOD's *Decree.*
"For as the sky soars high above earth,
  so the way I work surpasses the way you work,
  and the way I think is beyond the way you think.
Just as rain and snow descend from the skies
  and don't go back until they've watered the earth,
Doing their work of making things grow and blossom,
  producing seed for farmers and food for the hungry,
So will the words that come out of my mouth
  not come back empty-handed.
They'll do the work I sent them to do,
  they'll complete the assignment I gave them."

We who live in short spasms of time squander so much of it. God, who dwells in eternity, makes every moment matter and every word count. But God doesn't think as we do. God doesn't linger for a century over a video game saying, "I've earned this. I deserve a break this era." Even if eternity can spare the time, history can't. So what will we do with the next precious hour?

SIXTH READING » BARUCH 3:9-15, 32 – 4:4

Hear, O Israel, the commandments of life; keep your ears open, and you'll pick up some wisdom.

What's your story, O Israel? How come you find yourself in enemy territory so often?

You've grown gray hairs in a foreign land; you're as good as dead; you're written off as though you were already dwelling in the world below.

You've left behind the fountain of Lady Wisdom!

If you walked in the way of God, you'd live in peace forever.

Learn how to find prudence, fortitude, and understanding; once they are discovered, you'll know what life means, what wisdom means, what peace is.

Has anyone found where Lady Wisdom hangs out? Has anyone dipped a tentative hand into her treasury of insights?

But there's one person who truly knows where she is; he's the one who made the earth and filled it with four-footed beasts.

He turns the sun on and turns the sun off; it follows the path laid down for it; it dares not wander.

Stars twinkle and blink and seem quite happy in his company.

When he calls, they say, "We're already here," blinking and twinkling with joy at the one who made them.

This is our God; there's not another like him; he laid out the pathways to

Lady Wisdom and gave the directions to Jacob his faithful servant and Israel his beloved son.

Since then, she's been spotted regularly on earth, pausing now and then to chat with her admirers.

Lady Wisdom is an eternal book that contains the life-maps of God, which are also the Law of God. Everyone who follows the life-maps will live; those who don't will die.

Turn your life around, tribe of Jacob. Welcome Lady Wisdom while you can; let her be your lighthouse in the storm.

Don't waste your worship on some other god; don't spend your good offerings on a bad altar.

We're blessed, people of Israel, because we know what pleases God.

Lady Wisdom is handing out life-maps. What would you give to have one? Actually, you already do. The story of our faith is our life-map. We're already written into the plot. We can pretend we don't know where this plot is going, but if we've paid any attention at all, we do. We're like the stars of heaven, blinking and twinkling with the joy of knowing who we are: "We're already here!"

SEVENTH READING » EZEKIEL 36:16-17a, 18-28

GOD'S *Message came to me: "Son of man, when the people of Israel lived in their land, they polluted it by the way they lived. I poured out my anger on them because of the polluted blood they poured out on the ground. And so I got thoroughly angry with them polluting the country with their wanton murders and dirty gods. I kicked them out, exiled them to other countries. I sentenced them according to how they had lived. Wherever they went, they gave me a bad name. People said, 'These are* GOD'S *people, but they got kicked off his land.' I suffered much pain over my holy reputation, which the people of Israel blackened in every country they entered.*

"Therefore, tell Israel, 'Message of GOD, *the Master: I'm not doing this for you, Israel. I'm doing it for me, to save my character, my holy name, which you've blackened in every country where you've gone. I'm going to put my great and holy name on display, the name that has been ruined in so many countries, the name that you blackened wherever you went. Then the nations will realize who I really am, that I am* GOD, *when I show my holiness through you so that they can see it with their own eyes.*

"'For here's what I'm going to do: I'm going to take you out of these countries, gather you from all over, and bring you back to your own land. I'll pour pure water over you and scrub you clean. I'll give you a new heart, put a new spirit in you. I'll remove the stone heart from your body and replace it with a heart that's God-willed, not self-willed. I'll put my Spirit in you and make it possible for you to do what I tell you and live by my commands. You'll once again live in the land

I gave your ancestors. You'll be my people! I'll be your God!'"

Scriptures says: Once upon a time God chose a people to represent the holiness of God to the nations. But after a while, God wanted those same people off the divine résumé: Far from representing God, they were besmirching the Holy Name. Sadly, the church throughout history hasn't exactly been good for God's résumé either. Do you and I represent God's holiness, hour by hour, to a world that needs to see it?

EPISTLE » ROMANS 6:3-11

If we've left the country where sin is sovereign, how can we still live in our old house there? Or didn't you realize we packed up and left there for good? That is what happened in baptism. When we went under the water, we left the old country of sin behind; when we came up out of the water, we entered into the new country of grace—a new life in a new land!

That's what baptism into the life of Jesus means. When we are lowered into the water, it is like the burial of Jesus; when we are raised up out of the water, it is like the resurrection of Jesus. Each of us is raised into a light-filled world by our Father so that we can see where we're going in our new grace-sovereign country.

Could it be any clearer? Our old way of life was nailed to the cross with Christ, a decisive end to that sin-miserable life—no longer at sin's every beck and call! What we believe is this: If we get included in Christ's sin-conquering death, we also get included in his life-saving resurrection. We know that when Jesus was raised from the dead it was a signal of the end of death-as-the-end. Never again will death have the last word. When Jesus died, he took sin down with him, but alive he brings God down to us. From now on, think of it this way: Sin speaks a dead language that means nothing to you; God speaks your mother tongue, and you hang on every word. You are dead to sin and alive to God. That's what Jesus did.

Often when I've moved from one address to another, I'm still living in my old home. I look for things in the wrong cabinet, because that's where they used to be. I mourn the former mail carrier, the convenient corner store. I liked the way the light used to follow me around in the old rooms. But if I give it a chance, the new address will eventually become home. You have to give it time, the way every new habit needs time to become part of you.

GOSPEL » LUKE 24:1-12

At the crack of dawn on Sunday, the women came to the tomb carrying the burial spices they had prepared. They found the entrance stone rolled back from the tomb, so they walked in. But once inside, they couldn't find the body of the Master Jesus.

They were puzzled, wondering what to make of this. Then, out of nowhere it seemed, two men, light cascading over them, stood there. The women were awestruck and bowed down in worship. *The men said, "Why are you looking for the Living One in a cemetery? He is not here, but raised up. Remember how he told you when you were still back in Galilee that he had to be handed over to sinners, be killed on a cross, and in three days rise up?" Then they remembered Jesus' words.*

They left the tomb and broke the news of all this to the Eleven and the rest. Mary Magdalene, Joanna, Mary the mother of James, and the other women with them kept telling these things to the apostles, but the apostles didn't believe a word of it, thought they were making it all up.

But Peter jumped to his feet and ran to the tomb. He stooped to look in and saw a few grave clothes, that's all. He walked away puzzled, shaking his head.

Jesus is risen. So quit hanging around the cemetery! This is a message many of us still need to hear. Our religion is characterized by good news, not bad. The story has a happy ending, not a sad one. We've been invited to celebrate with Jesus, not to mourn him. Too many of us are better at Lent than we are at Easter. Let's put as much awareness into the next seven weeks as we did the last six!

From now on, think of it this way:
Sin speaks a dead language that means
nothing to you; God speaks your mother tongue,
and you hang on every word. You are dead
to sin and alive to God. That's what Jesus did.

EASTER SEASON

EASTER SUNDAY

FIRST READING » ACTS OF THE APOSTLES 10:34a, 37-43

Peter fairly exploded with his good news. "You know the story of what happened in Judea. It began in Galilee after John preached a total life-change. Then Jesus arrived from Nazareth, anointed by God with the Holy Spirit, ready for action. He went through the country helping people and healing everyone who was beaten down by the Devil. He was able to do all this because God was with him.

"And we saw it, saw it all, everything he did in the land of the Jews and in Jerusalem where they killed him, hung him from a cross. But in three days God had him up, alive, and out where he could be seen. Not everyone saw him—he wasn't put on public display. Witnesses had been carefully handpicked by God beforehand—us! We were the ones, there to eat and drink with him after he came back from the dead. He commissioned us to announce this in public, to bear solemn witness that he is in fact the One whom God destined as Judge of the living and dead. But we're not alone in this. Our witness that he is the means to forgiveness of sins is backed up by the witness of all the prophets."

We do indeed know the story, at least as well as the crowd of Gentiles around Peter in Jerusalem that morning. He was reminding them of the still-sensational topic around the city: about the man who had just been crucified for claiming more authority than Caesar. Or so the story went. Some said the man had even pretended to be God. Peter wanted to be sure they had more than the latest gossip, and as an eyewitness to it all, Peter was in the best position to deliver that testimony.

What about us? We know the story by heart, and in our own experience we're eyewitnesses to the way Jesus rescues us from death and restores us to new life. Is this a testimony we're likely to deliver to those who may not yet have heard it? As Saint Francis famously instructed, "Preach the gospel at all times. If necessary, use words."

> **How do we preach the gospel by our example, our choices, our behavior, our fidelity in relationship to the poor?**

SECOND READING » COLOSSIANS 3:1-4

So if you're serious about living this new resurrection life with Christ, act like it. Pursue the things over which Christ presides. Don't shuffle along, eyes to the ground, absorbed with the things right in front of you. Look up, and be alert to what is going on around Christ—that's where the action is. See things from his perspective.

Your old life is dead. Your new life, which is your real life—even though invisible to spectators—is with Christ in God. He is your life. When Christ (your real life, remember) shows up again on this earth, you'll show up, too—the real you, the glorious you. Meanwhile, be content with obscurity, like Christ.

It's easy for Saint Paul, maybe, to "look up" toward heaven and forget about earth. But my back hurts and I've got bills to pay. I'm behind in the tasks I set for today, and all of these things were true yesterday, too. How can I see things from Christ's perspective under these conditions?

For one thing, I doubt that Paul forgot about earth. His back hurt, too, from many beatings in the towns where his message was less than welcome. Paul sewed tents to pay for his keep, and we get the sense that such a zealous man always found himself behind in the master plan of bringing the gospel to the ends of the earth. At the same time, Paul bore in mind that he had "died to all that"; what was really important was his hidden life in Christ. Madly in love with the Jesus who frees sinners, Paul allowed that passion to carry him through each day with all its disappointments and failures. Paul saw earth, but through heaven's eyes.

What are the things of earth that occupy your thoughts?
How might viewing them "through heaven's eyes" change what you see?

GOSPEL » JOHN 20:1-9

Early in the morning on the first day of the week, while it was still dark, Mary Magdalene came to the tomb and saw that the stone was moved away from the entrance. She ran at once to Simon Peter and the other disciple, the one Jesus loved, breathlessly panting, "They took the Master from the tomb. We don't know where they've put him."

Peter and the other disciple left immediately for the tomb. They ran, neck and neck. The other disciple got to the tomb first, outrunning Peter. Stooping to look in, he saw the pieces of linen cloth lying there, but he didn't go in. Simon Peter arrived after him, entered the tomb, observed the linen cloths lying there, and the kerchief used to cover his head not lying with the linen cloths but separate, neatly folded by itself. Then the other disciple, the one who had gotten there first, went into the tomb, took one look at the evidence, and believed. No one yet knew from the Scripture that he had to rise from the dead.

Every Easter we wind up in the same place, staring into the empty tomb and trying to make sense out of it. Maybe it's a grisly case of theft. Maybe it's an incredible miracle. Maybe we should be horrified; or we should praise God. Maybe it's the same tragedy, different day. Or maybe, just maybe, this is the biggest transformation since creation came out of chaos, and we should all be dancing!

We hear the same story every year, but our hearts are in a different place each time so it meets us differently. Perhaps some years we're not moved at all: he is risen, what difference does it make? Other years, we may be moved to tears at what love can do. What we see as we peer into the empty tomb is up to us. Hope and life everlasting? Or a dark and hollow place that smells of death? Come and see.

What do you bring in your heart to the tomb this Easter?
How does what you bring affect what you see there?

WE RESPOND

Let your spirit go dancing this Easter. Visit a place of emptiness and bring abundance. Share love, delight, hope, peace where none exists. Don't shun the tombs, but look for the life waiting to emerge.

When Christ (your real life, remember)
shows up again on this earth,
you'll show up, too—the real you,
the glorious you.

SECOND SUNDAY OF EASTER

.... We Have Seen the Lord!

FIRST READING » ACTS OF THE APOSTLES 5:12-16

Through the work of the apostles, many God-signs were set up among the people, many wonderful things done. They all met regularly and in remarkable harmony on the Temple porch named after Solomon. But even though people admired them a lot, outsiders were wary about joining them. On the other hand, those who put their trust in the Master were added right and left, men and women both. They even carried the sick out into the streets and laid them on stretchers and bedrolls, hoping they would be touched by Peter's shadow when he walked by. They came from the villages surrounding Jerusalem, throngs of them, bringing the sick and bedeviled. And they all were healed.

Had Peter ever dared to imagine such a day? For three years he followed Jesus like a puppy around the countryside, watching miracles bloom like flowers as the Lord passed by. And now, desperate people hoped to be lucky enough to be touched by Peter's own shadow in the streets. He had finally attained the image of his Master and become a disciple worthy of the name.

When I was in parochial school, I thought this was the goal of becoming a saint: to rise to a level of holiness where miracles would spring from your fingertips for the good of the world. But getting to the point where people see Jesus in you is more like it. People ought to be able to look into the witness of our lives and say, "We have seen the Lord!" When people start to mistake you for Jesus, you know you're on the right track.

> Do you know people who could be "mistaken
> for Jesus" by their love and generosity?
> How does their witness challenge you
> to imitate Jesus more closely?

SECOND READING » REVELATION 1:9-11a, 12-13, 17-19

I, John, with you all the way in the trial and the Kingdom and the passion of patience in Jesus, was on the island called Patmos because of God's Word, the witness of Jesus. It was Sunday and I was in the Spirit, praying. I heard a loud voice behind me, trumpet-clear and piercing: "Write what you see into a book. Send it to the seven churches." I turned and saw the voice.

I saw a gold menorah
with seven branches,
And in the center, the Son of Man,
in a robe and gold breastplate.

I saw this and fainted dead at his feet. His right hand pulled me upright, his voice reassured me:

"Don't fear: I am First, I am Last, I'm Alive. I died, but I came to life, and my life is now forever. See these keys in my hand? They open and lock Death's doors, they open and lock Hell's gates. Now write down everything you see: things that are, things about to be."

The sight of the risen Lord must have been in some ways unbearable. Every time someone encounters Jesus after the resurrection, the first words out of his mouth are, "Don't fear." I can't remember who said it, but someone once observed, "Who's to say what's too awful to bear, and what is too beautiful to bear?" Dante imagined God like that: a Being too beautiful to gaze upon with the eyes of a sinner. When Absolute Love comes, would we not have to look away?

Jesus tells us there is nothing to fear. We look away, expecting reproach and condemnation, but that's because we really don't get it. Glory makes us ashamed, but because it IS glory, we're lifted up and redeemed by the encounter. We're afraid because of who we are, but we're urged to have hope because of who he is.

> Consider what's most beautiful to you: vistas, music,
> a child's trust in you, the face of one you love.
> How do these things reveal God's unseen nature?

GOSPEL » JOHN 20:19-31

Later on that day, the disciples had gathered together, but, fearful of the Jews, had locked all the doors in the house. Jesus entered, stood among them, and said, "Peace to you." Then he showed them his hands and side.

The disciples, seeing the Master with their own eyes, were exuberant. Jesus repeated his greeting: "Peace to you. Just as the Father sent me, I send you."

Then he took a deep breath and breathed into them. "Receive the Holy Spirit," he said. "If you forgive someone's sins, they're gone for good. If you don't forgive sins, what are you going to do with them?"

But Thomas, sometimes called the Twin, one of the Twelve, was not with them when Jesus came. The other disciples told him, "We saw the Master."

But he said, "Unless I see the nail holes in his hands, put my finger in the nail holes, and stick my hand in his side, I won't believe it."

Eight days later, his disciples were again in the room. This time Thomas was with them. Jesus came through the locked doors, stood among them, and said, "Peace to you."

Then he focused his attention on Thomas. "Take your finger and examine my hands. Take your hand and stick it in my side. Don't be unbelieving. Believe."

Thomas said, "My Master! My God!"

Jesus said, "So, you believe because you've seen with your own eyes. Even better blessings are in store for those who believe without seeing."

Jesus provided far more God-revealing signs than are written down in this book. These are written down so you will believe that Jesus is the Messiah, the Son of God, and in the act of believing, have real and eternal life in the way he personally revealed it.

Thomas missed it. The Lord came into their midst, tangibly and audibly. But Thomas wasn't there. Even after the most tumultuous week of their lives, Thomas was not about to sit and reflect. He had places to go, people to see. In my secret biblical dating service, I think Thomas would make a good husband for Martha. He was practical, a man of action, a good model of service. He may have been out verifying the account of the women from the morning, or getting supplies for the group, or checking out the streets to hear if there was talk of lynching the whole bunch of them. It was certainly a dangerous time to go out for a mere stroll. Thomas had reasons not to be among them. But just like Martha, his good intentions got in the way of the one thing that mattered. The only detail that escaped Thomas' attention that day was Jesus.

> **How does activity keep you from prayer, contemplation, and the quiet?**
> **How can you accommodate room in your day to "see" the Lord?**

WE RESPOND

Look for the Lord in the faces of others, those who are dear and especially those who are less so. Seek the Lord in beauty, in stillness, and behind locked doors most of all.

These are written down so you will believe that Jesus is the Messiah, the Son of God, and in the act of believing, have real and eternal life in the way he personally revealed it.

THIRD SUNDAY OF EASTER

FIRST READING » ACTS OF THE APOSTLES 5:27-32, 40b-41

The chief and his police went and got the apostles. Bringing them back, they stood them before the High Council. The Chief Priest said, "Didn't we give you strict orders not to teach in Jesus' name? And here you have filled Jerusalem with your teaching and are trying your best to blame us for the death of this man."

Peter and the apostles answered, "It's necessary to obey God rather than men. The God of our ancestors raised up Jesus, the One you killed by hanging him on a cross. God set him on high at his side, Prince and Savior, to give Israel the gift of a changed life and sins forgiven. And we are witnesses to these things. The Holy Spirit, whom God gives to those who obey him, corroborates every detail."

After giving them a thorough whipping, they warned them not to speak in Jesus' name and sent them off. The apostles went out of the High Council overjoyed because they had been given the honor of being dishonored on account of the Name.

There's authority, and then there are the authorities. The difference between the two is on display in this clash between the Sanhedrin and the apostles. Titular authority can be a bully, asserting itself by giving orders and making threats to those who don't buckle under. The other kind of authority knows that it derives from a higher source. The apostles choose to obey God, and exert divine authority by demonstrating the life they invite others to imitate. The Sanhedrin will arrest and rearrest the apostles, but it can only impose constraints on their bodies. Free hearts can't be imprisoned, and liberated spirits know no fear.

The most compelling leaders are those who show us how to live because they're compelled by an authority greater than themselves. They embody the vision, and show us how irresistibly beautiful it can be.

> **Give three examples of people you consider great leaders. What made them great, and why did people choose to follow them?**

SECOND READING » REVELATION 5:11-14

I looked again. I heard a company of Angels around the Throne, the Animals, and the Elders—ten thousand times ten thousand their number, thousand after thousand after thousand in full song:

> *The slain Lamb is worthy!*
> *Take the power, the wealth, the wisdom, the strength!*
> *Take the honor, the glory, the blessing!*

Then I heard every creature in Heaven and earth, in underworld and sea, join in, all voices in all places, singing:

To the One on the Throne! To the Lamb!
The blessing, the honor, the glory, the strength,
For age after age after age.

The Four Animals called out, "Oh, Yes!" The Elders fell to their knees and worshiped.

Here's a paradox if ever there was one! In the reign of God, who gets power and riches? The one who empties himself of power and takes on our poverty. Who gets wisdom and strength? The one who seems foolish in the eyes of the world, too weak to carry his own cross. Who gets honor? The humiliated one. Who gets glory? The one covered in shame. Who is blessed? The one called a blasphemer by religious-minded people. At the throne of God, things tend to look quite different than they do from here.

Kinda makes you shiver, doesn't it? Since the whole world as we know it is going to turn upside down, it's imperative to have upside down leaders, the sort who are followers first. Leaders who insist on others following them are going to end up at the back of the line, as will those who march right behind them. But if we follow the one who humbled himself for our sake, we may find that we have become leaders for others after all.

> **Think of ten ways to get rid of power, wealth, and honor.**
> **Be as creative as you can. Choose one of those**
> **ways and make it your specialty.**

GOSPEL » JOHN 21:1-19

After this, Jesus appeared again to the disciples, this time at the Tiberias Sea (the Sea of Galilee). This is how he did it: Simon Peter, Thomas (nicknamed "Twin"), Nathanael from Cana in Galilee, the brothers Zebedee, and two other disciples were together. Simon Peter announced, "I'm going fishing."

The rest of them replied, "We're going with you." They went out and got in the boat. They caught nothing that night. When the sun came up, Jesus was standing on the beach, but they didn't recognize him.

Jesus spoke to them: "Good morning! Did you catch anything for breakfast?"
They answered, "No."

He said, "Throw the net off the right side of the boat and see what happens."

They did what he said. All of a sudden there were so many fish in it, they weren't strong enough to pull it in.

Then the disciple Jesus loved said to Peter, "It's the Master!"

When Simon Peter realized that it was the Master, he threw on some clothes, for he was stripped for work, and dove into the sea. The other disciples came in by boat for they weren't far from land, a hundred yards or so, pulling along the net full of fish. When they got out of the boat, they saw a fire laid, with fish and bread cooking on it.

Jesus said, "Bring some of the fish you've just caught." Simon Peter joined them and pulled the net to shore—153 big fish! And even with all those fish, the net didn't rip.

Jesus said, "Breakfast is ready." Not one of the disciples dared ask, "Who are you?" They knew it was the Master.

Jesus then took the bread and gave it to them. He did the same with the fish. This was now the third time Jesus had shown himself alive to the disciples since being raised from the dead.

After breakfast, Jesus said to Simon Peter, "Simon, son of John, do you love me more than these?"

"Yes, Master, you know I love you."

Jesus said, "Feed my lambs."

He then asked a second time, "Simon, son of John, do you love me?"

"Yes, Master, you know I love you."

Jesus said, "Shepherd my sheep."

Then he said it a third time: "Simon, son of John, do you love me?"

Peter was upset that he asked for the third time, "Do you love me?" so he answered, "Master, you know everything there is to know. You've got to know that I love you."

Jesus said, "Feed my sheep. I'm telling you the very truth now: When you were young you dressed yourself and went wherever you wished, but when you get old you'll have to stretch out your hands while someone else dresses you and takes you where you don't want to go." He said this to hint at the kind of death by which Peter would glorify God. And then he commanded, "Follow me."

This image of Peter diving out of the boat always makes me smile. The evangelist describes Peter's preparations so discreetly, you might miss what he's saying: "Peter was in first-century underwear when the Lord arrived, so this was not an opportune time for a surprise visit." But Peter took his chances. He'd rather arrive in the Lord's presence in embarrassing disarray than not at all.

Peter follows with his heart and not with his head. Earlier, this led him to surrender to fear and deny his friend. But it also gives him the kind of passion that Jesus finds particularly endearing. If Peter is impetuous, he's also quick to repent and eager for another chance. In this sense he's like King David, who also won a lasting place in God's plan. Leaders with passion make mistakes. But perfection is rarely the quality God looks for in a future hero.

> Which is more important to you, your dignity or your service?
> Consider ways you're being called to be a "fool for Christ's sake."

WE RESPOND

Play a different game than the world is playing. Seek the lowest place. Give away wealth as it comes. Be weak when you're most tempted to make a show of strength. Let yourself be foolish to grownups.

FOURTH SUNDAY OF EASTER

FIRST READING » ACTS OF THE APOSTLES 13:14, 43-52

From Perga Paul and Barnabas traveled on to Antioch in Pisidia. On the Sabbath they went to the meeting place and took their places.

A good many Jews and converts to Judaism went along with Paul and Barnabas, who urged them in long conversations to stick with what they'd started, this living in and by God's grace.

When the next Sabbath came around, practically the whole city showed up to hear the Word of God. Some of the Jews, seeing the crowds, went wild with jealousy and tore into Paul, contradicting everything he was saying, making an ugly scene.

But Paul and Barnabas didn't back down. Standing their ground they said, "It was required that God's Word be spoken first of all to you, the Jews. But seeing that you want no part of it—you've made it quite clear that you have no taste or inclination for eternal life—the door is open to all the outsiders. And we're on our way through it, following orders, doing what God commanded when he said,

> *I've set you up*
> *as light to all nations.*
> *You'll proclaim salvation*
> *to the four winds and seven seas!"*

When the non-Jewish outsiders heard this, they could hardly believe their good fortune. All who were marked out for real life put their trust in God—they honored God's Word by receiving that life. And this Message of salvation spread like wildfire all through the region.

Some of the Jews convinced the most respected women and leading men of the town that their precious way of life was about to be destroyed. Alarmed, they turned on Paul and Barnabas and forced them to leave. Paul and Barnabas shrugged their shoulders and went on to the next town, Iconium, brimming with joy and the Holy Spirit, two happy disciples.

When was the last time you were truly delighted about something? Some folks live in a state of constant delight. And others don't even know why we're having this conversation. Delight is a condition that takes time to savor and appreciate. In our busy, productive, responsible world, it can seem childish to rejoice over a particularly nice flower, to feel glee at catching sight of an old friend on the street. But delight is more than a personality quirk. For Christians bearing good news, it's practically a vocation.

The Gentiles show delight when they discover that the good news of Jesus is open to them. Contrast this with the jealous, quarrelsome response of Paul's own countrymen, to whom the gospel is originally delivered. It takes very little heart space to be petty and miserable. Small hearts have little room for the expansive joy that good news yields. When we really hear the word of God for what it is, delight won't be an option, but a given.

How do you cultivate the joy of the gospel in your heart?
Do others suspect that good news is at the center of your life?

SECOND READING » REVELATION 7:9, 14b-17

I, John, saw a huge crowd, too huge to count. Everyone was there—all nations and tribes, all races and languages. And they were standing, dressed in white robes and waving palm branches, standing before the Throne and the Lamb.

Just then one of the Elders addressed me: "These are those who come from the great tribulation, and they've washed their robes, scrubbed them clean in the blood of the Lamb. That's why they're standing before God's Throne. They serve him day and night in his Temple. The One on the Throne will pitch his tent there for them: no more hunger, no more thirst, no more scorching heat. The Lamb on the Throne will shepherd them, will lead them to spring waters of Life. And God will wipe every last tear from their eyes."

A time beyond tears! In my young adulthood I did not believe in such a time. It was so far away from my own experience. Reality impressed me as hard, loveless, and full of suffering. In college my friends and I waxed philosophical about this. We suspected some people were born happy, and others born to sadness. That gave us some comfort, to accept our fate as it was written. In ten more years, this same passivity made me angry, and eventually I discarded it as an intolerable approach to life. Human nature is much too elastic, and grace too liberating a force, for predestination to hold any sway.

God doesn't create under a shadow, and no one is conceived for misery. Creation is originally named "good," and Easter is the restoration of original goodness. The sting of death has been withdrawn. Sin has lost its fatal force. In Luke's Beatitudes, we're promised that those who weep now will be given reason to laugh soon. Happiness is both the goal of our faith and also its outward sign: the unmistakable byproduct of a life delivered confidently into God's gentle hands.

In whose life have you seen authentic joy?
How does this differ from the transitory
satisfaction delivered by what we own or earn?

GOSPEL » JOHN 10:27-30

Jesus said: "My sheep recognize my voice. I know them, and they follow me. I give them real and eternal life. They are protected from the Destroyer for good. No one can steal them from out of my hand. The Father who put them under my care is so much greater than the Destroyer and Thief. No one could ever get them away from him. I and the Father are one heart and mind."

The slogan, "Think Different," reminds me that as Christians, we are called to "see different." We're invited to look at a world which seems to have gotten so out of hand and believe Jesus still has his sheep well in hand. We watch our loved ones die and still believe that only mortal life is passing away. We view the misery and poverty of folks on the streets and refuse to be paralyzed into inaction. We're aware that the violence in our society, and the violence we harbor in our hearts, is definitely related. We perceive that all the world's children are our children. Others may tell us that people get what they deserve, and not to waste our pity on the disadvantaged or marginalized ones. But we, who deserve condemnation and get mercy instead, can't be so smug. We're in the hands of a good Shepherd who speaks gentle words of life and hope. Promised an imperishable future, can we see those perishing all around us and NOT see how the world can and must be different?

> Make a short list of the world's problems.
> Create two columns of response:
> one for what conventional wisdom suggests we do,
> and the other for the response demanded by the gospels.
> What motives underlie each response?

WE RESPOND

Laugh often. Give someone a reason to smile. Greet strangers warmly. Play and have fun. Don't worry about how it looks to anyone else.

"My sheep recognize my voice.
I know them, and they follow me.
give them real and eternal life."

FIFTH SUNDAY OF EASTER

FIRST READING » ACTS OF THE APOSTLES 14:21-27

After proclaiming the Message in Derbe and establishing a strong core of disciples, Paul and Barnabas retraced their steps to Lystra, then Iconium, and then Antioch, putting muscle and sinew in the lives of the disciples, urging them to stick with what they had begun to believe and not quit, making it clear to them that it wouldn't be easy: "Anyone signing up for the kingdom of God has to go through plenty of hard times."

Paul and Barnabas handpicked leaders in each church. After praying—their prayers intensified by fasting—they presented these new leaders to the Master to whom they had entrusted their lives. Working their way back through Pisidia, they came to Pamphylia and preached in Perga. Finally, they made it to Attalia and caught a ship back to Antioch, where it had all started—launched by God's grace and now safely home by God's grace. A good piece of work.

On arrival, they got the church together and reported on their trip, telling in detail how God had used them to throw the door of faith wide open so people of all nations could come streaming in.

We can be pardoned for not getting visibly excited about the welcome mat being put out for the Gentiles. It's very hard to relate to the good fortune of those who lived in Asia Minor twenty centuries ago. But it's important to consider this fact as more than trivia, since we're the Gentiles they're talking about! For thousands of years the story of Abraham and Sarah, Moses, Deborah, Elijah, Isaiah, and the whole biblical gang had nothing to do with you and me. The story belonged to the people Israel and had no relevance to anyone outside that tribe. It was like news of the American Dream to someone on the far side of the world who could never hope to have a share in it.

And then God flung open the door and invited the rest of the world inside the story, so that you and I could take Israel's journey ourselves. When we make it to the book of Acts, we modern Gentiles should breathe a sigh of relief. At last! The Bible was almost over, but we made it in. Of course, the question remains: Having made it in by the skin of our teeth, are we now in any position to keep others out?

> **Who might you be tempted to identify as outside of salvation history?**
> **Would Saint Paul have fasted and prayed**
> **to get that person or group included?**
> **(See Acts 14:23.)**

THIS TRANSFORMING WORD

SECOND READING » REVELATION 21:1-5a

I, John, saw Heaven and earth new-created. Gone the first Heaven, gone the first earth, gone the sea.

I saw Holy Jerusalem, new-created, descending resplendent out of Heaven, as ready for God as a bride for her husband.

I heard a voice thunder from the Throne: "Look! Look! God has moved into the neighborhood, making his home with men and women! They're his people, he's their God. He'll wipe every tear from their eyes. Death is gone for good—tears gone, crying gone, pain gone—all the first order of things gone." The Enthroned continued, "Look! I'm making everything new."

What's new? Everything! At least that's what hear from the book that claims to reveal all. In the reign of God, everything we've come to expect cannot be expected anymore. No more bad news. No more loss. No more endings. I can't wait.

And theologians tell us we don't have to wait, in a manner of speaking. In the study of Last Things known as *eschatology*, scholars consider topics like the end of the world, final judgment, and the coming of the New Jerusalem—that great everlasting co-habitation of God and humanity. But scholars also speak of a "realized eschatology"—the claim that what God promises can be real for us right now. Why wait for a future reign of justice, peace, and love? Why not begin to live as if this were true right now?

I'd like to start a movement to realize our eschatology. Just think of the t-shirt possibilities. Confront bad news with Good News. Answer loss with gain. Look for what's being born in every death. Find the beginning lurking in endings. Heaven is too good to keep for the future, especially when it's right at hand.

> How has God "made all things new" in your life?
> How are you a message of good news to those
> who suffer the world's bad news?

GOSPEL » JOHN 13:31-33a, 34-35

When Judas had left, Jesus said, "Now the Son of Man is seen for who he is, and God seen for who he is in him. The moment God is seen in him, God's glory will be on display. In glorifying him, he himself is glorified—glory all around!

"Children, I am with you for only a short time longer. Let me give you a new command: Love one another. In the same way I loved you, you love one another. This is how everyone will recognize that you are my disciples—when they see the love you have for each other."

Everything is new in the Scriptures this week. Even the commandments! The big Ten are boiled down to one. A new law for a new and inclusive people: love.

For some folks, love is too small and vague and squishy to work as a commandment. How are we to keep law and order with mere sentimental feeling? This is a misunderstanding of the love command. It doesn't mean a return to bell-bottoms and peace signs. Love is a tall order, a mighty work that challenges the strong to be relentless, the brave to be even bolder. Love is not vague: It is precise to the last detail of our lives, eliciting very practical and direct responses to the corporal and spiritual needs of our community. And love is not squishy. It looks you right in the eye and dares you to claim an authority higher than its calling. The Ten Commandments are a walk in the park compared to the summons to love. It is always easier NOT to do something than to DO something.

How do you obey the command to love: in your relationships with others, in your stewardship of goods, in your fidelity to God?

WE RESPOND

Do ten things this week motivated by love and not by gain. If you love people who are REALLY hard to love, you only have to do five.

God has moved into the neighborhood,
making his home with men and women!
They're his people, he's their God.
He'll wipe every tear from their eyes.

SIXTH SUNDAY OF EASTER

FIRST READING » ACTS OF THE APOSTLES 15:1-2, 22-29

It wasn't long before some Jews showed up from Judea insisting that everyone be circumcised: "If you're not circumcised in the Mosaic fashion, you can't be saved." Paul and Barnabas were up on their feet at once in fierce protest. The church decided to resolve the matter by sending Paul, Barnabas, and a few others to put it before the apostles and leaders in Jerusalem.

Everyone agreed: apostles, leaders, all the people. They picked Judas (nicknamed Barsabbas) and Silas—they both carried considerable weight in the church—and sent them to Antioch with Paul and Barnabas with this letter:

> *From the apostles and leaders, your friends, to our friends in Antioch, Syria, and Cilicia:*
>
> *Hello!*
>
> *We heard that some men from our church went to you and said things that confused and upset you. Mind you, they had no authority from us; we didn't send them. We have agreed unanimously to pick representatives and send them to you with our good friends Barnabas and Paul. We picked men we knew you could trust, Judas and Silas— they've looked death in the face time and again for the sake of our Master Jesus Christ. We've sent them to confirm in a face-to-face meeting with you what we've written.*
>
> *It seemed to the Holy Spirit and to us that you should not be saddled with any crushing burden, but be responsible only for these bare necessities: Be careful not to get involved in activities connected with idols; avoid serving food offensive to Jewish Christians (blood, for instance); and guard the morality of sex and marriage.*
>
> *These guidelines are sufficient to keep relations congenial between us. And God be with you!*

This little meeting of Paul and Barnabas with the apostles and elders is historic. The council at Jerusalem was the first of a long line of church councils that weave through the centuries up to and including the Second Vatican Council of the last century. In Jerusalem, as with subsequent councils, the goal was to settle disputes both theological and practical. What is the true nature of the church, and how best to express that in the life of the community? Councils, then and now, seek to answer that question.

The decrees of the councils have never minced words when it came to their findings. Peter, James, and the Jerusalem elders send a message that holds the authority of both the leadership AND the Holy Spirit. The actual decree—that the community abstain from idol-tainted meat, from blood, from animals improperly killed, and from unlawful marriage (meaning marriage to close kin)—is not of much practical use today. But how we arrive at our self-understanding as church, universally and not in factions, through the Holy Spirit and not by personal inclination, is very much a part of our practice today.

> How did the Jerusalem council handle
> dissent in the formation of new decrees?
> How should a universal church deal with dissent today?

SECOND READING » REVELATION 21:10-14, 22-23

The angel took me away in the Spirit to an enormous, high mountain and showed me Holy Jerusalem descending out of Heaven from God, resplendent in the bright glory of God.

The City shimmered like a precious gem, light-filled, pulsing light. She had a wall majestic and high with twelve gates. At each gate stood an Angel, and on the gates were inscribed the names of the Twelve Tribes of the sons of Israel: three gates on the east, three gates on the north, three gates on the south, three gates on the west. The wall was set on twelve foundations, the names of the Twelve Apostles of the Lamb inscribed on them.

But there was no sign of a Temple, for the Lord God—the Sovereign-Strong— and the Lamb are the Temple. The City doesn't need sun or moon for light. God's Glory is its light, the Lamb its lamp!

When I was a teenager I saw my first city: Pittsburgh. The Greyhound pulled into the valley after dark, and the lights of the city glittered like stars for miles. To me, it looked like the nighttime sky had fallen to earth and made Pittsburgh. I thought it magnificent.

Since then I've seen lots of cities, and lived in a few. I've even seen the earthly Jerusalem, and thought it too was magnificent. But I've never seen a city like the heavenly Jerusalem, described in gleaming details with the Lamb as its light. A resplendent crystal city, with clarity as its fundamental design, would be something to see.

Most cities build on obscurity, hiding dark deeds, injustices, and poverty. There are parts you're supposed to visit, highlighted on tourist maps, and those you aren't meant to see, where nobody goes on purpose unless you have to live there. We're not quite ready for the crystal city, where all is brought to light by the illumination of Christ. In the meantime, we must pray for our cities, for all the hidden deeds and unseen misery.

> What percentage of your life is seen and known?
> How much of it is kept in darkness?

GOSPEL » JOHN 14:23-29

Judas (not Iscariot) said, "Master, why is it that you are about to make yourself plain to us but not to the world?"

"Because a loveless world," said Jesus, "is a sightless world. If anyone loves me, he will carefully keep my word and my Father will love him—we'll move right into the neighborhood! Not loving me means not keeping my words. The message you are hearing isn't mine. It's the message of the Father who sent me.

"I'm telling you these things while I'm still living with you. The Friend, the Holy Spirit whom the Father will send at my request, will make everything plain to you. He will remind you of all the things I have told you. I'm leaving you well and whole. That's my parting gift to you. Peace. I don't leave you the way you're used to being left—feeling abandoned, bereft. So don't be upset. Don't be distraught.

"You've heard me tell you, 'I'm going away, and I'm coming back.' If you loved me, you would be glad that I'm on my way to the Father because the Father is the goal and purpose of my life.

"I've told you this ahead of time, before it happens, so that when it does happen, the confirmation will deepen your belief in me."

In our search for clarity, we don't have to look far. As the mystics would say, look within: The Spirit of Truth dwells in you. It was obvious from the start that the disciples, left to themselves, would be seized with confusion, as indeed they were from the time Jesus was arrested. Jesus had traveled with this gang for a long time, so he understood their limitations very well. If he left them completely, there would be no church; there would be chaos. So he promised a Friend Spirit to be their guide until eternity.

Clarity is not a typical state of mind for humans, one must admit. We weigh pros and cons. We flip coins. Some of us angst, some look at horoscopes, some ask everyone advice and then take none of it. Sometimes, our only decision is to procrastinate until the decision is made by default. But there's another way for Christians to find their way: by consulting the Spirit. Discernment is a gift to the church. It works especially well in community. Pray. Ask. Listen. See.

> **What is your usual method for making decisions?**
> **What criteria do you use in choosing?**
> **What role does faith play in your choices?**

WE RESPOND

Practice clarity and discernment. Start by memorizing the corporal and spiritual works of mercy (you used to know them!) and exercising them regularly.

ASCENSION OF THE LORD

FIRST READING » ACTS OF THE APOSTLES 1:1-11

Dear Theophilus, in the first volume of this book I wrote on everything that Jesus began to do and teach until the day he said good-bye to the apostles, the ones he had chosen through the Holy Spirit, and was taken up to heaven. After his death, he presented himself alive to them in many different settings over a period of forty days. In face-to-face meetings, he talked to them about things concerning the kingdom of God. As they met and ate meals together, he told them that they were on no account to leave Jerusalem but "must wait for what the Father promised: the promise you heard from me. John baptized in water; you will be baptized in the Holy Spirit. And soon."

When they were together for the last time they asked, "Master, are you going to restore the kingdom to Israel now? Is this the time?"

He told them, "You don't get to know the time. Timing is the Father's business. What you'll get is the Holy Spirit. And when the Holy Spirit comes on you, you will be able to be my witnesses in Jerusalem, all over Judea and Samaria, even to the ends of the world."

These were his last words. As they watched, he was taken up and disappeared in a cloud. They stood there, staring into the empty sky. Suddenly two men appeared—in white robes! They said, "You Galileans!—why do you just stand here looking up at an empty sky? This very Jesus who was taken up from among you to heaven will come as certainly—and mysteriously—as he left."

Witnessing to the ends of the world sounds like hard work. There are days when I don't feel up to witnessing across the room. But the key part of this saying, easy to miss, is that the power of the Holy Spirit makes the church's mission to evangelize the world possible. If it were strictly up to you and me, Christianity would hardly make it down the block.

The vital role of the Holy Spirit doesn't imply, however, that we can sit back in our rocking chairs and watch the gospel spread. The Spirit dwells within us and moves in concert with our efforts. It's like those stories Jesus tells: The sower has to plant the seed, even while the one-hundredfold yield comes from God. We seed-sowers have to do our part for the Spirit to increase the yield. It's the best matching grant in the universe!

How can you witness to the truth of the gospel with your words, example, money, time, presence, vote, and service?

SECOND READING » EPHESIANS 1:17-23

I ask—ask the God of our Master, Jesus Christ, the God of glory—to make you intelligent and discerning in knowing him personally, your eyes focused and clear, so that you can see exactly what it is he is calling you to do, grasp the immensity of this glorious way of life he has for Christians, oh, the utter extravagance of his work in us who trust him—endless energy, boundless strength!

All this energy issues from Christ: God raised him from death and set him on a throne in deep heaven, in charge of running the universe, everything from galaxies to governments, no name and no power exempt from his rule. And not just for the time being, but forever. He is in charge of it all, has the final word on everything. At the center of all this, Christ rules the church. The church, you see, is not peripheral to the world; the world is peripheral to the church. The church is Christ's body, in which he speaks and acts, by which he fills everything with his presence.

What do you know about God? Try making a short list of things you would be willing to teach a child. Maybe you would begin by saying God is the source of everything in creation. And that God came to earth in Jesus, who lived and died and rose from the dead. Then you might want to say something about the Holy Spirit. But what would that be?

The first two Persons of the Trinity seem more tangible to most of us than the elusive Spirit, who often becomes the "poor relation" of the Trinity in our understanding. I find it easier to speak of the Spirit as a verb instead of a noun—in terms of what Spirit does than who Spirit is. The Spirit is the provider of seven wonderful gifts. The Spirit is revealed in nine blessed fruits. The Spirit moves and has being through the work of the community of faith. Follow the trail of holy people and good works, and see the Spirit in action!

> **Can you name the seven gifts of the Spirit?**
> **The nine fruits of the Spirit? (See Galatians 5:22-23.)**
> **How many of these are alive in you?**

GOSPEL » LUKE 24:46-53

Jesus said, "You can see now how it is written that the Messiah suffers, rises from the dead on the third day, and then a total life-change through the forgiveness of sins is proclaimed in his name to all nations—starting from here, from Jerusalem! You're the first to hear and see it. You're the witnesses. What comes next is very important: I am sending what my Father promised to you, so stay here in the city until he arrives, until you're equipped with power from on high."

He then led them out of the city over to Bethany. Raising his hands he blessed them, and while blessing them, took his leave, being carried up to heaven.

And they were on their knees, worshiping him. They returned to Jerusalem bursting with joy. They spent all their time in the Temple praising God. Yes.

Whenever we Christians are asked to "tell what we know" to those who don't share our faith, we should first speak of the mercy of God. Sometimes we're quicker to talk about God's rules and the church's. We're tempted to condemn and admonish the wayward. But when Jesus himself gave last-minute instructions to his disciples, he didn't say a word about how to behave. Instead, Jesus pointedly says that lives change when the forgiveness of sins is announced. Forgiveness comes first, not the change. Did any of us get that message growing up?

Forgiveness of sin and triumph over death are the core messages of Christianity. This is why Jesus came and taught and suffered and died and rose. If we forget to mention this in our rush to the rules, we withhold the fruit and offer the rind. People who know they've got a second chance may turn around. If there's no chance, why bother?

**Why is our witness a strong theme on the feast of the Ascension?
How do you testify to the forgiveness of sin?**

WE RESPOND

Reread the Apostles' Creed or Nicene Creed carefully to reflect on the faith of the church. Consider how each of these ideas affects your life.

*The church, you see, is not peripheral to the world;
the world is peripheral to the church.
The church is Christ's body,
in which he speaks and acts
by which he fills everything with his presence.*

SEVENTH SUNDAY OF EASTER
.... The Sleep of the Just

FIRST READING » ACTS OF THE APOSTLES 7:55-60

Stephen, full of the Holy Spirit, only had eyes for God, whom he saw in all his glory with Jesus standing at his side. He said, "Oh! I see heaven wide open and the Son of Man standing at God's side!"

Yelling and hissing, the mob drowned him out. Now in full stampede, they dragged him out of town and pelted him with rocks. The ringleaders took off their coats and asked a young man named Saul to watch them.

As the rocks rained down, Stephen prayed, "Master Jesus, take my life." Then he knelt down, praying loud enough for everyone to hear, "Master, don't blame them for this sin"—his last words. Then he died.

Something must be said about the sleep of the just. We use this term to denote the innocent rest of children, or how those with clean consciences drops off to sleep without anxiety. But when Stephen goes off to the sleep of the just, he gets there under a hail of stones and curses. Was he innocent? It depends on what you mean by that word. Stephen was guilty of proclaiming an unyielding bit of gospel. Was he anxious? Only that his murderers would suffer the effects of their sins. Stephen prays two short, all-he-had-time-for prayers as he dies. One is that Jesus would receive his life. The other was for the forgiveness of his killers. In these we hear the perfect imitation of Jesus on the cross. Stephen had learned his lessons well.

Stephen prayed for his murderers. The response to his prayer, as far as we can see, is the conversion of Saul. Saul guarded the cloaks of the killers, and though it never says that he picked up a stone, it's clear from the story that he approved the procedure. In the heart of this Saul who cried for Stephen's blood, an apostle named Paul lurked unsuspected. Stephen's prayer may have been just the thing to draw the saint out of hiding.

> **Have you ever prayed for an enemy
> or someone who caused you injury?
> What happened to them, or to you,
> through the power of this prayer?**

SECOND READING » REVELATION 22:12-14, 16-17, 20

I, John, heard a voice say to me, "Yes, I'm on my way! I'll be there soon! I'm bringing my payroll with me. I'll pay all people in full for their life's work. I'm A to Z, the First and the Final, Beginning and Conclusion.

"How blessed are those who wash their robes! The Tree of Life is theirs for good, and they'll walk through the gates to the City.

"I, Jesus, sent my Angel to testify to these things for the churches. I'm the Root and Branch of David, the Bright Morning Star."

"Come!" say the Spirit and the Bride.
Whoever hears, echo, "Come!"
Is anyone thirsty? Come!
All who will, come and drink,
Drink freely of the Water of Life!

He who testifies to all these things says it again: "I'm on my way! I'll be there soon!"
Yes! Come, Master Jesus!

In many ways the movie, *The Sixth Sense*, was just another ghost story. But a recurring line spoken by the child star—"I see dead people!"—became a hip phrase for awhile. The unfortunate child was able to communicate with the troubled spirits of those who died by violence. Within that experience he was able to discover a blessing: the ability to bring healing and peace to lost souls.

At a certain level a lot of us see dead people, and even deal with them from time to time. The communion of saints stretches between the realms of heaven and earth, and there's a whole lot of traffic going on, if we take the Bible and testimony of the saints seriously. Ask anyone who's lost a loved one, and he or she will tell you how their dear one has returned to reassure them in dreams, signs, and events. The power of our communion with those beyond death is felt in intercession, and more rarely in vision, as with Bernadette of Lourdes, or voices, like those heard by Joan of Arc. Second Coming is already in progress and Jesus will be here "soon." And all those dead people some folk see? We'll find out they're not dead at all.

> **We profess faith in the God of "the seen and unseen,"**
> **as well as "the communion of saints"**
> **composed of believers both living and dead.**
> **How do these articles of faith affect your prayer,**
> **and your thoughts about your own death?**

GOSPEL » JOHN 17:20-26

Raising his eyes in prayer, Jesus said:

"I'm praying not only for them
But also for those who will believe in me
Because of them and their witness about me.
The goal is for all of them to become one heart and mind—
Just as you, Father, are in me and I in you,
So they might be one heart and mind with us.
Then the world might believe that you, in fact, sent me.
The same glory you gave me, I gave them,
So they'll be as unified and together as we are—
I in them and you in me.
Then they'll be mature in this oneness,

And give the godless world evidence
That you've sent me and loved them
In the same way you've loved me.

Father, I want those you gave me
To be with me, right where I am,
So they can see my glory, the splendor you gave me,
Having loved me
Long before there ever was a world.
Righteous Father, the world has never known you,
But I have known you, and these disciples know
That you sent me on this mission.
I have made your very being known to them—
Who you are and what you do—
And continue to make it known,
So that your love for me
Might be in them
Exactly as I am in them."

A classical guitarist leased the apartment directly below mine. The first few nights he played the same few bars over and over, until two in the morning. I thought I'd have to move. But then one night, as I struggled to write the same sentence over and over, I suddenly appreciated my friend downstairs. He's engaged in the process of perfecting his music, so that he can play before his audience. I'm in the process of perfecting my discipleship. (The sentence can wait.) It's likely that neither of us will be perfect anytime soon. But we are one in the pursuit of the closer chord.

What makes us church is the shared pilgrimage toward a more perfect union with God's will. We struggle toward a goal that's not entirely attainable and yet we can, with patience and fidelity, draw closer to it over time. Jesus promises we'll know the same love of his Father that he knew, which is a thing we hardly dare to dream. With grateful hearts, then, we practice the same notes over and over, until we get it right.

> **Which aspects of your discipleship need more practice?**
> **How do you respond to the efforts of your neighbor,**
> **who may be less practiced than you?**

WE RESPOND

Choose someone to pray for from among your least favored list: an enemy, a critic, someone you find unsupportive or negative. Pray for that person regularly and earnestly, and see where prayer takes this relationship.

PENTECOST

FIRST READING » ACTS OF THE APOSTLES 2:1-11

When the Feast of Pentecost came, they were all together in one place. Without warning there was a sound like a strong wind, gale force—no one could tell where it came from. It filled the whole building. Then, like a wildfire, the Holy Spirit spread through their ranks, and they started speaking in a number of different languages as the Spirit prompted them.

There were many Jews staying in Jerusalem just then, devout pilgrims from all over the world. When they heard the sound, they came on the run. Then when they heard, one after another, their own mother tongues being spoken, they were thunderstruck. They couldn't for the life of them figure out what was going on, and kept saying, "Aren't these all Galileans? How come we're hearing them talk in our various mother tongues?

> *Parthians, Medes, and Elamites;*
> *Visitors from Mesopotamia, Judea, and Cappadocia,*
> *   Pontus and Asia, Phrygia and Pamphylia,*
> *   Egypt and the parts of Libya belonging to Cyrene;*
> *Immigrants from Rome, both Jews and proselytes;*
> *Even Cretans and Arabs!*

"They're speaking our languages, describing God's mighty works!"

What's the difference between a Christian and someone who simply goes to church? One answer might be the power of the Holy Spirit. Without reflection, we can be lulled into thinking that the point of religion is to go to church regularly, or to "be good," or at the very least, to feel guilty when we're "bad." We skim the surface of religion when we think this way. Being a disciple of Jesus is more challenging and more exciting than trying not to break too many rules.

Consider the experience of the first disciples. They listened to Jesus, day after day. They followed him around, stayed out of trouble, prayed when he prayed (and sometimes slept through the praying part, but hey). Yet nothing really changed for them or made much of an impact on their real lives until the Holy Spirit showed up. Suddenly they grew backbones, showed a lion's share of courage, spoke out what they believed and then lived what they spoke. And their 3-D testimony had power, and people were transformed by what they saw and heard. It puts mere church-going to shame.

> **Where do you see the Holy Spirit at work in the church?**
> **In your parish? In your own life?**

SECOND READING » 1 CORINTHIANS 12:3b-7, 12-13

Nobody would be inclined to say "Jesus is Master!" without the insight of the Holy Spirit.

God's various gifts are handed out everywhere; but they all originate in God's Spirit. God's various ministries are carried out everywhere; but they all originate in God's Spirit. God's various expressions of power are in action everywhere; but God himself is behind it all. Each person is given something to do that shows who God is: Everyone gets in on it, everyone benefits. All kinds of things are handed out by the Spirit, and to all kinds of people! The variety is wonderful!

You can easily enough see how this kind of thing works by looking no further than your own body. Your body has many parts—limbs, organs, cells—but no matter how many parts you can name, you're still one body. It's exactly the same with Christ. By means of his one Spirit, we all said good-bye to our partial and piecemeal lives. We each used to independently call our own shots, but then we entered into a large and integrated life in which he has the final say in everything. (This is what we proclaimed in word and action when we were baptized.) Each of us is now a part of his resurrection body, refreshed and sustained at one fountain—his Spirit—where we all come to drink. The old labels we once used to identify ourselves—labels like Jew or Greek, slave or free—are no longer useful. We need something larger, more comprehensive.

Sometimes we think ego trouble is a modern invention, but low self-esteem and jealousy have been with the human race for the long haul. Saint Paul has to deal with the conflicts in Corinth that arise because one person demonstrates a spiritual gift the next person doesn't have. Is it reasonable to be jealous that someone has a skill for leadership, teaching, persuasive speech, or prayer, particularly when the gift benefits the whole community? Reasonable, no; but human, yes. What you have may appear to diminish me, if I'm unsure of my own worth and gifts.

I remember watching a ballet dancer on a stage. The longer I watched, the sadder I felt about the condition of my own body and how uncoordinated and graceless I feel. The comparison I was making interfered with my ability to enjoy the dance and to share with the dancer his own joy in perfecting his vocation. Each gift, unique in itself, is given for all. Far from feeling diminished by the beauty in another, we might find in it cause for rejoicing.

**What kind of talent do you admire the most?
Which talents have you discovered in yourself so far?**

GOSPEL » JOHN 20:19-23

Later on that day, the disciples had gathered together, but, fearful of the Jews, had locked all the doors in the house. Jesus entered, stood among them, and said, "Peace to you." Then he showed them his hands and side.

The disciples, seeing the Master with their own eyes, were exuberant. Jesus repeated his greeting: "Peace to you. Just as the Father sent me, I send you."

Then he took a deep breath and breathed into them. "Receive the Holy Spirit," he said. "If you forgive someone's sins, they're gone for good. If you don't forgive sins, what are you going to do with them?"

What amazement we find in this little scene! Jesus presents to his disciples the wounds of his crucifixion, which caused such horror only days earlier. But this time, the sight of these wounds fills their hearts with joy. On Friday, that bruised body meant despair and defeat. By Sunday night, the sight of it is the greatest hope ever dared.

Pentecost is, in its own way, a second feast of Transfiguration. The disciples see things differently, and it's not only their perception that's new. They themselves are transformed from well-meaning but ineffective people into folks prepared to risk everything for the truth. The disciples (a term meaning "those who learn") become apostles ("those who are sent.") As apostles of the new millennium, we're summoned to this same new vision, and sent on behalf of this same truth. Jesus transforms death into life, darkness into light. We can help the world to see its own wounds in a whole new way.

> **Name some places you habitually go.**
> **How might you be "sent" there as an apostle of good news?**

WE RESPOND

The Holy Spirit is given to the church to bestow gifts to each for the sake of all. Pray about the gifts you possess and how to use them wisely in service to others. If you're unsure of your gifts, ask a friend, teacher, or spiritual director to help you to discern them.

TRINITY SUNDAY

FIRST READING » PROVERBS 8:22-31

Do you hear Lady Wisdom calling? She says:

"GOD sovereignly made me—the first, the basic—
*   before he did anything else.*
I was brought into being a long time ago,
*   well before Earth got its start.*
I arrived on the scene before Ocean,
*   yes, even before Springs and Rivers and Lakes.*
Before Mountains were sculpted and Hills took shape,
*   I was already there, newborn;*
Long before GOD stretched out Earth's Horizons,
*   and tended to the minute details of Soil and Weather,*
And set Sky firmly in place,
*   I was there.*
When he mapped and gave borders to wild Ocean,
*   built the vast vault of Heaven,*
*   and installed the fountains that fed Ocean,*
When he drew a boundary for Sea,
*   posted a sign that said, NO TRESPASSING,*
And then staked out Earth's foundations,
*   I was right there with him, making sure everything fit.*
Day after day I was there, with my joyful applause,
*   always enjoying his company,*
Delighted with the world of things and creatures,
*   happily celebrating the human family."*

The best-known story in the Bible is probably the creation story of Genesis. God made the world in six days and rested on the seventh. You may not be able to list the feats of creation in order—first light, then the firmament? first the chicken, then the egg?—but you get the general idea. God, who exists outside of time and isn't bound by place, designed creation to become an organized environment subject to time.

What Genesis doesn't tell us is that God is companioned through the process of creation by the presence of Wisdom. We imagine the colossal aloneness of God before creation, only to learn that a Triune God is never properly alone. Is Wisdom another name for "Jesus B.C.," the Son of God long before there was a Bethlehem? Is Wisdom a metaphor for the divine blueprint? Speculation goes in several directions, but the one thing we gain from this passage in Proverbs is that it is inappropriate to speak of the aloneness of God. Which is what today's feast is about: The nature of Trinity may be a mystery, but it's not a lonely one.

Is being alone a fearful or welcome idea to you?
What does companionship add or subtract from you?

SECOND READING » ROMANS 5:1-5

By entering through faith into what God has always wanted to do for us—set us right with him, make us fit for him—we have it all together with God because of our Master Jesus. And that's not all: We throw open our doors to God and discover at the same moment that he has already thrown open his door to us. We find ourselves standing where we always hoped we might stand—out in the wide open spaces of God's grace and glory, standing tall and shouting our praise.

There's more to come: We continue to shout our praise even when we're hemmed in with troubles, because we know how troubles can develop passionate patience in us, and how that patience in turn forges the tempered steel of virtue, keeping us alert for whatever God will do next. In alert expectancy such as this, we're never left feeling shortchanged. Quite the contrary—we can't round up enough containers to hold everything God generously pours into our lives through the Holy Spirit!

The Catholic calendar is chock full of feast days. We have special days to honor saints and martyrs and even a few angels. There are a few unusual feasts honoring important church buildings and the Chair of Peter itself. We set aside many days to honor Mary and the most significant events of the life of Jesus. But we have only one God feast: this one. This is the single opportunity we take each year to celebrate the reality of God that's been made known to us. We call this reality Trinity, but it's not a word that appears in the Bible. Trinity may not be God's name for what the divine essence is, but it's our way of expressing how we have come to know God through three major and unique revelations.

Christian tradition has called God by three names: Father, Son, and Holy Spirit. Others have suggested that God is more like a verb than a noun and prefer Creator, Redeemer, and Sanctifier, the three categories of divine activity. Saint Augustine, influenced by the writings of John, noted that God is love and therefore the Trinity is Lover, Beloved, and Love Itself. By whatever name we address the Divine, it's vital that we DO communicate. God is made known to us; it's time to return the favor.

What name do you use to address God in prayer?
How should God address you?

GOSPEL » JOHN 16:12-15

"I still have many things to tell you, but you can't handle them now. But when the Friend comes, the Spirit of the Truth, he will take you by the hand and guide you into all the truth there is. He won't draw attention to himself, but will make sense out of what is about to happen and, indeed, out of all that I have done and said. He will honor me; he will take from me and deliver it to you. Everything

the Father has is also mine. That is why I've said, 'He takes from me and delivers to you.'"

Jesus speaks of himself, the One he knows as Father, and the Friend Spirit interchangeably, at least in the Gospel of John. It can get a little confusing. Jesus and the Father are one, and the Spirit speaks for Jesus. Soon the disciples will share in this same unity when the Spirit comes to dwell in them. How can we tell where one Identity leaves off and another begins?

We can't. And we don't have to. That's the nature of mystery. God can't be sliced up like a pie and served across the table piece by piece. We want to be scientific, or at least mathematical, about Trinity: How much of Jesus is God? (All of him.) Then what's the difference between God and Jesus? (Full humanity.) How can Jesus be fully God and fully human? (Good question!) If Eucharist is Jesus, and we consume Eucharist, how much of us is Christ? (As much as we allow.) This last question is the only one that's no mystery at all. It's an invitation awaiting our response.

How much of your life is given over
to "being Christ," as the Eucharist invites us to be?
What can you do to increase the percentage of your surrender?

WE RESPOND

Celebrate God the Creator today. Enjoy the beauty of the natural world. Celebrate God the Redeemer in word and sacrament. Celebrate God the Sanctifier in prayer and praise.

*We can't round up enough containers
to hold everything God generously pours
into our lives through the Holy Spirit!*

BODY AND BLOOD OF CHRIST

FIRST READING » GENESIS 14:18-20

Melchizedek, king of Salem, brought out bread and wine—he was priest of The High God—and blessed him:

> *Blessed be Abram by The High God,*
> *Creator of Heaven and Earth.*
> *And blessed be The High God,*
> *who handed your enemies over to you.*

Abram gave him a tenth of all the recovered plunder.

Those of us who've been around the church awhile have heard the name Melchizedek a few times. He gets mentioned in Eucharistic Prayer I at Mass: "Accept these gifts, as once you were pleased to accept...the offering of your high priest Melchizedek." Or perhaps you remember the phrase, "You are a priest forever, according to the order of Melchizedek," which appears in Psalm 110 and is applied to Jesus in the Letter to the Hebrews. Melchizedek gets a lot of honor for an obscure king of Salem (an earlier version of Jeru-salem) and a Canaanite priest (a "pagan" priest, to use the old jargon).

But pagan is a relative term at this point in the Bible, since Abram has yet to become Abraham, the father of the Hebrew nation. Abram was a "pagan" himself when God first contacted him. So are many of us as we chase after the gods of material comfort and security on a regular basis. God is not described as unhappy to be blessed by Melchizedek, who recognizes Abram as a servant of the Most High. And the church is happy to honor this early priest of Canaan, who knew holiness when he saw it.

> **In what sense might you still be "pagan," honoring the gods of national or financial security, control of the agenda, or other powers?**

SECOND READING » 1 CORINTHIANS 11:23-26

Let me go over with you again exactly what goes on in the Lord's Supper and why it is so centrally important. I received my instructions from the Master himself and passed them on to you. The Master, Jesus, on the night of his betrayal, took bread. Having given thanks, he broke it and said,

> *This is my body, broken for you.*
> *Do this to remember me.*

After supper, he did the same thing with the cup:

> *This cup is my blood, my new covenant with you.*
> *Each time you drink this cup, remember me.*

What you must solemnly realize is that every time you eat this bread and every time you drink this cup, you reenact in your words and actions the death of the Master. You will be drawn back to this meal again and again until the Master returns.

Not long after we celebrate our God Feast on Trinity Sunday, we honor our communion with God through the Body and Blood of Christ. These feasts are naturally paired because knowing God through the triple revelation of Creation, Jesus, and the Spirit, leads us to seek union with the One who is so good to us. We consider the wonder of life around us—how exquisite and surprising and spectacular the world is. We meditate on the length to which God is willing to go to save life from the jaws of death by passing through them personally. We experience the power of the Spirit coursing through the church, the lives of the saints, and our own lives. How else can we respond, but to celebrate this feast of thanksgiving? Our Eucharist is an expression of God's ultimate self-giving, but it's also a vital response we make to what God has done and still does for us. The table is set, and the invitation is issued. We can say no. But what joy there is in saying yes!

> Would you characterize yourself as a grateful person?
> How do you express gratitude?
> What are the preconditions of a grateful heart?

GOSPEL » LUKE 9:11b-17

Jesus graciously welcomed them and talked to them about the kingdom of God. Those who needed healing, he healed.

As the day declined, the Twelve said, "Dismiss the crowd so they can go to the farms or villages around here and get a room for the night and a bite to eat. We're out in the middle of nowhere."

"You feed them," Jesus said.

They said, "We couldn't scrape up more than five loaves of bread and a couple of fish—unless, of course, you want us to go to town ourselves and buy food for everybody." (There were more than five thousand people in the crowd.)

But he went ahead and directed his disciples, "Sit them down in groups of about fifty." They did what he said, and soon had everyone seated. He took the five loaves and two fish, lifted his face to heaven in prayer, blessed, broke, and gave the bread and fish to the disciples to hand out to the crowd. After the people had all eaten their fill, twelve baskets of leftovers were gathered up.

Most of us would be as appalled as the Twelve if Jesus made this staggering demand of us. Feed five thousand people? On a fisherman's salary? In the middle of nowhere? Give us some lead-time, a boat, some nets, some fundraising expertise maybe. Give us fair odds. Five thousand to twelve is insurmountable by human standards. Five loaves and two fish would hardly make a satisfying meal for the dozen of them, much less for five thousand unexpected guests.

Two observations are useful here. #1: By human standards, it IS impossible, but Jesus never asks us to operate on human power alone. #2: In God's eyes, there's no such thing as unexpected guests. We should expect a guest at any moment, because the world is our neighbor. These two points dovetail. The world is our guest, and our hospitality can never be enough unless we ground ourselves absolutely in God's power to satisfy. Feed the world? Sure we can, and more than just bread. Right now? No better time to start, because our guests are getting mighty hungry while we argue about this.

Do you believe that with God all things are possible?
How do you demonstrate what you believe in how you live?

WE RESPOND

Take Jesus seriously. Begin feeding the world right now, starting with the next person you meet. Share your food, money, faith, time, company, laughter, and love. Decide on what seems a safe amount to share—then give more.

You will be drawn back to this meal
again and again
until the Master returns.

ORDINARY TIME

SECOND SUNDAY OF ORDINARY TIME

.... Mother Knows Best

FIRST READING » ISAIAH 62:1-5

Regarding Zion, I can't keep my mouth shut,
*   regarding Jerusalem, I can't hold my tongue,*
Until her righteousness blazes down like the sun
*   and her salvation flames up like a torch.*
Foreign countries will see your righteousness,
*   and world leaders your glory.*
You'll get a brand-new name
*   straight from the mouth of* GOD.
You'll be a stunning crown in the palm of GOD'S *hand,*
*   a jeweled gold cup held high in the hand of your God.*
 No more will anyone call you Rejected,
*   and your country will no more be called Ruined.*
You'll be called Hephzibah (My Delight),
*   and your land Beulah (Married),*
Because GOD *delights in you*
*   and your land will be like a wedding celebration.*
For as a young man marries his virgin bride,
*   so your builder marries you,*
And as a bridegroom is happy in his bride,
*   so your God is happy with you.*

We all know what vindication is: It's when the other guy is proven wrong! Vindication comes when the bully finally gets his. The unjustly accused is found innocent. It's a day to celebrate.

Our given names today may not be imbued with rich significance. Perhaps yours links you to a parent or reflects your heritage. It may have been chosen to honor a family friend. However you were named, imagine the name that God has for you: Beloved. Delightful. Mine. Consider God's name for you a mission to fulfill with your whole life.

The prophet says the rejected one isn't simply restored, but receives more glory than before. The Rejected becomes Delightful. The exonerated becomes a whole new person. Just as every newborn gets a name, a renewed person is renamed to reflect the transformation. So Abram, Jacob, Cephas, and Saul became Abraham, Israel, Peter, and Paul, the new names describing their relationship to God or a new mission. Vindication includes more than justice, but it's a new identity and purpose as well.

SECOND READING » 1 CORINTHIANS 12:4-11

God's various gifts are handed out everywhere; but they all originate in God's Spirit. God's various ministries are carried out everywhere; but they all originate in God's Spirit. God's various expressions of power are in action everywhere; but God himself is behind it all. Each person is given something to do that shows who God is: Everyone gets in on it, everyone benefits. All kinds of things are handed out by the Spirit, and to all kinds of people! The variety is wonderful:

> *wise counsel*
> *clear understanding*
> *simple trust*
> *healing the sick*
> *miraculous acts*
> *proclamation*
> *distinguishing between spirits*
> *tongues*
> *interpretation of tongues.*

All these gifts have a common origin, but are handed out one by one by the one Spirit of God. He decides who gets what, and when.

There are no super-Christians. Nobody has it all and does it all. Even Mother Teresa had her weaknesses, though they may not have been apparent from a distance. Talk to anyone who knew a saint, and they'll tell you the flip side of the story. Talk to the Franciscans about Francis. Read Thérèse of Lisieux's diary for her own self-criticism. None of us can attain the entirety of the Spirit's gifts. As far as we know, this is by design.

Why would the gifts of the Spirit be given out so piece-meal? You may have unshakeable faith. Your brother has a remarkable healing presence and touch. Your mentor is a giant of extraordinary deeds. Your spouse seems to see clearly to the truth in obscure situations. Your friend, much as you hate to admit it, cuts through your rationalization in every decision you make. How come you have something they don't have, and they all possess a sense that isn't in you?

To be the Body of Christ, we have to work together. Paragons of virtue and talent tend to stand apart, but those who recognize their incompleteness appreciate community. The interdependence of the Body of Christ is displayed in the scattering of the Spirit's gifts. Together, the community of the church assists and supports its members in claiming citizenship in the kingdom to come.

Identify the gifts of the Holy Spirit at work in every member of your family, faith community, or among your friends.

GOSPEL » JOHN 2:1-11

Three days later there was a wedding in the village of Cana in Galilee. Jesus' mother was there. Jesus and his disciples were guests also. When they started running low on wine at the wedding banquet, Jesus' mother told him, "They're just about out of wine."

Jesus said, "Is that any of our business, Mother—yours or mine? This isn't my time. Don't push me."

She went ahead anyway, telling the servants, "Whatever he tells you, do it."

Six stoneware water pots were there, used by the Jews for ritual washings. Each held twenty to thirty gallons. Jesus ordered the servants, "Fill the pots with water." And they filled them to the brim.

"Now fill your pitchers and take them to the host," Jesus said, and they did.

When the host tasted the water that had become wine (he didn't know what had just happened but the servants, of course, knew), he called out to the bridegroom, "Everybody I know begins with their finest wines and after the guests have had their fill brings in the cheap stuff. But you've saved the best till now!"

This act in Cana of Galilee was the first sign Jesus gave, the first glimpse of his glory. And his disciples believed in him.

Which of us has not had this conversation with a parent? At nine years old I was convinced I could only ride a two-wheeler bike IF it had training wheels. My mother said no; training wheels make you dependent. What I needed was just to get on the bike and go. So I mounted it, scowling to hide my uncertainty. As if to prove her wrong, I crashed head-on into a parked truck one block away. After dusting me off and assessing my bloody knees to be "nothing," Mom put me back on the bike. I rode effortlessly from that day on.

Mary gives birth to Jesus twice: once in Bethlehem, and again in Cana. She pushes Jesus into the destiny they both know awaits him, and like a woman in labor, she knows better than he does when "the hour has come." Jesus gives her a scowl and a brush-off at first. And then does as she directs. She knew he would. Her confidence leads her to grease the wheels with the servers even after being rebuffed. When we find ourselves hesitant, we might offer a prayer to the mother of Jesus for guidance. Even Jesus appreciated that her sense of timing could not be better.

> **In what part of your life may fear be holding you back, even though the time is right to act?**

WE RESPOND

Meditate on the particular name God has for you. Call yourself by that name in private, especially when you feel most uncertain.

THIRD SUNDAY OF ORDINARY TIME

FIRST READING » NEHEMIAH 8:2-4a, 5-6, 8-10

So Ezra the priest brought The Revelation to the congregation, which was made up of both men and women—everyone capable of understanding. It was the first day of the seventh month. He read it facing the town square at the Water Gate from early dawn until noon in the hearing of the men and women, all who could understand it. And all the people listened—they were all ears—to the Book of The Revelation.

The scholar Ezra stood on a wooden platform constructed for the occasion. Ezra opened the book. Every eye was on him (he was standing on the raised platform) and as he opened the book everyone stood. Then Ezra praised GOD, the great God, and all the people responded, "Oh Yes! Yes!" with hands raised high. And then they fell to their knees in worship of GOD, their faces to the ground.

They translated the Book of The Revelation of God so the people could understand it and then explained the reading.

Nehemiah the governor, along with Ezra the priest and scholar and the Levites who were teaching the people, said to all the people, "This day is holy to GOD, your God. Don't weep and carry on." They said this because all the people were weeping as they heard the words of The Revelation.

He continued, "Go home and prepare a feast, holiday food and drink; and share it with those who don't have anything: This day is holy to God. Don't feel bad. The joy of GOD is your strength!"

"Read 'em and weep." When you hear those words in a card game, you know you're defeated. The winning cards stare you in the face, and the game is out of your hands.

The Israelites had the same response to the long, long declaration of the law Ezra read before the assembly. The recently returned exiles were a different generation from the one propelled from Jerusalem. This was the first time they'd heard God's will proclaimed to them, since the manuscript had just been discovered in a forgotten archive. The crowd, standing from dawn till noon, was hearing for the first time of God's great love for them—and God's covenant of law, which they were so far from observing. Their shame and discouragement were so great, it broke their hearts.

Happily, God's will isn't a game of cards, and the odds are not stacked against them—or us. The discovery of the law made that day sacred, not a time for despair. But "church behavior" is hard to break. We're much more ready to wear our long faces in the name of religion than to celebrate and rejoice.

What's more common in your experience of religious people: the serious, grim face or the spirit of joy and laughter?

SECOND READING » 1 CORINTHIANS 12:12-30

You can easily enough see how this kind of thing works by looking no further than your own body. Your body has many parts—limbs, organs, cells—but no matter how many parts you can name, you're still one body. It's exactly the same with Christ. By means of his one Spirit, we all said good-bye to our partial and piecemeal lives. We each used to independently call our own shots, but then we entered into a large and integrated life in which he has the final say in everything. (This is what we proclaimed in word and action when we were baptized.) Each of us is now a part of his resurrection body, refreshed and sustained at one fountain—his Spirit—where we all come to drink. The old labels we once used to identify ourselves—labels like Jew or Greek, slave or free—are no longer useful. We need something larger, more comprehensive.

I want you to think about how all this makes you more significant, not less. A body isn't just a single part blown up into something huge. It's all the different-but-similar parts arranged and functioning together. If Foot said, "I'm not elegant like Hand, embellished with rings; I guess I don't belong to this body," would that make it so? If Ear said, "I'm not beautiful like Eye, limpid and expressive; I don't deserve a place on the head," would you want to remove it from the body? If the body was all eye, how could it hear? If all ear, how could it smell? As it is, we see that God has carefully placed each part of the body right where he wanted it.

But I also want you to think about how this keeps your significance from getting blown up into self-importance. For no matter how significant you are, it is only because of what you are a part of. An enormous eye or a gigantic hand wouldn't be a body, but a monster. What we have is one body with many parts, each its proper size and in its proper place. No part is important on its own. Can you imagine Eye telling Hand, "Get lost; I don't need you"? Or, Head telling Foot, "You're fired; your job has been phased out"? As a matter of fact, in practice it works the other way—the "lower" the part, the more basic, and therefore necessary. You can live without an eye, for instance, but not without a stomach. When it's a part of your own body you are concerned with, it makes no difference whether the part is visible or clothed, higher or lower. You give it dignity and honor just as it is, without comparisons. If anything, you have more concern for the lower parts than the higher. If you had to choose, wouldn't you prefer good digestion to full-bodied hair?

The way God designed our bodies is a model for understanding our lives together as a church: every part dependent on every other part, the parts we mention and the parts we don't, the parts we see and the parts we don't. If one part hurts, every other part is involved in the hurt, and in the healing. If one part flourishes, every other part enters into the exuberance.

You are Christ's body—that's who you are! You must never forget this. Only as you accept your part of that body does your "part" mean anything. You're familiar with some of the parts that God has formed in his church, which is his "body":

apostles
prophets
teachers
miracle workers
healers
helpers
organizers
those who pray in tongues.

But it's obvious by now, isn't it, that Christ's church is a complete Body and not a gigantic, unidimensional Part? It's not all Apostle, not all Prophet, not all Miracle Worker, not all Healer, not all Prayer in Tongues, not all Interpreter of Tongues. And yet some of you keep competing for so-called "important" parts.

Parishes can't exist without apostles: those sent out like rockets to the far corners of the parish or the world. And communities do need prophets who continually challenge our complacency. Parishes would fold without teachers and catechists—unpaid, underpaid, often unacclaimed—yet vital to the life of the church. Modern miracle workers may be writers of big checks or layers of concrete; their mighty deeds are the cornerstones of each new ministry. Those present to the sick deserve more praise and recognition than this space can hold in. Even folks who bring the language of heaven to our ears with the gift of tongues or music need our thanks.

But how about a word for administration, among the most thankless jobs in the church? I'm talking about folks who answer phones, type letters, balance budgets. Envelope stuffers and bazaar organizers, committee leaders, and yes, even pastors. Paul claims administration as a gift of the Spirit given to the church. It may seem like so much paperwork, but out from under endless meetings, the work of the church rises and takes flight.

> **How many gifts and roles on Paul's list can you identify within your community?**

GOSPEL » LUKE 1:1-4; 4:14-21

So many others have tried their hand at putting together a story of the wonderful harvest of Scripture and history that took place among us, using reports handed down by the original eyewitnesses who served this Word with their very lives. Since I have investigated all the reports in close detail, starting from the story's beginning, I decided to write it all out for you, most honorable Theophilus, so you can know beyond the shadow of a doubt the reliability of what you were taught.

Jesus returned to Galilee powerful in the Spirit. News that he was back spread through the countryside. He taught in their meeting places to everyone's acclaim and pleasure.

He came to Nazareth where he had been reared. As he always did on the Sabbath, he went to the meeting place. When he stood up to read, he was handed the scroll of the prophet Isaiah. Unrolling the scroll, he found the place where it was written,

> *God's Spirit is on me;*
> > *he's chosen me to preach the Message of good news to the poor,*
> *Sent me to announce pardon to prisoners and*
> > *recovery of sight to the blind,*
> *To set the burdened and battered free,*
> > *to announce, "This is God's year to act!"*

He rolled up the scroll, handed it back to the assistant, and sat down. Every eye in the place was on him, intent. Then he started in, "You've just heard Scripture make history. It came true just now in this place."

Sixty percent of the stories in Luke are told nowhere else in the New Testament. This year the church focuses this gospel, so it's worth taking a closer look at what makes it unique. Did the church really need a third gospel?

Scholars say Luke, a Greek follower of Paul, has a special commitment to "redefining" Israel. Consider: A Gentile might have little natural interest in the savior of a small Jewish country. Luke focuses on how Jesus might be relevant to outsiders. Luke fashions his story of the Jewish messiah to be significant to his Greek readers.

So we hear how Jesus extends sympathy and healing toward Roman soldiers. Jesus tells the story of a Samaritan and calls him good and of a son who strays into Gentile territory and yet is welcomed back by his father. Pilate seems more sympathetic in Luke's depiction. And women, more visible in Greek culture, get much more attention from Luke. Luke reinvents "the chosen people of Israel" as anyone who embraces the good news of Jesus. Luke also goes on to tell of the exploits of the church beyond Israel in Acts—but that's another story.

> **What features distinguish the four gospels**
> **and their testimonies in your understanding?**

WE RESPOND

Read the introduction to Luke in your Bible. Flip through the gospel and get familiar with its stories. Notice stories about outsiders: foreigners, the despised, women, and the poor.

FOURTH SUNDAY OF ORDINARY TIME

FIRST READING » JEREMIAH 1:4-5, 17-19

This is what GOD said:

"Before I shaped you in the womb,
I knew all about you.
Before you saw the light of day,
I had holy plans for you:
A prophet to the nations—
that's what I had in mind for you.

But you—up on your feet and get dressed for work!
Stand up and say your piece. Say exactly what I tell you to say.
Don't pull your punches
or I'll pull you out of the lineup.

Stand at attention while I prepare you for your work.
I'm making you as impregnable as a castle,
Immovable as a steel post,
solid as a concrete block wall.
You're a one-man defense system
against this culture,
Against Judah's kings and princes,
against the priests and local leaders.
They'll fight you, but they won't
even scratch you.
I'll back you up every inch of the way."
GOD's Decree.

If we act according to God's will, there's a sure way to know we're on the right track: We'll feel hostile push-back from some direction. If all we experience is the esteem of others, we're probably doing something wrong.

Jesus says no servant is greater than the master. If the world disapproves of you, know that it hated Jesus first. Approval is earned by those who conform to worldly values. To earn social approval, believe what the pundits say. Hold the opinions spoon-fed by the media. Want the things advertisers are selling. If you're wearing the right sneakers, the system is working and you're part of it. But if you make people think uncomfortable thoughts—say, by championing the oppressed or humanizing the agreed-upon enemy—the growl of disapproval will be evident. The more successfully you challenge the popular mindset, the more likely you'll be crucified.

The point isn't to be hated but to be truthful. Jeremiah was so truthful, to a culture like ours which is glad to be lied to, that he was persecuted. We all prefer approval. The truth is a high price to pay for it.

Where are you tempted to conform to popular values? Where do you feel the pushback that comes with adhering to Christ?

SECOND READING » 1 CORINTHIANS 12:31 – 13:13

But now I want to lay out a far better way for you.

If I speak with human eloquence and angelic ecstasy but don't love, I'm nothing but the creaking of a rusty gate.

If I speak God's Word with power, revealing all his mysteries and making everything plain as day, and if I have faith that says to a mountain, "Jump," and it jumps, but I don't love, I'm nothing.

If I give everything I own to the poor and even go to the stake to be burned as a martyr, but I don't love, I've gotten nowhere. So, no matter what I say, what I believe, and what I do, I'm bankrupt without love.

Love never gives up.
Love cares more for others than for self.
Love doesn't want what it doesn't have.
Love doesn't strut,
Doesn't have a swelled head,
Doesn't force itself on others,
Isn't always "me first,"
Doesn't fly off the handle,
Doesn't keep score of the sins of others,
Doesn't revel when others grovel,
Takes pleasure in the flowering of truth,
Puts up with anything,
Trusts God always,
Always looks for the best,
Never looks back,
But keeps going to the end.

Love never dies. Inspired speech will be over some day; praying in tongues will end; understanding will reach its limit. We know only a portion of the truth, and what we say about God is always incomplete. But when the Complete arrives, our incompletes will be canceled.

When I was an infant at my mother's breast, I gurgled and cooed like any infant. When I grew up, I left those infant ways for good.

We don't yet see things clearly. We're squinting in a fog, peering through a mist. But it won't be long before the weather clears and the sun shines bright! We'll see it all then, see it all as clearly as God sees us, knowing him directly just as he knows us!

But for right now, until that completeness, we have three things to do to lead us toward that consummation: Trust steadily in God, hope unswervingly, love extravagantly. And the best of the three is love.

If the last Bible in the world were about to be burned, snatch this page from the flames. Paul's stirring words about the true nature of love are unrivaled by all the sonnets of Shakespeare. Do you want to know how to love? Read 1 Corinthians 13. Do you want to know how to live? Read it again. Loving God, self, and neighbor are the sum of law and prophecy.

Refining our love is the work of a lifetime. Eliminating prejudice, judgmentalism, and cynicism is merely the first stage, and that's no picnic. Developing patience takes constant vigilance, and to be kind—just that—is a wonder. When was the last time someone was kind to you? When were you kind?

Love aims toward the future. Love isn't about nostalgia but about hope. If what we love is long gone, we aren't talking about Christian love, but mere sentimentality. Love means to "hope unswervingly." Love trusts in God, a kingdom coming, good news, and the peace that springs from justice. Until our hearts are on fire for the future, our love is still a work in progress.

> **Make a pie chart of your love.**
> **What percentage of your love is attached to the past,**
> **and what's directed toward the future?**

GOSPEL » LUKE 4:21-30

Jesus rolled up the scroll, handed it back to the assistant, and sat down. Every eye in the place was on him, intent. Then he started in, "You've just heard Scripture make history. It came true just now in this place."

All who were there, watching and listening, were surprised at how well he spoke. But they also said, "Isn't this Joseph's son, the one we've known since he was a youngster?"

He answered, "I suppose you're going to quote the proverb, 'Doctor, go heal yourself. Do here in your hometown what we heard you did in Capernaum.' Well, let me tell you something: No prophet is ever welcomed in his hometown. Isn't it a fact that there were many widows in Israel at the time of Elijah during that three and a half years of drought when famine devastated the land, but the only widow to whom Elijah was sent was in Sarepta in Sidon? And there were many lepers in Israel at the time of the prophet Elisha but the only one cleansed was Naaman the Syrian."

That set everyone in the meeting place seething with anger. They threw him out, banishing him from the village, then took him to a mountain cliff at the edge of the village to throw him to his doom, but he gave them the slip and was on his way.

Jesus' first recorded homily doesn't go over well with the hometown crowd. At first they're surprised by his poise. A fine reading from the carpenter's son! Imagine that!

But then Jesus pokes them in the eye with Luke's gospel theme: God champions outsiders. God stands with the people we don't care about. It's the foreign widow who gets help, someone else's lepers who are healed.

The crowd's admiration melts. Their fury propels Jesus out of the meeting place, out of town, out to the cliff's edge! The ministry of Jesus might have concluded right there in Chapter 4. But he passes through their hands like sand.

Do we blame Nazareth's citizens for behaving this way? Aren't we reluctant to send medical supplies to the Third World when we can't afford to see our own doctors? Don't we balk at supporting tutors for center-city kids as we struggle to get our own children through school? The diocese closes our parish and opens a ministry to migrant families: Where's the justice in that?

It's hard to point a finger at Nazareth.

Do you give more of your heart over to love or to fury?

WE RESPOND

Take one line from 1 Corinthians 13 that challenges you in a personal way. Write it out and tape it to your computer or bathroom mirror or dashboard. Meditate on it until it enters your heart and your life.

Trust steadily in God, hope unswervingly, love extravagantly.

FIFTH SUNDAY IN ORDINARY TIME

FIRST READING » ISAIAH 6:1-2a, 3-8

In the year that King Uzziah died, I saw the Master sitting on a throne—high, exalted!—and the train of his robes filled the Temple. Angel-seraphs hovered above him, each with six wings. And they called back and forth one to the other,

> *Holy, Holy, Holy is GOD-of-the-Angel-Armies.*
> *His bright glory fills the whole earth.*

The foundations trembled at the sound of the angel voices, and then the whole house filled with smoke. I said,

"Doom! It's Doomsday!
  I'm as good as dead!
Every word I've ever spoken is tainted—
  blasphemous even!
And the people I live with talk the same way,
  using words that corrupt and desecrate.
And here I've looked God in the face!
  The King! GOD-of-the-Angel-Armies!"

Then one of the angel-seraphs flew to me. He held a live coal that he had taken with tongs from the altar. He touched my mouth with the coal and said,

"Look. This coal has touched your lips.
  Gone your guilt,
  your sins wiped out."
And then I heard the voice of the Master:
  "Whom shall I send?
  Who will go for us?"
I spoke up,
  "I'll go.
  Send me!"

Some folks are privileged to be baptized as adults. But that decision was made for most of us long ago by our parents when we were in no position to argue. Still, every Christian faces a moment when the decision to follow Christ or not is placed squarely in our hands. We choose. And God will not override our choice.

Whom shall I send, God asks, when a family is evicted for falling behind on the rent? Who will cry out when the environment is threatened by economic greed; when a child is beaten; when a neighborhood is endangered by drug dealers; when an elderly person is ill and alone? No one can do everything but each of us can do something. Every voice not raised for justice is part of the grand silence that assents to injustice.

Perhaps we've felt shy about entering the arena of social conflict. Heroism is a difficult fit in our no-drama little lives. Yet in Baptism, we're initiated to a share in Christ's death. Under those conditions, heroism may be hard to avoid.

In what way might you be moved at this time to answer God's call: Whom shall I send?

SECOND READING » 1 CORINTHIANS 15:1-11

Friends, let me go over the Message with you one final time—this Message that I proclaimed and that you made your own; this Message on which you took your stand and by which your life has been saved. (I'm assuming, now, that your belief was the real thing and not a passing fancy, that you're in this for good and holding fast.)

The first thing I did was place before you what was placed so emphatically before me: that the Messiah died for our sins, exactly as Scripture tells it; that he was buried; that he was raised from death on the third day, again exactly as Scripture says; that he presented himself alive to Peter, then to his closest followers, and later to more than five hundred of his followers all at the same time, most of them still around (although a few have since died); that he then spent time with James and the rest of those he commissioned to represent him; and that he finally presented himself alive to me. It was fitting that I bring up the rear. I don't deserve to be included in that inner circle, as you well know, having spent all those early years trying my best to stamp God's church right out of existence.

But because God was so gracious, so very generous, here I am. And I'm not about to let his grace go to waste. Haven't I worked hard trying to do more than any of the others? Even then, my work didn't amount to all that much. It was God giving me the work to do, God giving me the energy to do it. So whether you heard it from me or from those others, it's all the same: We spoke God's truth and you entrusted your lives.

Many of us could easily come forward with a litany of our faults. Among them might be procrastination, unruly temper, impulsive behavior, laziness, judgmentalism, cynicism, or timidity. In and of themselves, these components of our character may not be "sins" in the technical sense. But they may predispose us to choose wrong or fail to do good: the sins of commission and omission. Our little character flaws, as we like to think of them, may not be so harmless after all.

Saint Paul was aware of the defects in his character, both large and small. He knew he had a tendency to be proud and boastful, and to judge others who were not as morally perfect as he strove to be. His boasting and judging led him to persecute the early church brutally—before he was moved by Christ to join it. Ever after, Paul's boasting was in the power of Christ, and his passion for perfection led him to weave the theology of Christianity that supports the church to this day. Through the grace of God, even our flaws can be useful.

How might your personal flaws lead
to real avenues of sinful behavior?
How does your faith address
these flaws and transform them?

GOSPEL » LUKE 5:1-11

*Once when Jesus was standing on the shore of Lake Gennesaret, the crowd was
pushing in on him to better hear the Word of God. He noticed two boats tied up.
The fishermen had just left them and were out scrubbing their nets. He climbed
into the boat that was Simon's and asked him to put out a little from the shore.
Sitting there, using the boat for a pulpit, he taught the crowd.*

*When he finished teaching, he said to Simon, "Push out into deep water and
let your nets out for a catch."*

*Simon said, "Master, we've been fishing hard all night and haven't caught
even a minnow. But if you say so, I'll let out the nets." It was no sooner said
than done—a huge haul of fish, straining the nets past capacity. They waved to
their partners in the other boat to come help them. They filled both boats, nearly
swamping them with the catch.*

*Simon Peter, when he saw it, fell to his knees before Jesus. "Master, leave. I'm
a sinner and can't handle this holiness. Leave me to myself." When they pulled
in that catch of fish, awe overwhelmed Simon and everyone with him. It was the
same with James and John, Zebedee's sons, coworkers with Simon.*

*Jesus said to Simon, "There is nothing to fear. From now on you'll be fishing
for men and women." They pulled their boats up on the beach, left them, nets
and all, and followed him.*

In a short time Jesus had become wildly popular. In a town where, admittedly, not
much ever happened, it was now dangerous for Jesus to speak in public. For his own
safety he waded over and sat in the boat of a fisherman whose nightshift had just
ended. Jesus asked if Simon would be so kind as to give him a little distance from
the shore to buffer him from the press of the crowds. It's important to note they had
just met. Simon the fisherman had yet to become Peter the disciple, the Lord's right-
hand man.

As Jesus preached from his boat, Simon washed his nets and couldn't help but
hear what Jesus was saying. Exhausted from a fruitless night's work, Simon wondered if such fine words could make any difference to his life. When Jesus asked
him to take the boat out deeper and fish again, it was as if the preacher had read
his thoughts. The resulting catch was so astonishing, it nearly sank two boats. But
if Simon thought he could make a buck off this gospel, he was in for a surprise. He'd
just signed on to serve a different fleet entirely.

WE RESPOND

God is calling you, with your gifts and flaws, to serve in the catch of your life. Pray the prayer of Isaiah: Here I am, Lord, send me!

Even then, my work didn't amount to all that much.
It was God giving me the work to do,
God giving me the energy to do it.

SIXTH SUNDAY IN ORDINARY TIME

.... Standing on Level Ground

FIRST READING » JEREMIAH 17:5-8

GOD's Message:

"Cursed is the strong one
who depends on mere humans,
Who thinks he can make it on muscle alone
and sets GOD aside as dead weight.
He's like a tumbleweed on the prairie,
out of touch with the good earth.
He lives rootless and aimless
in a land where nothing grows.

"But blessed is the man who trusts me, GOD,
the woman who sticks with GOD.
They're like trees replanted in Eden,
putting down roots near the rivers—
Never a worry through the hottest of summers,
never dropping a leaf,
Serene and calm through droughts,
bearing fresh fruit every season."

In God we trust. At least that's what it says on our money. It's harder to find evidence of that trust in the way we arrange our lives. How many kinds of insurance do you carry? Do you have a savings account? In how many directions do you pledge your allegiance? Our security rests on many practical pillars. How does trusting God fit into that?

It's not necessary to close your IRA to prove your loyalty to God. But it's useful to reflect on how we depend on ourselves and our systems to carry us through. We profess faith in God but, as with our major medical policy, we hope we won't have to tap into it. When it comes to the matters that shape our lives, we count heavily on our own initiative. This works well much of the time. But when we come up against our mortality in loss, sickness, disability, or other crises, we find out quickly what a short plank we walk to the end of our own resources. In such hours we learn whether we really do trust in God—or if that phrase just looks good on the money.

> **When has trusting in God gotten you**
> **where trust in things failed to take you?**

SECOND READING » 1 CORINTHIANS 15:12, 16-20

Now, let me ask you something profound yet troubling. If you became believers because you trusted the proclamation that Christ is alive, risen from the dead, how can you let people say that there is no such thing as a resurrection?

If corpses can't be raised, then Christ wasn't, because he was indeed dead. And if Christ wasn't raised, then all you're doing is wandering about in the dark, as lost as ever. It's even worse for those who died hoping in Christ and resurrection, because they're already in their graves. If all we get out of Christ is a little inspiration for a few short years, we're a pretty sorry lot. But the truth is that Christ has been raised up, the first in a long legacy of those who are going to leave the cemeteries.

Philosophers and playwrights of ancient Greece—Aristotle, Plato, Homer, Virgil—put learning within reach of the popular mind. While in our culture we use entertainment largely to avoid thinking, Greek culture encouraged creative thinking as the greatest parlor game of all. Plato writes of Socrates, who gathered gangs of youths on street corners and taught them to think for themselves—much to the outrage of their elders. It should be no surprise that Christians of Corinth, after considering Paul's teachings about Jesus, tried to shape this story into another wisdom teaching, conveniently leaving out scary parts like the crucifixion and mystical parts like resurrection.

The Christian story needs its scary and mystical parts. They're at the heart of the message, what the church calls the kerygma of our faith. "Christ has died, Christ is risen, Christ will come again" is shorthand for the gospel. If you hang on to the moral teachings alone, you may have a system of ethics. You don't have Christianity.

Are you more comfortable with Jesus the teacher or Jesus the savior?
How do you incorporate both into your faith as a Christian?

GOSPEL » LUKE 6:17, 20-26

Coming down off the mountain with them, he stood on a plain surrounded by disciples, and was soon joined by a huge congregation from all over Judea and Jerusalem, even from the seaside towns of Tyre and Sidon. Then he spoke:

You're blessed when you've lost it all.
God's kingdom is there for the finding.

You're blessed when you're ravenously hungry.
Then you're ready for the Messianic meal.

You're blessed when the tears flow freely.
Joy comes with the morning.

"Count yourself blessed every time someone cuts you down or throws you out, every time someone smears or blackens your name to discredit me. What it means is that the truth is too close for comfort and that that person is uncomfortable. You can be glad when that happens—skip like a lamb, if you like! —for even though they don't like it, I do...and all heaven applauds. And know

that you are in good company; my preachers and witnesses have always been treated like this.

But it's trouble ahead if you think you have it made.
What you have is all you'll ever get.

And it's trouble ahead if you're satisfied with yourself.
Your self will not satisfy you for long.

And it's trouble ahead if you think life's all fun and games.
There's suffering to be met, and you're going to meet it.

"There's trouble ahead when you live only for the approval of others, saying what flatters them, doing what indulges them. Popularity contests are not truth contests—look how many scoundrel preachers were approved by your ancestors! Your task is to be true, not popular."

The Sermon on the Mount is the most recognized passage of the gospel. Matthew's gospel pictures Jesus on a hillside preaching. Luke tells us Jesus delivered this famous sermon on a plain. Does it matter whether this is the Sermon on the Mount or the Plain? Scholars have speculated that Luke didn't know any better. As a Greek convert to the faith, he may never have been close enough to the geography of Israel to know the difference.

But in the context of Luke's whole story, it's a shrewd move to have Jesus preaching on level ground. Jesus literally levels the playing field by blessing the poor with the advantages of the rich, promising satisfaction to the hungry, and laughter to those who grieve. He likewise assures those who've made it that "it's trouble ahead." If Jesus stands on a par with the crowds and doesn't enjoy a privileged place, we can be sure the justice of the kingdom will make no exceptions.

How are you, at this time in life,
poor, hungry, sorrowing, or excluded?
How are you rich, satisfied, celebrating, and admired?

WE RESPOND

Commit yourself to leveling the playing field. Share your surplus: money, time, love, joy, faith, talent, attention, respect.

SEVENTH SUNDAY IN ORDINARY TIME

FIRST READING » 1 SAMUEL 26:2, 7-9, 12-13, 22-23

Saul was on his way to the wilderness of Ziph, taking three thousand of his best men, the pick of the crop, to hunt for David in that wild desert.

So David and Abishai entered the encampment by night, and there he was—Saul, stretched out asleep at the center of the camp, his spear stuck in the ground near his head, with Abner and the troops sound asleep on all sides.

Abishai said, "This is the moment! God has put your enemy in your grasp. Let me nail him to the ground with his spear. One hit will do it, believe me; I won't need a second!"

But David said to Abishai, "Don't you dare hurt him! Who could lay a hand on GOD's anointed and even think of getting away with it?"

David took the spear and water jug that were right beside Saul's head, and they slipped away. Not a soul saw. Not a soul knew. No one woke up! They all slept through the whole thing. A blanket of deep sleep from GOD had fallen on them.

Then David went across to the opposite hill and stood far away on the top of the mountain. With this safe distance between them he said, "See what I have here? The king's spear. Let one of your servants come and get it. It's GOD's business to decide what to do with each of us in regard to what's right and who's loyal. GOD put your life in my hands today, but I wasn't willing to lift a finger against GOD's anointed."

Revenge is supposed to be sweet. Anyone familiar with the stories of David and Saul appreciates Abishai's desire for vengeance. King Saul, who once loved David as a son, used to be soothed by the music David played for him to calm his nerves. But Saul's descent into paranoia made David a marked man, constantly in fear of his life. David's loyal nephew Abishai only wants to protect the man who will be the next king of Israel. Just one thrust, loyal Abishai guarantees, and this campaign of terror will be over.

David won't allow it. He has a chance to destroy his enemy and will not take it. Instead, David recalls how Saul was once God's chosen and anointed king over Israel. That same anointing has come upon David. To question God's choice in the first instance might cast doubt in the second. When we have a chance to defeat an opponent, do we stop to think that God has a plan for that person too? David defers to God's judgment. We're often only too happy to follow ours.

> How have you dealt with opponents?
> How might David's way shape
> our future response to sources of conflict?

SECOND READING » 1 CORINTHIANS 15:45-49

We follow this sequence in Scripture: The First Adam received life, the Last Adam is a life-giving Spirit. Physical life comes first, then spiritual—a firm base shaped from the earth, a final completion coming out of heaven. The First Man was made out of earth, and people since then are earthy; the Second Man was made out of heaven, and people now can be heavenly. In the same way that we've worked from our earthy origins, let's embrace our heavenly ends.

Back in college, I took a grisly course called Structures of English. It involved grammar and phonics and Noam Chomsky and all sorts of things I never could sort out. But the professor earned my respect when he guessed where I was from, within twenty miles, based on the sounds of my vowels alone. It seems our use of language is so parochial that we betray our origins in a couple of words.

As people of earth, we wear our origins as clearly as the tags in our clothes, spelling out where we come from and of what stuff we are made. Though we may think of ourselves as 100% clay—that is, fully Adam—we're really a blend of mortal and eternal materials. We may be "Made in USA," but we're made FOR the reign of God. The clay part will wear thin, but the eternal part has a warranty that's hard to believe. We give evidence to the heavenly part of ourselves when we seek forgiveness instead of revenge, generosity in place of possessiveness. People can tell we are "Made for Heaven" when our Christian dialect is showing.

What have you done today that gives evidence that you are made for heaven?

GOSPEL » LUKE 6:27-38

Jesus said to his disciples:

"To you who are ready for the truth, I say this: Love your enemies. Let them bring out the best in you, not the worst. When someone gives you a hard time, respond with the energies of prayer for that person. If someone slaps you in the face, stand there and take it. If someone grabs your shirt, giftwrap your best coat and make a present of it. If someone takes unfair advantage of you, use the occasion to practice the servant life. No more tit-for-tat stuff. Live generously.

"Here is a simple rule of thumb for behavior: Ask yourself what you want people to do for you; then grab the initiative and do it for them! If you only love the lovable, do you expect a pat on the back? Run-of-the-mill sinners do that. If you only help those who help you, do you expect a medal? Garden-variety sinners do that. If you only give for what you hope to get out of it, do you think that's charity? The stingiest of pawnbrokers does that.

"I tell you, love your enemies. Help and give without expecting a return. You'll never—I promise—regret it. Live out this God-created identity the way our Father lives toward us, generously and graciously, even when we're at our worst. Our Father is kind; you be kind.

"Don't pick on people, jump on their failures, criticize their faults—unless, of course, you want the same treatment. Don't condemn those who are down; that hardness can boomerang. Be easy on people; you'll find life a lot easier. Give away your life; you'll find life given back, but not merely given back—given back with bonus and blessing. Giving, not getting, is the way. Generosity begets generosity."

"Be nice to Brenda," the grownups said. Then they left us alone in the yard together. At the age of seven, the idea of being nice to Brenda was nauseating to me. Brenda was the antithesis of the girl I was. She never got dirty. She wore pink ankle socks. She had naturally curly hair that never mussed and an annoying little yappy dog. No matter what sort of play I suggested, she always backed off in horror saying, "I can't do that." Brenda was a complete mess.

What Jesus asks us to do goes far beyond being nice to Brenda. We aren't asked merely to tolerate our enemies, to make nice with them under mandatory social situations. We're asked to take them into our hearts, to make room for them in our prayers, to offer them kindness for unkindness. We have to open our minds and change our hearts in regard to them. And the yappy dog too. We love our enemies because the act of loving transforms us and could transform them too. It's the only thing that can. The only acceptable enemy in the reign of God is no enemy at all.

How could Jesus' formula for dealing with enemies change your life?

WE RESPOND

Choose an enemy in your life (hint: an intolerable relative, a grating co-worker, maybe even yourself) and consider taking three steps to peace. Ask Jesus to help you, since this is his idea.

EIGHTH SUNDAY IN ORDINARY TIME

.... Heart Fruit

FIRST READING » SIRACH 27:4-7

As sifting flour leaves dust behind, so sifting ideas leaves lint of their own. As pottery needs a furnace, so the just need suffering. As fruit trees need pruning, so people's words need censoring. Hear people out before you praise them; opinions reveal real values.

Abraham Lincoln said it a little differently than Ben Sira, the author of Sirach: "It is better to remain silent and thought a fool, than to speak up and remove all doubt." We scrutinize our candidates in every election year to hear how their words confirm or betray their character. When we talk we give ourselves away too, despite our best intentions. That's why there's a law that says, "You have the right to remain silent."

The words we speak not only reveal us, but they have a way of deepening who we are. This shouldn't surprise believers in an incarnate God. Remember the story of "My Fair Lady"? In an era ruled by class, Eliza Doolittle is not a lady at the start of the story. Once she learns to talk like one, however, the identity blooms in her and takes over. When you and I speak bitterly, we harden into cynics. When we think violent thoughts, it's only a matter of time before we indulge violent actions. Words take on flesh, the way God's word of love becomes the baby of Bethlehem, and Jesus' stories of forgiveness become the man on the cross.

How do your words reveal the person you are,
and the person you're becoming?

SECOND READING » 1 CORINTHIANS 15:54-58

In the resurrection scheme of things, this has to happen: everything perishable taken off the shelves and replaced by the imperishable, this mortal replaced by the immortal. Then the saying will come true:

> *Death swallowed by triumphant Life!*
> *Who got the last word, oh, Death?*
> *Oh, Death, who's afraid of you now?*

It was sin that made death so frightening and law-code guilt that gave sin its leverage, its destructive power. But now in a single victorious stroke of Life, all three—sin, guilt, death—are gone, the gift of our Master, Jesus Christ. Thank God!

With all this going for us, my dear, dear friends, stand your ground. And don't hold back. Throw yourselves into the work of the Master, confident that nothing you do for him is a waste of time or effort.

First the bad news: Everything we create, organize, dream, and love in this world is bound for destruction. This includes your house, your career, all your best plans, and the people you care about. This isn't just bad news: this is a catastrophe.

Now the good news: Everything that serves the kingdom of God remains forever. How much of that includes the above list is up to you.

Of course, we'd all like to think that most...at least, much...well, that some of what we do serves God more than it does our own interests. I can count whole minutes that I was on God's payroll today! But even with my shaky math skills, it seems that a day containing 1,440 minutes is still unevenly weighted with self-promoting activities. My friend clearly wanted more time from me today than I was willing to give. I didn't write that letter to my aunt I've been putting off for weeks. I spent considerably more time eating than I did in prayer. The score so far today? Bound for destruction: 1,400 minutes. Serving the kingdom? You do the math.

> How much of your labor
> serves self-interest vs. eternal values?
> Do the proportions satisfy you?

GOSPEL » LUKE 6:39-45

Jesus quoted a proverb: "'Can a blind man guide a blind man?' Wouldn't they both end up in the ditch? An apprentice doesn't lecture the master. The point is to be careful whom you follow as your teacher.

"It's easy to see a smudge on your neighbor's face and be oblivious to the ugly sneer on your own. Do you have the nerve to say, 'Let me wash your face for you,' when your own face is distorted by contempt? It's this I-know-better-than-you mentality again, playing a holier-than-thou part instead of just living your own part. Wipe that ugly sneer off your own face and you might be fit to offer a washcloth to your neighbor.

"You don't get wormy apples off a healthy tree, nor good apples off a diseased tree. The health of the apple tells the health of the tree. You must begin with your own life-giving lives. It's who you are, not what you say and do, that counts. Your true being brims over into true words and deeds."

How can we develop healthy hearts? First off, clear the decks of all that causes hearts to go rotten: lingering on past injuries, blaming others for who we are now, presuming ill intentions of others, judging according to well-worn prejudices. Unforgiveness has got to go, as well as any hint of self-righteousness.

Then, once our hearts are clean and fresh—I realize I'm glossing over some real hard work here like counseling, confession, grief work, and huge helpings of honesty—only then can we open our hearts to the good things they're intended for. Things like the fruits of the Holy Spirit elsewhere listed as "love, joy, peace, patience, kindness, generosity, faithfulness, gentleness, and self-control." (See Galatians 5:22-23.) If we try to take good fruit in before we discharge any heart-rot we've built up over the years—well, you know how it works with apples. Start with a healed, new-born heart, and virtue will cling to us like butterflies on flowers. It may sound like an awful lot of work, but what will happen to our hearts if we don't do it?

What kind of heart-work do you need to do to rid yourself of the damage of the past?

WE RESPOND

Don't let anything keep you from the goodness God desires for you. Take your heart to a specialist: a priest, counselor, spiritual director, someone who loves you. Let go of what binds you, and seek only goodness.

"It's who you are, not what you say and do, that counts. Your true being brims over into true words and deeds."

TENTH SUNDAY IN ORDINARY TIME

.... The Gift of a Son

FIRST READING » 1 KINGS 17:17-24

The jar of meal didn't run out and the bottle of oil didn't become empty: GOD's promise fulfilled to the letter, exactly as Elijah had delivered it!

Later on the woman's son became sick. The sickness took a turn for the worse—and then he stopped breathing.

The woman said to Elijah, "Why did you ever show up here in the first place—a holy man barging in, exposing my sins, and killing my son?"

Elijah said, "Hand me your son."

He then took him from her bosom, carried him up to the loft where he was staying, and laid him on his bed. Then he prayed, "O GOD, my God, why have you brought this terrible thing on this widow who has opened her home to me? Why have you killed her son?"

Three times he stretched himself out full-length on the boy, praying with all his might, "GOD, my God, put breath back into this boy's body!" GOD listened to Elijah's prayer and put breath back into his body—he was alive! Elijah picked the boy up, carried him downstairs from the loft, and gave him to his mother. "Here's your son," said Elijah, "alive!"

The woman said to Elijah, "I see it all now—you are a holy man. When you speak, GOD speaks—a true word!"

The death of a son was the death of hope in the ancient world. This was especially true for a widow, who would have no man to protect her interests now or in the future. If women had no place outside the home, who would speak for them in the world beyond their door? A son guaranteed the esteem of the community, a home always open to you, and a future of grandchildren.

In the stories of mystics and prophets, widows are often the beneficiaries of attention and kindness. Certainly this is because "the Lord hears the cry of the poor." But also because mystics deal in symbols, and children are metaphors of the future. The healing of a child restores the hope of a future. Our God is always the Lord of present tense, with an eye to future possibility.

> **Do you characterize yourself as a person of hope?**
> **How does hope affect the decisions you make today?**

SECOND READING » GALATIANS 1:11-19

Know this—I am most emphatic here, friends—this great Message I delivered to you is not mere human optimism. I didn't receive it through the traditions, and I wasn't taught it in some school. I got it straight from God, received the Message directly from Jesus Christ.

I'm sure that you've heard the story of my earlier life when I lived in the

Jewish way. In those days I went all out in persecuting God's church. I was systematically destroying it. I was so enthusiastic about the traditions of my ancestors that I advanced head and shoulders above my peers in my career. Even then God had designs on me. Why, when I was still in my mother's womb he chose and called me out of sheer generosity! Now he has intervened and revealed his Son to me so that I might joyfully tell non-Jews about him.

Immediately after my calling—without consulting anyone around me and without going up to Jerusalem to confer with those who were apostles long before I was—I got away to Arabia. Later I returned to Damascus, but it was three years before I went up to Jerusalem to compare stories with Peter. I was there only fifteen days—but what days they were! Except for our Master's brother James, I saw no other apostles.

Paul is a man of many mistakes, freely admitted. What makes him an attractive role model is that despite serious past errors of thinking and behaving, he turns himself around and goes a new way in good cheer. Paul claims his brutal past but doesn't drag it around in shame and false humility, beating himself up about it. He'd been there, done that. After Jesus is revealed to him, Paul sits with his new sight for three years before doing anything. Perhaps he's dumbfounded to have been so wrong—or so forgiven. Or maybe it takes him that long to sift through the ramifications of what he saw. After that, he makes a smooth, severe course correction and never looks back.

Most of us have to do some course correction over the years: a lot or a little, depending on where we started. The most dangerous stance is to imagine we've arrived and need no fine tuning. The mature Christian is never a static one.

> Draw a map of your life indicating moments
> when new information affected your direction.
> Which three life revelations affected your faith the most?

GOSPEL » LUKE 7:11-17

Jesus went to the village Nain. His disciples were with him, along with quite a large crowd. As they approached the village gate, they met a funeral procession— a woman's only son was being carried out for burial. And the mother was a widow. When Jesus saw her, his heart broke. He said to her, "Don't cry." Then he went over and touched the coffin. The pallbearers stopped. He said, "Young man, I tell you: Get up." The dead son sat up and began talking. Jesus presented him to his mother.

They all realized they were in a place of holy mystery; that God was at work among them. They were quietly worshipful—and then noisily grateful, calling out among themselves, "God is back, looking to the needs of his people!" The news of Jesus spread all through the country.

When we think resurrection, we think Easter. Yet three other stories in the gospels merit some attention in this category: Jairus' daughter, Lazarus, and this son of

Nain. A daughter, a brother, and a son. These are all very different cases. Jairus is a synagogue official, regarded as worthy of the attention of Jesus. Yet he pleads for the life of a daughter, among the least esteemed members of a household. Lazarus of course is a friend of Jesus, the brother-protector of his other friends Martha and Mary. Personal affection alone drew Jesus to act.

In the story of Nain, it's the mother's grief that compels Jesus to the scene. Perhaps Jesus previews his own mother's sorrow at his death, which was always present to him. He gave this son back to his mother. One day, he would give his mother to a disciple.

> **We are given to each other as children, siblings,
> and parents, literally and in the spirit.
> How does the human family honor,
> or dishonor, these ties?**

WE RESPOND

Recognize the "place of holy mystery" right where you are. God is capable of restoring anything lost, dead, or missing here. Pray for what is needed.

*They all realized they were
in a place of holy mystery;
that God was at work among them.*

ELEVENTH SUNDAY IN ORDINARY TIME

FIRST READING » 2 SAMUEL 12:7-10, 13

"You're the man!" said Nathan. "And here's what GOD, the God of Israel, has to say to you: I made you king over Israel. I freed you from the fist of Saul. I gave you your master's daughter and other wives to have and to hold. I gave you both Israel and Judah. And if that hadn't been enough, I'd have gladly thrown in much more. So why have you treated the word of GOD with brazen contempt, doing this great evil? You murdered Uriah the Hittite, then took his wife as your wife. Worse, you killed him with an Ammonite sword! And now, because you treated God with such contempt and took Uriah the Hittite's wife as your wife, killing and murder will continually plague your family.

Then David confessed to Nathan, "I've sinned against GOD."

Nathan pronounced, "Yes, but that's not the last word. GOD forgives your sin. You won't die for it."

If you had to choose between throwing a life preserver to a drowning person or to someone doing the backstroke, to whom would you respond? This question is obviously not an ethical stumper. What applies here most certainly has implications for rescues in general. When one fellow is in desperate need and another is just fine, the person to rescue is clearly the one screaming.

Why is it harder to imagine that God engineers all of salvation history for the sake of sinners and not the righteous? And yet many who consider themselves quite good Christians are the first to suspect they've earned God's mercy, and are disgruntled to hear that God might hand it over to folks who, most sincerely, don't have a prayer of deserving it. King David was an adulterer and a murderer—a breaker of two serious commandments, as we might all agree. Yet when confronted with his sins, David admits them, and the prophet Nathan does not hesitate to offer him God's forgiveness. David screamed, and God rescued.

Who is "screaming" for rescue in your family or community?

SECOND READING » GALATIANS 2:16, 19-21

We know very well that we are not set right with God by rule-keeping but only through personal faith in Jesus Christ. How do we know? We tried it—and we had the best system of rules the world has ever seen! Convinced that no human being can please God by self-improvement, we believed in Jesus as the Messiah so that we might be set right before God by trusting in the Messiah, not by trying to be good.

What actually took place is this: I tried keeping rules and working my head off to please God, and it didn't work. So I quit being a "law man" so that I could be God's man. Christ's life showed me how, and enabled me to do it. I identified myself completely with him. Indeed, I have been crucified with Christ. My ego is no longer central. It is no longer important that I appear righteous before you or have your good opinion, and I am no longer driven to impress God. Christ lives in me. The life you see me living is not "mine," but it is lived by faith in the Son of God, who loved me and gave himself for me. I am not going back on that.

Is it not clear to you that to go back to that old rule-keeping, peer-pleasing religion would be an abandonment of everything personal and free in my relationship with God? I refuse to do that, to repudiate God's grace. If a living relationship with God could come by rule-keeping, then Christ died unnecessarily.

No person of faith would dare to look Jesus in the face and say, "Your crucifixion was pointless." The cross is the ultimate sacrifice of ultimate love. How in heaven's name could that be pointless? Yet so many of us have spent our lives trying to be "good enough" to get into heaven. Such an idea renders the death of Jesus irrelevant to our salvation. Sure, we're saying, it was a very generous thing Jesus did—but once I clear up these few bad habits of mine, THEN the gates of heaven will spring open for me!

This is what Saint Paul means by saying we're set right with God not by rule-keeping but by trust in Christ. Even if we kept every rule perfectly, even if that were possible, it wouldn't purchase heaven for us. God rescues us because, honestly folks, God is the only one who can. Getting our moral ducks in a row is our response to God's grace, not what earns us grace. Good moral behavior is not the thing that compels God to be nice to us.

> **When has someone been good to you
> even when you didn't deserve it?**

GOSPEL » LUKE 7:36 – 8:3

One of the Pharisees asked him over for a meal. He went to the Pharisee's house and sat down at the dinner table. Just then a woman of the village, the town harlot, having learned that Jesus was a guest in the home of the Pharisee, came with a bottle of very expensive perfume and stood at his feet, weeping, raining tears on his feet. Letting down her hair, she dried his feet, kissed them, and anointed them with the perfume. When the Pharisee who had invited him saw this, he said to himself, "If this man was the prophet I thought he was, he would have known what kind of woman this is who is falling all over him."

Jesus said to him, "Simon, I have something to tell you."

"Oh? Tell me."

"Two men were in debt to a banker. One owed five hundred silver pieces, the other fifty. Neither of them could pay up, and so the banker canceled both debts. Which of the two would be more grateful?"

Simon answered, "I suppose the one who was forgiven the most."

"That's right," said Jesus. Then turning to the woman, but speaking to Simon, he said, "Do you see this woman? I came to your home; you provided no water for my feet, but she rained tears on my feet and dried them with her hair. You gave me no greeting, but from the time I arrived she hasn't quit kissing my feet. You provided nothing for freshening up, but she has soothed my feet with perfume. Impressive, isn't it? She was forgiven many, many sins, and so she is very, very grateful. If the forgiveness is minimal, the gratitude is minimal."

Then he spoke to her: "I forgive your sins."

That set the dinner guests talking behind his back: "Who does he think he is, forgiving sins!"

He ignored them and said to the woman, "Your faith has saved you. Go in peace."

He continued according to plan, traveled to town after town, village after village, preaching God's kingdom, spreading the Message. The Twelve were with him. There were also some women in their company who had been healed of various evil afflictions and illnesses: Mary, the one called Magdalene, from whom seven demons had gone out; Joanna, wife of Chuza, Herod's manager; and Susanna—along with many others who used their considerable means to provide for the company.

Sinners and prophets have nothing in common. That's what the Pharisee at supper with Jesus is thinking. If Jesus is so holy, he wouldn't accept contact with a sinner. He wouldn't want her in the same room! To Simon, it's proof positive that Jesus isn't so great after all. He should have shrugged off "that sort of woman" like vermin.

This sort of woman, to Jesus, is *forgiven*. Her tears demonstrate the depth of her regret. Her tender service reveals her great love. To reject this woman would deny the ends of a saving God. She's already repented her sin. Time to set her free of it! What Jesus also sees is Simon's lack of love. His host hadn't served the most basic needs of a traveler or greeted him with real affection. Simon's lovelessness shows that his sins are still very close to his heart. It's hard to save someone who doesn't know he's in trouble.

Have you ever refused help even when you needed it very much?

WE RESPOND

Consider times when you've failed to love God, others, and yourself. Seek reconciliation where necessary. Forgive as you are forgiven.

TWELFTH SUNDAY IN ORDINARY TIME

FIRST READING » ZECHARIAH 12:10-11; 13:1

"I'll deal with the family of David and those who live in Jerusalem. I'll pour a spirit of grace and prayer over them. They'll then be able to recognize me as the One they so grievously wounded—that piercing spear-thrust! And they'll weep— oh, how they'll weep! Deep mourning as of a parent grieving the loss of the firstborn child. The lamentation in Jerusalem that day will be massive, as famous as the lamentation over Hadad-Rimmon on the fields of Megiddo.

"On the Big Day, a fountain will be opened for the family of David and all the leaders of Jerusalem for washing away their sins, for scrubbing their stained and soiled lives clean."

For many Catholics our first sense of Jesus is that he is the Man-on-the-Cross. The crucifix is central to our religious consciousness: at the head of the sanctuary in our churches, at the start of every set of rosary beads, affixed to the wall in our homes. Our emphasis on the crucified Lord can seem alien to many of our Protestant friends, who prefer an empty cross reminding them that Jesus is risen and no longer held bound to anything.

But we choose to hold fast to this image of the still-suffering Lord because, in our world, Jesus is in agony every day. In the news we see him in tragic figures war-torn and battle scarred. We see him hungry and thirsty and in need of shelter. We see him sick and lonely, in nursing homes and prisons. We see him as a member of a despised race or an unwanted foreigner. Until the last man, woman, and child is relieved of such suffering, we cannot take the crucifix down and forget our suffering Lord.

**Where in your family or community
do you see signs of suffering?**

SECOND READING » GALATIANS 3:26-29

By faith in Christ you are in direct relationship with God. Your baptism in Christ was not just washing you up for a fresh start. It also involved dressing you in an adult faith wardrobe—Christ's life, the fulfillment of God's original promise.

In Christ's family there can be no division into Jew and non-Jew, slave and free, male and female. Among us you are all equal. That is, we are all in a common relationship with Jesus Christ. Also, since you are Christ's family, then you are Abraham's famous "descendant," heirs according to the covenant promises.

Here's another Catholic understanding of Jesus: that he and his Body, the church, are one. The church's unity is one of our most precious gifts. Many things divide us as individuals before we come into the church from the parking lot. But once inside and gathered around Christ's Word and Sacrament, our unity is the only thing that matters.

We no longer divide the assembly according to who's "Jew or Greek" among us. But how about who speaks English or Spanish or Vietnamese? "Slave and free" may be categories of the past, but how about addictions, mental illness, poverty, and other conditions that make a person decidedly unfree? Gender—"male and female"—remains a fracture in the church that's far from healed. And new cracks in our community pose threats to unity: conservative vs. progressive. Those who want a flag in the sanctuary and those who fear the blending of church and state. However tempted we are to make other things ultimate, our union in Christ remains the bottom line.

What attitudes and issues are especially divisive in your parish today?

GOSPEL » LUKE 9:18-24

One time when Jesus was off praying by himself, his disciples nearby, he asked them, "What are the crowds saying about me, about who I am?"

They said, "John the Baptizer. Others say Elijah. Still others say that one of the prophets from long ago has come back."

He then asked, "And you—what are you saying about me? Who am I?"

Peter answered, "The Messiah of God." Jesus then warned them to keep it quiet. They were to tell no one what Peter had said.

He went on, "It is necessary that the Son of Man proceed to an ordeal of suffering, be tried and found guilty by the religious leaders, high priests, and religion scholars, be killed, and on the third day be raised up alive."

Then he told them what they could expect for themselves: "Anyone who intends to come with me has to let me lead. You're not in the driver's seat—I am. Don't run from suffering; embrace it. Follow me and I'll show you how. Self-help is no help at all. Self-sacrifice is the way, my way, to finding yourself, your true self."

Naming Jesus has never been easy. There are many popular ways to identify him: King, Lord, Messiah, Teacher, Christ, Savior, Son of God, friend, and brother are a few of the titles and roles assigned to him in religious ed classes. To the crowds in his own day, Jesus was ardently debated as the reincarnation of John the Baptist, the returned prophet Elijah, or some other ancient prophet risen from the dead. But the most important answer to the question, "Who is Jesus?" remains the reply you and I give in the privacy of our hearts.

When we call someone by name, we often establish the terms of our relationship in that same address. For example, if we call someone "Mom," "Mrs. Walsh," or "Honey," those names reveal something about the nature of our dealings with that person. The name we use for Jesus does the same thing. Who is he really to us? What do we hope for in this relationship? How close are we willing to get to Jesus?

Choose three names for Jesus that are especially meaningful for you. What does each tell you about your relationship with Jesus?

WE RESPOND

Spend an intentional hour with Jesus this week. It could be in contemplation before the tabernacle, time spent reading the gospels, a visit to a nursing home, or full attention given to someone who needs you.

"Self-help is no help at all.
Self-sacrifice is the way, my way,
to finding yourself, your true self."

THIRTEENTH SUNDAY IN ORDINARY TIME

FIRST READING » 1 KINGS 19:16b, 19-21

GOD said to Elijah, "Anoint Elisha son of Shaphat from Abel Meholah to succeed you as prophet."

Elijah went straight out and found Elisha son of Shaphat in a field where there were twelve pairs of yoked oxen at work plowing; Elisha was in charge of the twelfth pair. Elijah went up to him and threw his cloak over him.

Elisha deserted the oxen, ran after Elijah, and said, "Please! Let me kiss my father and mother good-bye—then I'll follow you."

"Go ahead," said Elijah, "but, mind you, don't forget what I've just done to you."

So Elisha left; he took his yoke of oxen and butchered them. He made a fire with the plow and tackle and then boiled the meat—a true farewell meal for the family. Then he left and followed Elijah, becoming his right-hand man.

God is calling you. This call fulfills the reason for which you were born. Embracing this call leads to the only real joy the human heart can know. What keeps you from running into the arms of your true purpose with all the passion in your being?

We have our excuses. There's no time right now; maybe later, when the pace of life slows down. Maybe we have intriguing choices before us at the moment, and what God asks of us sounds too limiting. Maybe we're so distracted that we can't quite tune in to what God is saying long enough to hear what's being offered. The prophet-to-be Elisha is not unwilling to follow Elijah, the great prophet he'll be replacing. But he just wants a moment to say goodbye to the old life. Elisha already shows a prophetic sensibility: He knows his new call will take him far away from everything he's known.

> **How has God "thrown a cloak" over you,**
> **inviting you to come on a journey of faith?**
> **What keeps you from responding**
> **more fully to that invitation?**

SECOND READING » GALATIANS 5:1, 13-18

Christ has set us free to live a free life. So take your stand! Never again let anyone put a harness of slavery on you.

It is absolutely clear that God has called you to a free life. Just make sure that you don't use this freedom as an excuse to do whatever you want to do and destroy your freedom. Rather, use your freedom to serve one another in love; that's how freedom grows. For everything we know about God's Word is summed up in a single sentence: Love others as you love yourself. That's an act of true freedom. If you bite and ravage each other, watch out—in no time at all you will be annihilating each other, and where will your precious freedom be then?

My counsel is this: Live freely, animated and motivated by God's Spirit. Then you won't feed the compulsions of selfishness. For there is a root of sinful self-interest in us that is at odds with a free spirit, just as the free spirit is incompatible with selfishness. These two ways of life are antithetical, so that you cannot live at times one way and at times another way according to how you feel on any given day. Why don't you choose to be led by the Spirit and so escape the erratic compulsions of a law-dominated existence?

Freedom is a big word in our national vocabulary. We Americans celebrate our liberty and pledge to champion those around the world deprived of theirs. Our Constitution spells out in detail the many forms our liberty takes. We're not a nation that accepts chains readily, as we remember too keenly the price of a human soul bound on either side of slavery.

The story of the Jewish people is much the same. Having known slavery in Egypt, submission in Babylonian exile, and Roman occupation of their land, freedom became a fiery word in Israel's vocabulary. When Saint Paul speaks of the freedom of Christ, he's mindful of how powerful this word is. Law was intended to keep people from sin, yet paradoxically it chained them to an awareness of sin they couldn't escape. The way of the Spirit liberates our hearts to move purposefully in the direction of grace.

> Has religion so far prompted you more
> to avoid sin or seek grace?

GOSPEL » LUKE 9:51-62

When it came close to the time for his Ascension, he gathered up his courage and steeled himself for the journey to Jerusalem. He sent messengers on ahead. They came to a Samaritan village to make arrangements for his hospitality. But when the Samaritans learned that his destination was Jerusalem, they refused hospitality. When the disciples James and John learned of it, they said, "Master, do you want us to call a bolt of lightning down out of the sky and incinerate them?"

Jesus turned on them: "Of course not!" And they traveled on to another village.

On the road someone asked if he could go along. "I'll go with you, wherever," he said.

Jesus was curt: "Are you ready to rough it? We're not staying in the best inns, you know."

Jesus said to another, "Follow me."

He said, "Certainly, but first excuse me for a couple of days, please. I have to make arrangements for my father's funeral."

Jesus refused. "First things first. Your business is life, not death. And life is urgent: Announce God's kingdom!"

Then another said, "I'm ready to follow you, Master, but first excuse me while I get things straightened out at home."

Jesus said, "No procrastination. No backward looks. You can't put God's kingdom off till tomorrow. Seize the day."

Sometimes Jesus can seem a little uncaring in the clipped tone of gospel stories. A would-be disciple asks to do the duty of a son to his father: to bury him. While it's not apparent in this translation, the father may not need burying right away. Chances are he's ill or old, however, and the son is simply asking permission to delay his discipleship to a time when his father no longer needs him. It seems a reasonable request.

But Jesus knows how we use parents, children, spouses, work, or health to excuse ourselves from discipleship. All excuses meet the same response: God's kingdom won't wait. Present circumstances can never be obstacles to following Jesus. The life engaging us so deeply is the very place where our mission logically begins. We keep thinking vocations are for folks who can clear away enough personal agenda to pursue one. Nice try. Our personal agenda is where vocation is happening.

> **Name the main areas of concern in your life:**
> **work, relationships, or special burdens.**
> **How does Jesus call you to**
> **"announce the kingdom" in each of these?**

WE RESPOND

Consider local ways to announce the kingdom to the poor, afflicted, oppressed. Don't miss even a small chance to make kingdom "come" for others.

FOURTEENTH SUNDAY IN ORDINARY TIME

FIRST READING » ISAIAH 66:10-14c

GOD'S *Message:*

"Rejoice, Jerusalem,
and all who love her, celebrate!
And all you who have shed tears over her,
join in the happy singing.
You newborns can satisfy yourselves
at her nurturing breasts.
Yes, delight yourselves and drink your fill
at her ample bosom."

GOD'S *Message:*

"I'll pour robust well-being into her like a river,
the glory of nations like a river in flood.
You'll nurse at her breasts,
nestle in her bosom,
and be bounced on her knees.
As a mother comforts her child,
so I'll comfort you.
You will be comforted in Jerusalem."

You'll see all this and burst with joy
—you'll feel ten feet tall—
As it becomes apparent that GOD *is on your side.*

The fate of Jerusalem mirrors the fate of the nation. It helps to think "Washington" when you read passages about the significance of Jerusalem. What happens in the capital affects us all, from the lowliest to the most powerful person in the land. But unlike Washington, Jerusalem is not only the center of political power for the people: It is also the designated meeting ground between the community and their God. The Temple in Jerusalem is the center of worship, petition, and sacrifice. It is holy ground in a way Washington can only be to the political idealist. When things go right in Jerusalem, it's as if "God's in his Temple, all's right with the world." When things go awry with Jerusalem, the whole nation must tremble.

Which center of authority affects your welfare the most?
How do you benefit from or might you be oppressed by it?

SECOND READING » GALATIANS 6:14-18

For my part, I am going to boast about nothing but the Cross of our Master, Jesus Christ. Because of that Cross, I have been crucified in relation to the world, set free from the stifling atmosphere of pleasing others and fitting into the little patterns that they dictate. Can't you see the central issue in all this? It is not what you and I do—submit to circumcision, reject circumcision. It is what God is doing, and he is creating something totally new, a free life! All who walk by this standard are the true Israel of God—his chosen people. Peace and mercy on them!

Quite frankly, I don't want to be bothered anymore by these disputes. I have far more important things to do—the serious living of this faith. I bear in my body scars from my service to Jesus.

May what our Master Jesus Christ gives freely be deeply and personally yours, my friends. Oh, yes!

Paul makes a fascinating claim in saying he bears the scars of his service to Jesus in his flesh. Many people have wondered if that means Paul had the stigmata, the five wounds of Christ from the cross impressed miraculously into his body. Most likely Paul is contrasting scars from his many beatings on mission with the simple mark of circumcision, normally viewed as a sign of true covenant with God. Paul insists circumcision is neither good nor bad as a sign of relationship with God. The Christian mark must go deeper than the flesh.

Blood covenants have always been popular as a means of sealing relationships. We don't have to look farther than the playground to see that. But the little girl-friends I once sealed to myself in friendship belong to a past life and loyalty. The new covenant of blood in the Eucharist goes deeper, with roots not only in the past but also in the future.

> How has your relationship with Jesus marked you?
> Can others see the markings of Christianity
> on your life and your decisions?

GOSPEL » LUKE 10:1-12, 17-20

Later the Master selected seventy and sent them ahead of him in pairs to every town and place where he intended to go. He gave them this charge:

"What a huge harvest! And how few the harvest hands. So on your knees; ask the God of the Harvest to send harvest hands.

"On your way! But be careful—this is hazardous work. You're like lambs in a wolf pack.

"Travel light. Comb and toothbrush and no extra luggage.

"Don't loiter and make small talk with everyone you meet along the way.

"When you enter a home, greet the family, 'Peace.' If your greeting is received, then it's a good place to stay. But if it's not received, take it back and get out. Don't impose yourself.

"Stay at one home, taking your meals there, for a worker deserves three square meals. Don't move from house to house, looking for the best cook in town.

"When you enter a town and are received, eat what they set before you, heal anyone who is sick, and tell them, 'God's kingdom is right on your doorstep!'

"When you enter a town and are not received, go out in the street and say, 'The only thing we got from you is the dirt on our feet, and we're giving it back. Did you have any idea that God's kingdom was right on your doorstep?' Sodom will have it better on Judgment Day than the town that rejects you."

The seventy came back triumphant. "Master, even the demons danced to your tune!"

Jesus said, "I know. I saw Satan fall, a bolt of lightning out of the sky. See what I've given you? Safe passage as you walk on snakes and scorpions, and protection from every assault of the Enemy. No one can put a hand on you. All the same, the great triumph is not in your authority over evil, but in God's authority over you and presence with you. Not what you do for God but what God does for you—that's the agenda for rejoicing."

Your name in lights—imagine that! The ego is drawn to the idea of being seen as special. Only the pathologically shy among us don't like a little attention now and then. Growing up in a large family, my siblings and I would stand on our heads to get a little extra parental attention. The disciples were subject to the same impulses. Once they found out that the power of Jesus "worked" in them, too, they rushed back to Jesus to claim his approval. Aren't we great? Did you see what we did?

Jesus is like the good parent. He assures them they did good work, and he did see it. Then he reminds them that none of this makes them more special since the success belongs to God. Their names are written in heaven simply because they are his. Who needs neon, when we've got celestial celebrity? We may be forgotten in this life, but we're known and remembered where it counts.

> How much does your appetite for attention
> or approval shape your behavior?
> How does your relationship with God
> involve the quest for approval?

WE RESPOND

God loves us, who we are, as we are, right now. Breathe in the love of God, slowly and deeply. Exhale the insecurity that keeps you from accepting this love. Repeat daily as needed.

FIFTEENTH SUNDAY IN ORDINARY TIME

FIRST READING » DEUTERONOMY 30:10-14

Moses said, "But only if you listen obediently to GOD, your God, and keep the commandments and regulations written in this Book of Revelation. Nothing halfhearted here; you must return to GOD, your God, totally, heart and soul, holding nothing back.

"This commandment that I'm commanding you today isn't too much for you, it's not out of your reach. It's not on a high mountain—you don't have to get mountaineers to climb the peak and bring it down to your level and explain it before you can live it. And it's not across the ocean—you don't have to send sailors out to get it, bring it back, and then explain it before you can live it. No. The word is right here and now—as near as the tongue in your mouth, as near as the heart in your chest. Just do it!"

People are always looking for a guru to make sense of the inexplicable for them. I employ a tax guy for this reason, but others may look to accountants, lawyers, realtors, social workers, priests, spiritual directors, or big sisters for varying degrees of hand-holding during life's more confusing moments. Making decisions is tough, and the consequences of our actions are not always clear on the business end of a choice.

Moses, the unintentional guru of a new nation, wants to make clear on the eve of their parting that the people need not look to him nor to any spiritual guide to discern God's will. Though he once handed them God's law on tablets of stone, he assures them God's desire is imprinted on their hearts. Religion is as easy or as complicated as we want it to be. We can treat God like the unknowable and fearful Wizard of Oz if it suits us. Or we can accept the idea that being God's people is as natural, familiar, and life-giving as breathing.

> **Do you see the spiritual life**
> **as easy or hard, confusing or clear?**

SECOND READING » COLOSSIANS 1:15-20

We look at this Son and see the God who cannot be seen. We look at this Son and see God's original purpose in everything created. For everything, absolutely everything, above and below, visible and invisible, rank after rank after rank of angels—everything got started in him and finds its purpose in him. He was there before any of it came into existence and holds it all together right up to this moment. And when it comes to the church, he organizes and holds it together, like a head does a body.

He was supreme in the beginning and—leading the resurrection parade—he is supreme in the end. From beginning to end he's there, towering far above everything, everyone. So spacious is he, so roomy, that everything of God finds its proper place in him without crowding. Not only that, but all the broken and dislocated pieces of the universe—people and things, animals and atoms—get properly fixed and fit together in vibrant harmonies, all because of his death, his blood that poured down from the Cross.

"Lord, show us the Father." Philip once made this request of Jesus, inadvertently exposing the fact that he'd been with Jesus all this while and still didn't understand who he was following. (See John 14:8-9.) Paul once made a similar mistake, seeing Jesus as a threat to faith in God rather than the fulfillment of it. But after the resurrection, Philip saw Jesus for who he really was, and was willing to be martyred for him. And when Paul heard the voice of Jesus speaking his name, he changed lanes from persecuting Christians to sharing their mission far and wide.

Jesus makes God's love visible and tangible within human history. Since the revelation of Jesus, we don't have to guess anymore who God is or what God wants or what we're supposed to do. If we listen to the voice of Jesus calling our name, we'll have no trouble pursuing our best and happiest path.

> **List ten things you learn about God from listening to the story of Jesus.**

GOSPEL » LUKE 10:25-37

Then a religion scholar stood up with a question to test Jesus. "Teacher, what do I need to do to get eternal life?"

He answered, "What's written in God's Law? How do you interpret it?"

He said, "That you love the Lord your God with all your passion and prayer and muscle and intelligence—and that you love your neighbor as well as you do yourself."

"Good answer!" said Jesus. "Do it and you'll live."

Looking for a loophole, he asked, "And just how would you define 'neighbor'?"

Jesus answered by telling a story. "There was once a man traveling from Jerusalem to Jericho. On the way he was attacked by robbers. They took his clothes, beat him up, and went off leaving him half-dead. Luckily, a priest was on his way down the same road, but when he saw him he angled across to the other side. Then a Levite religious man showed up; he also avoided the injured man.

"A Samaritan traveling the road came on him. When he saw the man's condition, his heart went out to him. He gave him first aid, disinfecting and bandaging his wounds. Then he lifted him onto his donkey, led him to an inn, and made him comfortable. In the morning he took out two silver coins and gave them to the innkeeper, saying, 'Take good care of him. If it costs any more, put it on my bill—I'll pay you on my way back.'

"What do you think? Which of the three became a neighbor to the man attacked by robbers?"

"The one who treated him kindly," the religion scholar responded. Jesus said, "Go and do the same."

In his first inaugural address, President George W. Bush used the metaphor of the road to Jericho in pledging our nation to a goal of personal responsibility for the welfare of all. We would not cross to the side of the road to avoid getting involved in our neighbor's suffering. Americans would not be guilty bystanders, unwilling to risk the dirty, messy business of human compassion. This speech made some folks uncomfortable. Not everyone wants to invest in human misery just because it's there. If only being a Good Samaritan were always as simple and sanitary as writing a check!

But the Samaritan in the parable does a lot more than pick up the tab for a stranger's misfortune. He ministers to him personally, investing time and care and human feeling into someone who happens to be an enemy of his people. The business of compassion smears the neat categories of responsibility. It leads where we may not expect or want to go.

Is there someone who may need your compassion at this time? How may you have to go across "enemy lines" to help?

WE RESPOND

Pray for the courage to get your hands dirty when you encounter human suffering.

"The word is right here and now—
as near as the tongue in your mouth,
as near as the heart in your chest.
Just do it!"

SIXTEENTH SUNDAY IN ORDINARY TIME

FIRST READING » GENESIS 18:1-10a

God appeared to Abraham at the Oaks of Mamre while he was sitting at the entrance of his tent. It was the hottest part of the day. He looked up and saw three men standing. He ran from his tent to greet them and bowed before them.

He said, "Master, if it please you, stop for a while with your servant. I'll get some water so you can wash your feet. Rest under this tree. I'll get some food to refresh you on your way, since your travels have brought you across my path."

They said, "Certainly. Go ahead."

Abraham hurried into the tent to Sarah. He said, "Hurry. Get three cups of our best flour; knead it and make bread."

Then Abraham ran to the cattle pen and picked out a nice plump calf and gave it to the servant who lost no time getting it ready. Then he got curds and milk, brought them with the calf that had been roasted, set the meal before the men, and stood there under the tree while they ate.

The men said to him, "Where is Sarah your wife?"

He said, "In the tent."

One of them said, "I'm coming back about this time next year. When I arrive, your wife Sarah will have a son."

Abraham shows himself to be the consummate host. He offers the common courtesies of desert hospitality to the strangers who pass his tent: water to bathe the feet, the shade of a tree to rest under, some food and drink. Hospitality is a principal virtue of Middle Eastern culture, and it means more than the willingness to pour some tea. Desert people understand that travelers can spend a day walking from well to well, through wild lands under a fierce sun, at the mercy of outlaws every step of the way. Hospitality toward strangers can mean the difference between life and death, so it moves beyond courtesy into the category of duty. In Jewish law, hospitality to the stranger was elevated to the status of an obligation due to God. The Giver of life did not create us to perish within reach of an outstretched hand. Can we say, in our global economy, that anyone is beyond the grasp of our hospitality?

How do you show hospitality to friends and strangers, both near and far?

SECOND READING » COLOSSIANS 1:24-28

I want you to know how glad I am that it's me sitting here in this jail and not you. There's a lot of suffering to be entered into in this world—the kind of suffering Christ takes on. I welcome the chance to take my share in the church's part of that suffering. When I became a servant in this church, I experienced this suffering as a sheer gift, God's way of helping me serve you, laying out the whole truth.

This mystery has been kept in the dark for a long time, but now it's out in the open. God wanted everyone, not just Jews, to know this rich and glorious secret inside and out, regardless of their background, regardless of their religious standing. The mystery in a nutshell is just this: Christ is in you, therefore you can look forward to sharing in God's glory. It's that simple. That is the substance of our Message. We preach Christ, warning people not to add to the Message. We teach in a spirit of profound common sense so that we can bring each person to maturity. To be mature is to be basic. Christ! No more, no less.

Listening to a friend rant and rave the other night about injustices he's suffered from many hands, it occurred to me that his story is often one of victimhood. It's easy to get stuck on proclaiming ourselves in a variety of ways, whether the theme be our strengths, victories, or injuries. Paul made a commitment throughout his ministry to proclaim "only Christ, and him crucified" (as he phrased it in 1 Corinthians 2:2). It makes a difference whose story dominates center stage in our lives. If we're locked into a recitation of our woes or our righteousness, we're reinforcing a self-centered view of the universe that confines and limits us. If we focus instead on counting our blessings, or contemplating how God is healing us and helping us forward, we put God at the center, just as it should be in the life of a believer.

> **Who claims the center of your life, you or Christ?**
> **Give examples.**

GOSPEL » LUKE 10:38-42

As they continued their travel, Jesus entered a village. A woman by the name of Martha welcomed him and made him feel quite at home. She had a sister, Mary, who sat before the Master, hanging on every word he said. But Martha was pulled away by all she had to do in the kitchen. Later, she stepped in, interrupting them. "Master, don't you care that my sister has abandoned the kitchen to me? Tell her to lend me a hand."

The Master said, "Martha, dear Martha, you're fussing far too much and getting yourself worked up over nothing. One thing only is essential, and Mary has chosen it—it's the main course, and won't be taken from her."

People who think of themselves as "pray-ers" love the story of Mary and Martha, while others who characterize themselves as "do-ers" are irritated by it. After all, Martha is an exemplary model of hospitality. She is serving her guest and honoring God in the process, just like Abraham did in the first reading today. So why is Abraham so esteemed and Martha seemingly admonished for exhibiting precisely the same behavior?

Martha has done nothing wrong, and Jesus does not put her down for her generous service—though plenty of homilists this Sunday will make it sound that way. Martha fulfills the cultural and religious obligation of hospitality admirably. Mary has chosen to follow another imperative, one that sprang from within her own desire: to be in the company of Jesus. If Martha errs, it's only in passing judgment over Mary's choice. Hospitality takes many forms. One of them is presence.

How do you serve the Lord by doing?
How do you serve the Lord by being present?

WE RESPOND

Make a commitment to hospitality. Cultivate the spirit of welcome. Risk becoming known as a source of refuge.

The mystery in a nutshell is just this:
Christ is in you, therefore you can look
forward to sharing in God's glory.
It's that simple.

FIRST READING » GENESIS 18:20-32

GOD continued, "*The cries of the victims in Sodom and Gomorrah are deafening; the sin of those cities is immense. I'm going down to see for myself, see if what they're doing is as bad as it sounds. Then I'll know.*"

The men set out for Sodom, but Abraham stood in GOD's path, blocking his way.

Abraham confronted him, "Are you serious? Are you planning on getting rid of the good people right along with the bad? What if there are fifty decent people left in the city; will you lump the good with the bad and get rid of the lot? Wouldn't you spare the city for the sake of those fifty innocents? I can't believe you'd do that, kill off the good and the bad alike as if there were no difference between them. Doesn't the Judge of all the Earth judge with justice?"

GOD said, "*If I find fifty decent people in the city of Sodom, I'll spare the place just for them.*"

Abraham came back, "Do I, a mere mortal made from a handful of dirt, dare open my mouth again to my Master? What if the fifty fall short by five— would you destroy the city because of those missing five?"

He said, "I won't destroy it if there are forty-five."

Abraham spoke up again, "What if you only find forty?"

"Neither will I destroy it if for forty."

He said, "Master, don't be irritated with me, but what if only thirty are found?"

"No, I won't do it if I find thirty."

He pushed on, "I know I'm trying your patience, Master, but how about for twenty?"

"I won't destroy it for twenty."

He wouldn't quit, "Don't get angry, Master—this is the last time. What if you only come up with ten?"

"For the sake of only ten, I won't destroy the city."

Sodom and Gomorrah are popularly known as places where lust and debauchery had risen to an outrageous crescendo. The most serious sin of these cities, by biblical standards, was the abuse of a stranger. As we saw in last week's readings, hospitality toward the traveler was God's own law. Violence perpetrated on the guest of a community deeply violated the duty to protect and care for the wanderer. In these dangerous cities, far from being guaranteed automatic protection, a visitor could easily get killed. The spirit of these two cities, indifferent to the obligations of one human being to another, stank to high heaven.

One has to wonder what the judgment will be on the cities we live in today. Are our streets safe for strangers? Do we welcome the foreigner among us? Are wanderers protected or persecuted by our laws? Do we treat human life with respect or indifference? How much violence are we willing to tolerate, in film and in fact, before it's too much?

> Rate the level of violence in your life:
> in words, behavior, attitudes, and opinions;
> in stories you hear, tell, read, and watch.
> What is the net impact on you?

SECOND READING » COLOSSIANS 2:12-14

If it's an initiation ritual you're after, you've already been through it by submitting to baptism. Going under the water was a burial of your old life; coming up out of it was a resurrection, God raising you from the dead as he did Christ. When you were stuck in your old sin-dead life, you were incapable of responding to God. God brought you alive—right along with Christ! Think of it! All sins forgiven, the slate wiped clean, that old arrest warrant canceled and nailed to Christ's Cross.

Many of us learned the paperwork on sin as children: a ledger on us is kept somewhere with "credit" and "debit" columns. An angel keeps the sum of our charities and offenses for some future day of reckoning. It's a simplistic image. It disregards the power of forgiveness. But it has the merit of being easy to understand and it appeals to human standards of justice.

Paul does the paperwork on sin too. He imagines sin as a contract with the devil, legally binding us to death and destruction. The saving act of Jesus is to snatch that piece of paper from hell's in-box and nail it to the cross, staking a new claim on our souls. It's not unlike Abraham's haggle with the angel of destruction in the first reading, bartering for innocent lives in Sodom and Gomorrah who were about to face annihilation. So here's the difference. Abraham as lawyer makes a case for the innocent; Jesus is willing to advocate for the guilty. Which is a good thing for sinners like me.

> If salvation depended on acts of charity,
> do you think you would be saved or lost?

GOSPEL » LUKE 11:1-13

One day he was praying in a certain place. When he finished, one of his disciples said, "Master, teach us to pray just as John taught his disciples."

So he said, "When you pray, say,

Father,
Reveal who you are.
Set the world right.
Keep us alive with three square meals.

Keep us forgiven with you and forgiving others.
Keep us safe from ourselves and the Devil."

Then he said, *"Imagine what would happen if you went to a friend in the middle of the night and said, 'Friend, lend me three loaves of bread. An old friend traveling through just showed up, and I don't have a thing on hand.'*

"The friend answers from his bed, 'Don't bother me. The door's locked; my children are all down for the night; I can't get up to give you anything.'

"But let me tell you, even if he won't get up because he's a friend, if you stand your ground, knocking and waking all the neighbors, he'll finally get up and get you whatever you need.

"Here's what I'm saying:

Ask and you'll get;
Seek and you'll find;
Knock and the door will open.

"Don't bargain with God. Be direct. Ask for what you need. This is not a cat-and-mouse, hide-and-seek game we're in. If your little boy asks for a serving of fish, do you scare him with a live snake on his plate? If your little girl asks for an egg, do you trick her with a spider? As bad as you are, you wouldn't think of such a thing—you're at least decent to your own children. And don't you think the Father who conceived you in love will give the Holy Spirit when you ask him?"

Prayer requires courage. Imagine the flutter in Abraham's heart when he asked God to consider the innocent who would suffer with the guilty in the destruction of evil cities! Who is Abraham to tell God what's just? Yet our every prayer of petition is roughly the same. With hearts fluttering, we ask God to act according to our perception. It's a bold thing to do.

Jesus encourages his disciples to pray with daring. He tells us to ask for God to reveal divinity to us! That's a big request. Jesus also teaches us to ask for more immediate and practical concerns like food, forgiveness, and to be spared the tug of sin on our hearts. Jesus says we can ask for anything in prayer, big or small, trusting that the One who loves us desires our welfare more than we do. With confidence, then, let us pray.

> **What are the most common obstacles you face in prayer,**
> **and how do you overcome them?**

WE RESPOND

Renew your dedication to prayer. Consider what works for you—meditation, ritual prayer, song, movement—and which environment is most conducive, whether indoors, outdoors, a pew, a favorite chair. Be there for the conversation!

EIGHTEENTH SUNDAY IN ORDINARY TIME

FIRST READING » ECCLESIASTES 1:2; 2:21-23

Smoke, nothing but smoke. [That's what the Quester says.]
There's nothing to anything—it's all smoke.

What's the point of working your fingers to the bone if you hand over what you worked for to someone who never lifted a finger for it? Smoke, that's what it is. A bad business from start to finish. So what do you get from a life of hard labor? Pain and grief from dawn to dusk. Never a decent night's rest. Nothing but smoke.

Death DOES have a sting. Despite what we say in our more pious moments, we're painfully aware of how much it hurts to leave this world or to say goodbye to those whom we love. Most of us have lost many wonderful friends and family members to death—and if you haven't, you will. The finality of death can make us bitter with its unfairness, taking babies along with the elderly, the innocent with the guilty, those who eat right and work out as blithely as those who wantonly abuse their health. Death has no sense of justice. That's why the Quester, the speaker in Ecclesiastes, sounds so discouraged.

Because death is such a grim reality for the living, we find ways to talk around it. We say "if I should die" or "in case I die"—as if there were any question about the matter! Death stops for all of us, as Emily Dickinson says. Whatever we're doing with our lives, no matter how important it is to us or to others, all of that will stop too. So the question remains not IF I should die, but how I should live out the time that is given to me.

> **What difference does the inevitability**
> **of death make to your life?**
> **If you knew you'd die tonight,**
> **what would you be sure to do or not do today?**

SECOND READING » COLOSSIANS 3:1-5, 9-11

So if you're serious about living this new resurrection life with Christ, act like it. Pursue the things over which Christ presides. Don't shuffle along, eyes to the ground, absorbed with the things right in front of you. Look up, and be alert to what is going on around Christ—that's where the action is. See things from his perspective.

Your old life is dead. Your new life, which is your real life—even though invisible to spectators—is with Christ in God. He is your life. When Christ (your real life, remember) shows up again on this earth, you'll show up, too—the real you, the glorious you. Meanwhile, be content with obscurity, like Christ.

And that means killing off everything connected with that way of death: sexual promiscuity, impurity, lust, doing whatever you feel like whenever you feel like it, and grabbing whatever attracts your fancy.

Don't lie to one another. You're done with that old life. It's like a filthy set of ill-fitting clothes you've stripped off and put in the fire. Now you're dressed in a new wardrobe. Every item of your new way of life is custom-made by the Creator, with his label on it. All the old fashions are now obsolete. Words like Jewish and non-Jewish, religious and irreligious, insider and outsider, uncivilized and uncouth, slave and free, mean nothing. From now on everyone is defined by Christ, everyone is included in Christ.

Many people think of death as a dreary thing that happens at the far end of our attention. But today we hear about the death that occurs right under our noses, at the center of our interest, in the midst of life. For the Christian, alive to the reality of eternity, death is in a sense already behind us.

So how does this work? We might define life as the land of possibility. As long as we're alive there are choices to be made, and the last word on what CAN be done has not yet been spoken. Death, on the other hand, closes the door on choice and will. In a different way, as we embrace the new life Jesus offers, some doors also close. Falseness and division and privileged status are not compatible with our new state of being. We're dead to all that.

The new life in Christ may shut the door on some old possibilities, but no one will be sorry when heaven opens and hell closes its gates. Death still waits around the last bend in the road, but even death isn't death anymore. Without the sting, it's more like a change of address.

> Would you be willing to die to greed, dishonesty,
> and prejudice, to embrace life in Christ?
> How would your life change if you did?

GOSPEL » LUKE 12:13-21

Someone out of the crowd said, "Teacher, order my brother to give me a fair share of the family inheritance."

He replied, "Mister, what makes you think it's any of my business to be a judge or mediator for you?"

Speaking to the people, he went on, "Take care! Protect yourself against the least bit of greed. Life is not defined by what you have, even when you have a lot."

Then he told them this story: "The farm of a certain rich man produced a terrific crop. He talked to himself: 'What can I do? My barn isn't big enough for this harvest.' Then he said, 'Here's what I'll do: I'll tear down my barns and build bigger ones. Then I'll gather in all my grain and goods, and I'll say to myself, Self, you've done well! You've got it made and can now retire. Take it easy and have the time of your life!'

"*Just then God showed up and said, 'Fool! Tonight you die. And your barnful of goods—who gets it?'*

"*That's what happens when you fill your barn with Self and not with God.*"

Forget the death tax. There's something creepier out there than what happens to our inheritance after we expire. What's really hair-raising is that everything we're currently gripping is going to be taken out of our hands, all in a moment. Between one breath in this world and the next drawn in the great beyond, everything we hang onto will not be "ours" anymore.

Well, not quite everything. We do lose money, houses, cars, internet access, and everything in the garage and storage unit. We can't hang onto popularity, prestige, or what's on our résumés. We can't cling to roles and relationships, as Jesus assures those who argue over whose wife a much-married woman will be in heaven. We can't even hold onto what we'll look like in eternity. But we do get to keep what we did "for the least of our brothers and sisters." So make a note: The real death tax is steep. Investing in the poor is the best way to make a killing.

**How much have you saved up
in the account of things that matter to God?**

WE RESPOND

Assign a number to the percentage of your resources (material and personal) currently invested in the poor Christ. The traditional tithe is ten percent. Think of ways to increase your contribution to meet the tithe.

*Every item of your new way of life
is custom-made by the Creator,
with his label on it.
All the old fashions are now obsolete.*

NINETEENTH SUNDAY IN ORDINARY TIME
.... Holy Children of the Good

FIRST READING » WISDOM 18:6-9

Our ancestors had some intimation of what would happen the night of that first Passover, but they had confidence in their commitments to you and were confident in yours to them. When things actually happened as you had said, it brought them some measure of relief, stiffening their resolve to rely on the promises you'd already made them.

Thus a measure of justice was restored and the enemies of your people were being annihilated. You punished them and rewarded your people in one fell swoop; indeed, you went out of your way to do it. All during this wretched time, your good people maintained their sacrificial schedule; they even managed to get complete agreement on the Law of Moses. They'd be faithful in good time and bad, and they'd retain the ancient hymns of praise.

A lot of really important things happen in the first half of the Bible, but arguably the most pivotal event for the Hebrew nation is the story of their exodus from Egypt. Passover becomes the central feast for Jews ever after, a meal as significant in its own way as the Eucharist is for us. Passover tells Jewish believers who they are and what their covenant with God is about. It binds them to God and to one another. It reveals who the children of goodness are, those who remain faithful to the God of sure rescue.

On that special night of the first Passover, those who ate the meal put their lives on the line to do it. They put their future in the hands of a mysterious God who would curiously relieve their burden by bringing them into the harsh desert. Today, anyone can sit down to a Seder meal—even Christians do it—and risk very little. In the same way our Eucharist has become an all-too-easy meal to share. The children of goodness are not those who simply celebrate with a meal. We also have to become the bread we eat.

> How do you become the Body of Christ
> blessed, broken, and shared for the sake of others?

SECOND READING » HEBREWS 11:1-2, 8-19

The fundamental fact of existence is that this trust in God, this faith, is the firm foundation under everything that makes life worth living. It's our handle on what we can't see. The act of faith is what distinguished our ancestors, set them above the crowd.

By an act of faith, Abraham said yes to God's call to travel to an unknown place that would become his home. When he left he had no idea where he was going. By an act of faith he lived in the country promised him, lived as a stranger camping in tents. Isaac and Jacob did the same, living under the same promise. Abraham did it by keeping his eye on an unseen city with real, eternal foundations—the City designed and built by God.

By faith, barren Sarah was able to become pregnant, old woman as she was at the time, because she believed the One who made a promise would do what he said. That's how it happened that from one man's dead and shriveled loins there are now people numbering into the millions.

Each one of these people of faith died not yet having in hand what was promised, but still believing. How did they do it? They saw it way off in the distance, waved their greeting, and accepted the fact that they were transients in this world. People who live this way make it plain that they are looking for their true home. If they were homesick for the old country, they could have gone back any time they wanted. But they were after a far better country than that—heaven country. You can see why God is so proud of them, and has a City waiting for them.

By faith, Abraham, at the time of testing, offered Isaac back to God. Acting in faith, he was as ready to return the promised son, his only son, as he had been to receive him—and this after he had already been told, "Your descendants shall come from Isaac." Abraham figured that if God wanted to, he could raise the dead. In a sense, that's what happened when he received Isaac back, alive from off the altar.

When I was a kid I watched the Jerry Lewis telethon every Labor Day weekend. It was a ritual as deeply engrained in me as going back to school. The promotional ad, voiced over by George Burns, appeared continually for weeks in advance: "Watch Jerry, and see the stars come out." He meant the movie stars, of course, who showed up throughout the wee hours of this extravaganza to keep viewers tuned in.

I was fascinated by the stars, but even more fascinated by the rolling numbers as pledges for the fundraiser grew higher and higher. To me, the dollars seemed to symbolize the compassion of the nation. I could almost read how many good people there are in the mounting contribution—people who were stars in their own right shining through the darkness of a disease they were pledging to fight.

The list of biblical heroes rolls on and on through Noah, Abraham, Sarah, Moses, the prophets, and the apostles. And where the Bible ends the canon of the saints begins to the present day. You want to see stars? They still shine in our communities wherever goodness is happening.

Where do you see "stars" shining in your family or your community?

GOSPEL » LUKE 12:32-48

"Don't be afraid of missing out. You're my dearest friends! The Father wants to give you the very kingdom itself.

"Be generous. Give to the poor. Get yourselves a bank that can't go bankrupt, a bank in heaven far from bankrobbers, safe from embezzlers, a bank you can bank on. It's obvious, isn't it? The place where your treasure is, is the place you will most want to be, and end up being.

"Keep your shirts on; keep the lights on! Be like house servants waiting for

their master to come back from his honeymoon, awake and ready to open the door when he arrives and knocks. Lucky the servants whom the master finds on watch! He'll put on an apron, sit them at the table, and serve them a meal, sharing his wedding feast with them. It doesn't matter what time of the night he arrives; they're awake—and so blessed!

"You know that if the house owner had known what night the burglar was coming, he wouldn't have stayed out late and left the place unlocked. So don't you be slovenly and careless. Just when you don't expect him, the Son of Man will show up."

Peter said, "Master, are you telling this story just for us? Or is it for everybody?"

The Master said, "Let me ask you: Who is the dependable manager, full of common sense, that the master puts in charge of his staff to feed them well and on time? He is a blessed man if when the master shows up he's doing his job. But if he says to himself, 'The master is certainly taking his time,' begins maltreating the servants and maids, throws parties for his friends, and gets drunk, the master will walk in when he least expects it, give him the thrashing of his life, and put him back in the kitchen peeling potatoes.

"The servant who knows what his master wants and ignores it, or insolently does whatever he pleases, will be thoroughly thrashed. But if he does a poor job through ignorance, he'll get off with a slap on the hand. Great gifts mean great responsibilities; greater gifts, greater responsibilities."

Most of the folks we know aren't bad people, by any means. They're not hopelessly corrupted by greed, sacrificing their children to their own ambitions, or cheating on their spouses. Most people we keep company with are not cruel, careless of the poor, bigoted, or addicted to power for its own sake. But in the same way, most people we know aren't what we'd call "holy" either. That is, their lives and choices aren't centered on God and the desire for goodness above all else.

But we probably do know some holy people, and they're marvelous! They seem to breathe the Holy Spirit and seek God's will as naturally as the rest of us seek our next meal. They're wonderfully kind; not cynical or suspicious of others' motives; not quick to criticize or pass judgment. They show mercy to people who don't "deserve" it. They do good not because they're being watched, but because it gives them pleasure to do it. We want to be like these people. As we watch holiness in action, our hearts ache for it.

**Where have you seen holiness in action?
How might you fall short of the example of holiness you see?**

WE RESPOND

Sign up to become one of the "children of goodness." Consider what you might say or do if you were in the presence of God, and then live as if that were always true. Which it is.

TWENTIETH SUNDAY IN ORDINARY TIME

.... Setting the World on Fire

FIRST READING » JEREMIAH 38:4-6, 8-10

These officials told the king, "Please, kill this man Jeremiah. He's got to go! He's ruining the resolve of the soldiers who are still left in the city, as well as the people themselves, by spreading these words. This man isn't looking after the good of this people. He's trying to ruin us!"

King Zedekiah caved in: "If you say so. Go ahead, handle it your way. You're too much for me."

So they took Jeremiah and threw him into the cistern of Malkijah the king's son that was in the courtyard of the palace guard. They lowered him down with ropes. There wasn't any water in the cistern, only mud. Jeremiah sank into the mud.

While the king was holding court in the Benjamin Gate, Ebed-melek went immediately from the palace to the king and said, "My master, O king—these men are committing a great crime in what they're doing, throwing Jeremiah the prophet into the cistern and leaving him there to starve. He's as good as dead, There isn't a scrap of bread left in the city."

So the king ordered Ebed-melek the Ethiopian, "Get three men and pull Jeremiah the prophet out of the cistern before he dies."

Jeremiah was a troublemaker. Prophets generally are. He got people mad because he unsettled their complacency. He messed with their minds and their resignation to bad times. He sowed the seed of doubt about the authorities to whom they readily capitulated. This caused problems for the folks in power; they in turn caused problems for the troublemaker. That business about being tossed in the cistern wasn't the half of it.

Young readers of Scripture love Jeremiah, and no wonder: he wasn't more than a teenager himself when he accepted the call to prophesy. "Accepted" isn't quite the right word for it: Jeremiah was drafted by God's irresistible will. And though the prophet complained soulfully about his commission throughout his career, Jeremiah was exceptional at what he did. He predicted the exile of his nation, and it went down in exile. Jeremiah didn't quit no matter how hard or hopeless the matter seemed. He had fire in his heart, imprisoned in his bones, and he had to let it out. His passion for God's truth was his greatness. His example continues to set fires in many hearts.

> **How can you tell the difference between a normal troublemaker and a prophetic one?**

SECOND READING » HEBREWS 12:1-4

Do you see what this means—all these pioneers who blazed the way, all these veterans cheering us on? It means we'd better get on with it. Strip down, start running—and never quit! No extra spiritual fat, no parasitic sins. Keep your eyes on Jesus, who both began and finished this race we're in. Study how he did it. Because he never lost sight of where he was headed—that exhilarating finish in and with God—he could put up with anything along the way: cross, shame, whatever. And now he's there, in the place of honor, right alongside God. When you find yourselves flagging in your faith, go over that story again, item by item, that long litany of hostility he plowed through. That will shoot adrenaline into your souls!

In this all-out match against sin, others have suffered far worse than you, to say nothing of what Jesus went through—all that bloodshed!

One thing ought to be clear by now to those who hold worldly power. If people oppose you, the worst thing you can do is kill them! Martyrs only serve to inspire new leaders willing to risk everything for the cause.

Martyrdom played a powerful role in the life of the early church. Because the Lord himself "put up with anything...cross, shame, whatever," early followers were willing to risk crucifixion for the gospel. Hope in the resurrection being central to their faith, the thought of death was no deterrent. The more martyrs were created, the more Christianity caught fire in the imagination and fascination of the populace.

Unable to defeat Christianity, secular powers were obliged to do a merger with it by making it an official religion of the empire. Christianity became "Christendom," a domesticated and more controllable creature. The prolific era of martyrs ceased. Yet in pockets of the world to the present day, people of faith still put their lives on the line, gambling on Jesus.

> **How much of your life and comfort would you be willing to "gamble" on Jesus?**

GOSPEL » LUKE 12:49-53

"I've come to start a fire on this earth—how I wish it were blazing right now! I've come to change everything, turn everything rightside up—how I long for it to be finished! Do you think I came to smooth things over and make everything nice? Not so. I've come to disrupt and confront! From now on, when you find five in a house, it will be—

Three against two,
and two against three;
Father against son,
and son against father;
Mother against daughter,
and daughter against mother;

Mother-in-law against bride,
and bride against mother-in-law."

Was Jesus a troublemaker? You betcha. Today Christianity is invoked as the flagship for the armada of Family Values, Patriotism, and other political bulwarks. History might sound a cough of protest. The Jesus people were originally deemed a threat to social mores. Romans saw Christianity as subversive of civic responsibility. Christians caused a tremor in established hierarchies, divisions, and alliances in the culture. Christian leaders worked hard to dispel such charges, even including Hellenistic household codes in Paul's letters to assure people that "wives [would be] submissive to their husbands," as children would be to parents, and slaves to owners.

Yet Jesus says plainly that his message causes division and dissension. His gospel leads to shattered families, as each member chooses for or against his way. Marriages will end. Different generations may find a chasm of meaning yawn between them. The Christian community redefines home, family, and social responsibility for those who believe. Those who take Jesus seriously, and those who don't, still find Jesus to be trouble.

> **Do you think church and government should be allied?**
> **How might that partnership affect the church's mission?**

WE RESPOND

Reflect on the source of your passions: family, work, creative endeavors, or other pursuits. Find ways to make your passions work together for God's purposes.

TWENTY-FIRST SUNDAY IN ORDINARY TIME

FIRST READING » ISAIAH 66:18-21

GOD's decree: "I know everything they've ever done or thought. I'm going to come and then gather everyone—all nations, all languages. They'll come and see my glory. I'll set up a station at the center. I'll send the survivors of judgment all over the world: Spain and Africa, Turkey and Greece, and the far-off islands that have never heard of me, who know nothing of what I've done nor who I am. I'll send them out as missionaries to preach my glory among the nations. They'll return with all your long-lost brothers and sisters from all over the world. They'll bring them back and offer them in living worship to GOD. They'll bring them on horses and wagons and carts, on mules and camels, straight to my holy mountain Jerusalem," says GOD. "They'll present them just as Israelites present their offerings in a ceremonial vessel in the Temple of GOD. I'll even take some of them and make them priests and Levites," says GOD.

It will surprise no one that many Scripture commentators do not moonlight as sports legends. I was one of those kids who was rarely chosen for a team until all other picks were made. I would be drafted into the game sometime after the boy with the cast on his arm, and the child who weighed fifty pounds. My lack of coordination was notorious, not to mention my indifference to the spirit of competition, a notion I could never quite get the sense of. How could the outcome of a game matter?

Still, when my sister Sue was playing, I got on her team every time. Sue WAS a sports legend—tough, determined, as strong and as fast as any boy on the block. And since everybody wanted Sue on their team, when she was playing, I was playing, period. My hapless performance couldn't offset her brilliant one. If a team would not agree to take me, Sue wouldn't play, so that cinched the deal.

Sue did what God does, according to prophecy. God makes the playing field of truth open to all comers, regardless of standards and suitability. God's clout is irresistible. Whom God invites, no one can exclude.

Who gets excluded in your family, or where you live or work?
What can you do to include them?

SECOND READING » HEBREWS 12:5-7, 11-13

So don't feel sorry for yourselves. Or have you forgotten how good parents treat children, and that God regards you as his children?

> *My dear child, don't shrug off God's discipline,*
> *but don't be crushed by it either.*
> *It's the child he loves that he disciplines;*

the child he embraces, he also corrects.

God is educating you; that's why you must never drop out. He's treating you as dear children. This trouble you're in isn't punishment; it's training. At the time, discipline isn't much fun. It always feels like it's going against the grain. Later, of course, it pays off handsomely, for it's the well-trained who find themselves mature in their relationship with God.

So don't sit around on your hands! No more dragging your feet! Clear the path for long-distance runners so no one will trip and fall, so no one will step in a hole and sprain an ankle. Help each other out. And run for it!

We know what happens to children who grow up lawless. Children deprived of structure and guidance suffer the lack of boundaries within which to gain the traction of maturity. Like plants without stakes to guide their growth, they list and can't find the sun.

Civil and religious laws function as supportive structure for adults, too, who need to touch a few boundaries now and then. The purpose of all discipline is the same: to establish the voice of conscience to guide our direction and choices. If we don't internalize these outward disciplines, then we'll be ego-driven instead, trying to cheat the system for the rest of our lives. What can I get away with, without getting caught? How far can I go, before I go too far? How many times will my family forgive me, before I lose their trust? How bad can I be, before God makes me pay? If we regularly engage this debate within ourselves, it may be time to revisit our moral center and find a new teacher.

> **Do you seek to do good, or what you can get away with?**
> **Where do you turn for moral guidance?**

GOSPEL » LUKE 13:22-30

He went on teaching from town to village, village to town, but keeping on a steady course toward Jerusalem.

A bystander said, "Master, will only a few be saved?"

He said, "Whether few or many is none of your business. Put your mind on your life with God. The way to life—to God!—is vigorous and requires your total attention. A lot of you are going to assume that you'll sit down to God's salvation banquet just because you've been hanging around the neighborhood all your lives. Well, one day you're going to be banging on the door, wanting to get in, but you'll find the door locked and the Master saying, 'Sorry, you're not on my guest list.'

"You'll protest, 'But we've known you all our lives!' only to be interrupted with his abrupt, 'Your kind of knowing can hardly be called knowing. You don't know the first thing about me.'

"That's when you'll find yourselves out in the cold, strangers to grace. You'll watch Abraham, Isaac, Jacob, and all the prophets march into God's kingdom.

You'll watch outsiders stream in from east, west, north, and south and sit down at the table of God's kingdom. And all the time you'll be outside looking in—and wondering what happened. This is the Great Reversal: the last in line put at the head of the line, and the so-called first ending up last."

Is there an end to God's love for us? Scripture and tradition say no. God is love, by definition. And God is infinite, also by definition. So the boundaries of divine love would be impossible to circumscribe.

The question often hidden behind that query is: Is there an end to our chances to be with God forever? The answer to that seems to be yes. Or, as a local priest often says in his homilies, "Hey, time forecloses!" Time is among the first creatures God made to serve the divine purpose. Time and space make up the matrix that enables the rest of creation to exist. Yet Scripture tells us that all of creation, time and space included, will one day be rolled up like a carpet. Entering eternity necessitates the abandonment of time.

Time does foreclose. The door which has stood open since the dawn of the first day will one day be shut. Now's the time to choose the rich embrace of God's companionship and desire. If we choose to be strangers to this love, God will not insist.

> **Would people describe you as a loving person?**
> **How do you show your love to God and to others?**

WE RESPOND

Open the door on love. Love generously, even when you're not loved back. Put your love to work for people who will never meet you. Make your love an invitation for others to pursue love.

TWENTY-SECOND SUNDAY IN ORDINARY TIME
.... Have a Seat!

FIRST READING » SIRACH 3:17-18, 20, 28-29

Child, work hard but don't trumpet your success; you'll be ranked above the one who gives but expects something in return. No matter how great you become, humble yourself at every opportunity; you'll find appreciation in the presence of God.

Things beyond your reach—don't spend much time on. Things too complicated for you—don't waste energy on. The wise heart understands the words of the wise, the cocked ear desires wisdom.

Water puts out fire; charitable giving pays off sins.

A word to the wise is sufficient? A recent bumper sticker read: "A word to the wise is UNNECESSARY." Funny, perhaps. But it can't beat the truth of the original. The wise seek wisdom. People who think they know-it-all, don't. The wise also teach wisdom, not hoarding it as an advantage over others. The wise know wisdom involves an ongoing exchange through centuries, among generations, from many sources. You can't afford to pass up wisdom even if the source is unacceptable to you. When you meet a person who is truly wise, do everything possible to apprentice yourself!

We're mentored by wisdom throughout our lives. At different times I've been guided by priests, religious sisters, elderly relatives, professors, a janitor, a taxi driver, a dying man, and a stranger I met while hiking. The wise may be Buddhists, Protestants, Jews, and people who don't have a name for God. When wisdom speaks, take a seat.

Who were some of your past mentors?
Identify wise people to whom you give your attention today.

SECOND READING » HEBREWS 12:18-19, 22-24a

Unlike your ancestors, you didn't come to Mount Sinai—all that volcanic blaze and earthshaking rumble—to hear God speak. The earsplitting words and soul-shaking message terrified them and they begged him to stop.

No, that's not your experience at all. You've come to Mount Zion, the city where the living God resides. The invisible Jerusalem is populated by throngs of festive angels and Christian citizens. It is the city where God is Judge, with judgments that make us just. You've come to Jesus, who presents us with a new covenant, a fresh charter from God. He is the Mediator of this covenant.

The murder of Jesus, unlike Abel's—a homicide that cried out for vengeance—became a proclamation of grace.

What's a theophany? It's a thing God does to get our attention. Such a manifestation of divine presence and power is usually described in pretty scary terms. The

Bible is full of theophanies, not the least being the events around Mount Sinai. The writer of this letter reminds his readers that Sinai, as scary as it was for everyone involved, isn't the sort of experience of God we find in Jesus.

Christian theophanies reveal less terror, more glory. God is described as fully present in a beautiful city to come. We see God in the radiance of our transfigured Lord, and in the Risen One of Easter. But not all Christian epiphanies are soft and lovely. God is also manifested in the sorrowful cross, and in the faces of the poor in parts of our own cities where glory is the last thing you can expect to see. The face of Christ is revealed in the refugee, the orphan, the natural disaster victim. Theophanies happen every day. They're not always identified accurately.

Name three times or places where you've seen God.
What do your theophanies teach you about what God is like?

GOSPEL » LUKE 14:1, 7-14

One time when Jesus went for a Sabbath meal with one of the top leaders of the Pharisees, all the guests had their eyes on him, watching his every move.

He went on to tell a story to the guests around the table. Noticing how each had tried to elbow into the place of honor, he said, "When someone invites you to dinner, don't take the place of honor. Somebody more important than you might have been invited by the host. Then he'll come and call out in front of everybody, 'You're in the wrong place. The place of honor belongs to this man.' Red-faced, you'll have to make your way to the very last table, the only place left.

"When you're invited to dinner, go and sit at the last place. Then when the host comes he may very well say, 'Friend, come up to the front.' That will give the dinner guests something to talk about! What I'm saying is, If you walk around with your nose in the air, you're going to end up flat on your face. But if you're content to be simply yourself, you will become more than yourself."

Then he turned to the host. "The next time you put on a dinner, don't just invite your friends and family and rich neighbors, the kind of people who will return the favor. Invite some people who never get invited out, the misfits from the wrong side of the tracks. You'll be—and experience—a blessing. They won't be able to return the favor, but the favor will be returned—oh, how it will be returned!—at the resurrection of God's people."

True story: I attended a meeting held in a conference room. The chairs arranged in the usual circle looked typically uncomfortable except for one large, ornate, padded chair which no one had yet claimed. I had walked far to be there and was tired, but the idea of taking that particular chair seemed selfish. So I passed on it, choosing a tin folding chair instead. More folks arrived. They eyed the beautiful chair wistfully. Each chose another place to sit. Finally a pert little woman walked in and without hesitation made a beeline for the best chair in the room. As she plopped into it, there was a creaking sound, and the bottom fell out and she went through it! As we helped the poor woman up—bruised only in the ego—we all laughed at having coveted that precarious chair. We named it the Chair of Humiliation. It looked appealing, but led to embarrassment. Sometimes the comforts we seek and the honors we claim have a way of backfiring. Humility beats humiliation by a mile!

Who is your best teacher of true humility?

WE RESPOND

Practice humility. Surrender the larger portion. Let someone get ahead of you. Allow the quiet person to speak. Seek wise teachers. Listen to their words, watch their actions, imitate their example.

"Invite some people who never get invited out,
the misfits from the wrong side of the tracks.
You'll be—and experience—a blessing."

TWENTY-THIRD SUNDAY IN ORDINARY TIME
.... What's Your Plan?

FIRST READING » WISDOM 9:13-18b

How does the mind of God work? Who can follow the directions from the Lord's recipe? Our reasoning processes are cumbersome; our philosophical constructs are complicated; our bodies grind the soul down; our existence messes the mind up. It's hard to make sense out of what's going on in the world; harder still to understand what's happening right under our noses.

As for what's in the heavens, who'll figure it out? Who'll know what your counsel might be? We won't, unless you send your divine spirit by sharing Wisdom with us. How else will you keep us on the straight and narrow? Lady Wisdom has helped us know your pleasure throughout history.

"The Woman Without a Plan!" That's how Sam mocked Amanda when he was especially annoyed. Sam was unquestionably The Man With the Plan. He'd always known which college he'd attend, where he'd get his Ph.D., when he would acquire university tenure, and how he'd make his move into politics. Sam will be President of the United States one day. Just you watch!

Compared with Sam, Amanda was innocent of motives. She changed schools and subjects, moved here and there, worked white collar one year, blue collar the next. It drove Sam nuts to watch her make her seemingly random sideways course through life. And Sam was right. Amanda had no plan. But that was the plan: not to push, but to explore. She walked through doors that opened, rather than forcing her way into each room. She was trying to listen to life, instead of doing all the talking. She allowed herself to be shaped to a Will other than her own. She doesn't know where it's all going. This journey may be the destination.

> **What plans have you made for your life?**
> **How willing are you to incorporate surprises?**

SECOND READING » PHILEMON 9-10, 12-17

I have a favor to ask of you. As Christ's ambassador and now a prisoner for him, I wouldn't hesitate to command this if I thought it necessary but I'd rather make it a personal request.

While here in jail, I've fathered a child, so to speak. And here he is, hand-carrying this letter—Onesimus!

I'm sending him back to you, but it feels like I'm cutting off my right arm in doing so. I wanted in the worst way to keep him here as your stand-in to help out while I'm in jail for the Message. But I didn't want to do anything behind your back, make you do a good deed that you hadn't willingly agreed to.

Maybe it's all for the best that you lost him for a while. You're getting him back now for good—and no mere slave this time, but a true Christian brother!

That's what he was to me—he'll be even more than that to you.

So if you still consider me a comrade-in-arms, welcome him back as you would me.

The Letter to Philemon is so unusual that it deserves a little attention. It's the shortest independent piece of Scripture in the Bible. (The prophecy of Obadiah in the Old Testament has fewer verses but is slightly longer.) Most of Paul's letters are instructions to communities he has left behind; this one is of a rare personal nature. Sandwiched between greetings and the usual salutatory prayer, Paul asks for a favor from his friend Philemon. He wants Philemon to give the slave Onesimus his freedom. We ask: A Christian owns a slave? A rich one might: Religious conversion and social revolution don't always go hand-in-hand all at once. Paul doesn't preach at Philemon or command him to do anything. Paul prefers to persuade his friend to see the matter for himself in a new light. This short letter is an early indication that Christianity promises to be the quiet little religion that rocks the world.

> **What has more influence in your life, a reproach or a suggestion?**
> **How do you persuade others to choose the good?**

GOSPEL » LUKE 14:25-33

One day when large groups of people were walking along with him, Jesus turned and told them, "Anyone who comes to me but refuses to let go of father, mother, spouse, children, brothers, sisters—yes, even one's own self!—can't be my disciple. Anyone who won't shoulder his own cross and follow behind me can't be my disciple.

"Is there anyone here who, planning to build a new house, doesn't first sit down and figure the cost so you'll know if you can complete it? If you only get the foundation laid and then run out of money, you're going to look pretty foolish. Everyone passing by will poke fun at you: 'He started something he couldn't finish.'

"Or can you imagine a king going into battle against another king without first deciding whether it is possible with his ten thousand troops to face the twenty thousand troops of the other? And if he decides he can't, won't he send an emissary and work out a truce?

"Simply put, if you're not willing to take what is dearest to you, whether plans or people, and kiss it good-bye, you can't be my disciple."

We are a society of planners. We've got calendars scrawled black and blue with appointments; smart phones in our pockets; magnets holding up lists all over the fridge. Our budgets tell us where the money's gone to, and copious records are filed for the taxman. I can tell you where I'm going to be and what I'll be doing on most days a year from now! This can all be a little intense.

Jesus has no dispute with careful schedules and records. But he wonders aloud that we take such care to plan dental appointments six months ahead, and show far less concern for the responsibilities of discipleship. Which will last longer: our teeth or our souls? We know where our money's invested and how much our next paycheck will bring in, but what spiritual riches have we stored for ourselves? I know where I'll be on Sunday a year from now. But where will I be when God's kingdom comes?

How would you go about planning a spiritual budget for a year? For today?

WE RESPOND

Add these items to your spiritual budget: Weekly Eucharist. Regular personal prayer. Time with Scripture. Seasonal self-examination and reconciliation. Annual retreat time. A spiritual audit of what you do with your time and money.

*"Simply put, if you're not willing
to take what is dearest to you,
whether plans or people,
and kiss it good-bye,
you can't be my disciple."*

TWENTY-FOURTH SUNDAY IN ORDINARY TIME

FIRST READING » EXODUS 32:7-11, 13-14

GOD spoke to Moses, "Go! Get down there! Your people whom you brought up from the land of Egypt have fallen to pieces. In no time at all they've turned away from the way I commanded them: They made a molten calf and worshiped it. They've sacrificed to it and said, 'These are the gods, O Israel, that brought you up from the land of Egypt!'"

GOD said to Moses, "I look at this people—oh! what a stubborn, hard-headed people! Let me alone now, give my anger free reign to burst into flames and incinerate them. But I'll make a great nation out of you."

Moses tried to calm his GOD down. He said, "Why, GOD, would you lose your temper with your people? Why, you brought them out of Egypt in a tremendous demonstration of power and strength. Think of Abraham, Isaac, and Israel, your servants to whom you gave your word, telling them 'I will give you many children, as many as the stars in the sky, and I'll give this land to your children as their land forever.'"

And GOD did think twice. He decided not to do the evil he had threatened against his people.

After the Golden Calf Incident, God is reputed to have been pretty angry. And we all know what that means! Up to now in the story, the presentation of God's anger has been fairly consistent: Adam and Eve, expelled from paradise for a seriously bad decision. The people of the earth, cursed with languages due to an architectural miscalculation concerning a tower. Noah and his family, floating alone above the land where their wicked neighbors used to reside. And we don't even have to mention that at the bottom of the Dead Sea are the remains of two other municipalities named Sodom and Gomorrah. Getting God angry is a bad idea.

But this time, Moses is on site to protest. Abraham once dickered for the innocent lives of Sodom; here, Moses bargains for the lives of the truly guilty. Do these people deserve mercy? According to human justice, no way. Moses holds God to a higher standard, however. And God, thank God, agrees.

> **Do you think "God changed his mind"**
> **about punishment due to sinners,**
> **or that Moses changed his own mind**
> **about the nature of God's relationship to us?**

SECOND READING » 1 TIMOTHY 1:12-17

I'm so grateful to Christ Jesus for making me adequate to do this work. He went out on a limb, you know, in trusting me with this ministry. The only credentials I brought to it were invective and witch hunts and arrogance. But I was treated mercifully because I didn't know what I was doing—didn't know Who I was doing it against! Grace mixed with faith and love poured over me and into me. And all because of Jesus.

Here's a word you can take to heart and depend on: Jesus Christ came into the world to save sinners. I'm proof—Public Sinner Number One—of someone who could never have made it apart from sheer mercy. And now he shows me off—evidence of his endless patience—to those who are right on the edge of trusting him forever.

> Deep honor and bright glory
> to the King of All Time—
> One God, Immortal, Invisible,
> ever and always. Oh, yes!

Think of something you've done in your life that you're heartily ashamed of. You may have hurt someone dear to you. Or perhaps you took something valuable that wasn't yours. Maybe you broke one of the commandments that seems bigger than the others. Or you exacted revenge, way out of proportion, on an enemy.

Would you change what you did, if you could? Would you make another decision, if you knew then what you know now?

Paul persecuted Christians before he became one. He was probably responsible for the death of several important local leaders of the early church. There was a time when he spat at the name of Jesus. None of this stands in the way of us calling him Saint Paul today. A great sinner became one of the greatest saints because he believed in God's mercy, and let it transform his life.

> **Do you accept mercy from others,**
> **and show mercy toward those who injure or offend you?**

GOSPEL » LUKE 15:1-32

By this time a lot of men and women of doubtful reputation were hanging around Jesus, listening intently. The Pharisees and religion scholars were not pleased, not at all pleased. They growled, "He takes in sinners and eats meals with them, treating them like old friends." Their grumbling triggered this story.

"Suppose one of you had a hundred sheep and lost one. Wouldn't you leave the ninety-nine in the wilderness and go after the lost one until you found it? When found, you can be sure you would put it across your shoulders, rejoicing, and when you got home call in your friends and neighbors, saying, 'Celebrate with me! I've found my lost sheep!' Count on it—there's more joy in heaven over one sinner's rescued life than over ninety-nine good people in no need of rescue.

"Or imagine a woman who has ten coins and loses one. Won't she light a lamp and scour the house, looking in every nook and cranny until she finds it? And when she finds it you can be sure she'll call her friends and neighbors: 'Celebrate with me! I found my lost coin!' Count on it—that's the kind of party

God's angels throw every time one lost soul turns to God."

Then he said, "There was once a man who had two sons. The younger said to his father, 'Father, I want right now what's coming to me.'

"So the father divided the property between them. It wasn't long before the younger son packed his bags and left for a distant country. There, undisciplined and dissipated, he wasted everything he had. After he had gone through all his money, there was a bad famine all through that country and he began to hurt. He signed on with a citizen there who assigned him to his fields to slop the pigs. He was so hungry he would have eaten the corncobs in the pig slop, but no one would give him any.

"That brought him to his senses. He said, 'All those farmhands working for my father sit down to three meals a day, and here I am starving to death. I'm going back to my father. I'll say to him, Father, I've sinned against God, I've sinned before you; I don't deserve to be called your son. Take me on as a hired hand.' He got right up and went home to his father.

"When he was still a long way off, his father saw him. His heart pounding, he ran out, embraced him, and kissed him. The son started his speech: 'Father, I've sinned against God, I've sinned before you; I don't deserve to be called your son ever again.'

"But the father wasn't listening. He was calling to the servants, 'Quick. Bring a clean set of clothes and dress him. Put the family ring on his finger and sandals on his feet. Then get a grain-fed heifer and roast it. We're going to feast! We're going to have a wonderful time! My son is here—given up for dead and now alive! Given up for lost and now found!' And they began to have a wonderful time.

"All this time his older son was out in the field. When the day's work was done he came in. As he approached the house, he heard the music and dancing. Calling over one of the houseboys, he asked what was going on. He told him, 'Your brother came home. Your father has ordered a feast—barbecued beef!— because he has him home safe and sound.'

"The older brother stalked off in an angry sulk and refused to join in. His father came out and tried to talk to him, but he wouldn't listen. The son said, 'Look how many years I've stayed here serving you, never giving you one moment of grief, but have you ever thrown a party for me and my friends? Then this son of yours who has thrown away your money on whores shows up and you go all out with a feast!'

"His father said, 'Son, you don't understand. You're with me all the time, and everything that is mine is yours—but this is a wonderful time, and we had to celebrate. This brother of yours was dead, and he's alive! He was lost, and he's found!'"

Lost sheep, lost coins, lost sons. In the parables of Jesus, things and people get lost and found a lot. In our experience, a lot gets lost along the way of life. Everything from socks and keys, to health and love. And some things stay lost.

The value of what gets lost in our lives varies incalculably, just as it does in Jesus' stories. Sometimes we lose money or a job, and that can have serious consequences. But those losses are not even in the same category as losing someone you love to death, or losing your independence as your body fails. As we suffer the great losses in our lives, even when someone or something seems hopelessly and irretrievably lost, Jesus assures us he's on the other end, retrieving and rescuing. That's God's job in a nutshell, according to the Christian tradition: to save what was lost. To redeem a world. To make sure that everything lost gets found.

Which kinds of losses have you faced?
Do you trust God to find and restore the rest?

WE RESPOND

When friends lose their faith, encourage them. When people you know lose heart, support them. When strangers lose their homes in disaster, contribute toward their rescue. When members of your community lose a loved one, mourn with them. And when those around you experience restoration of a loss, celebrate with them.

"Count on it—there's more joy in heaven
over one sinner's rescued life
than over ninety-nine good people
in no need of rescue."

TWENTY-FIFTH SUNDAY IN ORDINARY TIME
.... Can We Be Trusted?

FIRST READING » AMOS 8:4-7

Listen to this, you who walk all over the weak,
*   you who treat poor people as less than nothing,*
Who say, "When's my next paycheck coming
*   so I can go out and live it up?*
How long till the weekend
*   when I can go out and have a good time?"*
Who give little and take much,
*   and never do an honest day's work.*
You exploit the poor, using them—
*   and then, when they're used up, you discard them.*

GOD swears against the arrogance of Jacob:
*   "I'm keeping track of their every last sin."*

How do you do business? Can people take you at your word, or do you promise and fail to deliver? Do you cheat a little around the edges: at cards, at work, at tax time, at fidelity? Is your integrity a thing to marvel, or a thing of the past?

When we have our regular national conversations about "character," we're really talking about integrity. We want our leaders to be trustworthy. We want their appearance and their inner conviction to match up. We want their words and their actions to be on the same page. We want these people to be "real," and not fictions drummed up by handlers and spin-doctors. But it's silly, really, for us to expect our leaders to be better people than we're willing to be ourselves. How real are you? Are you everything you pretend to be, or is your life a "spin" of rationalizations, boasts, and justifications?

> **Answer the questions above as honestly as you can, at least to yourself.**
> **How can you begin to make your life more real, and less a work of fiction?**

SECOND READING » 1 TIMOTHY 2:1-8

The first thing I want you to do is pray. Pray every way you know how, for everyone you know. Pray especially for rulers and their governments to rule well so we can be quietly about our business of living simply, in humble contemplation. This is the way our Savior God wants us to live.

He wants not only us but everyone saved, you know, everyone to get to know the truth we've learned: that there's one God and only one, and one Priest-Mediator between God and us—Jesus, who offered himself in exchange for everyone held captive by sin, to set them all free. Eventually the news is going to get out. This and this only has been my appointed work: getting this news to those who have never heard of God, and explaining how it works by simple faith and plain truth.

Since prayer is at the bottom of all this, what I want mostly is for men to pray—not shaking angry fists at enemies but raising holy hands to God.

What is truth? Pilate once asked this simple-seeming question of Jesus. He may or may not have been sincere in the asking. But it's a good question for leaders to ask. Would that all world leaders were motivated by the desire to seek and act on the truth!

In this letter, Timothy gets some great advice regarding community leadership, and so do we. We're advised to pray for those who hold authority because their relationship to the truth—intimate, distant, or non-existent—has ramifications for all of us. It makes me wonder: How many of us prayed for past leaders with integrity issues? How many of us were praying for Richard Nixon or Bill Clinton; for the U.S. bishops or fill-in-the-blank with the latest headline-maker? We're quick to condemn leaders who fail us, but are less committed to lending spiritual support for the vital role they play in leading us. Do we pray for world leaders, our pastors, our bosses? What about parents and teachers? Does authority have to "deserve" our prayers in order to get them?

> Which are you more likely to do,
> scorn authorities or pray for them?
> Do you believe your prayers "matter"?

GOSPEL » LUKE 16:1-13

Jesus said to his disciples, "There was once a rich man who had a manager. He got reports that the manager had been taking advantage of his position by running up huge personal expenses. So he called him in and said, 'What's this I hear about you? You're fired. And I want a complete audit of your books.'

"The manager said to himself, 'What am I going to do? I've lost my job as manager. I'm not strong enough for a laboring job, and I'm too proud to beg.... Ah, I've got a plan. Here's what I'll do...then when I'm turned out into the street, people will take me into their houses.'

"Then he went at it. One after another, he called in the people who were in debt to his master. He said to the first, 'How much do you owe my master?'

"He replied, 'A hundred jugs of olive oil.'

"The manager said, 'Here, take your bill, sit down here—quick now—write fifty.'

"To the next he said, 'And you, what do you owe?'

"He answered, 'A hundred sacks of wheat.'

"He said, 'Take your bill, write in eighty.'

"Now here's a surprise: The master praised the crooked manager! And why? Because he knew how to look after himself. Streetwise people are smarter in this regard than law-abiding citizens. *They are on constant alert, looking for angles, surviving by their wits. I want you to be smart in the same way—but for what is* right—*using every adversity to stimulate you to creative survival, to concentrate your attention on the bare essentials, so you'll live, really live, and not complacently just get by on good behavior."*

Jesus went on to make these comments:

> *If you're honest in small things,*
> > *you'll be honest in big things;*
> *If you're a crook in small things,*
> > *you'll be a crook in big things.*
> *If you're not honest in small jobs,*
> > *who will put you in charge of the store?*
> *No worker can serve two bosses:*
> > *He'll either hate the first and love the second*
> *Or adore the first and despise the second.*
> > *You can't serve both God and the Bank.*

A red-spined book sat on the shelf of my parents' home while I was growing up. It was titled: *You Can Trust the Communists.* Believe me, my parents were not subversive characters by any means, so this title tended to startle the casual browser. Should you pick up this book and look at the face of it, however, you would see the subtitle: *(To Be Communists).* I admit I never read the book, but the deceptive title reminds me of the parable of the unjust steward. Is Jesus praising the actions of the steward, as the master in the story does? Are we to presume "the ends justify the means" in Jesus' evaluation? Of course not. Jesus is saying you can trust the unjust steward (to be unjust). And to be good at it. This guy is a pro.

Can you trust Christians, to be Christians? Not always. We don't live up to our name every time. We aren't "professionals" about our faith, skilled and dedicated, fully identified with our vocation. Many of us are hobbyists, at best, playing at Christianity in our spare time, when it doesn't get in the way. Jesus asks for more.

> **Consider the gifts that God has entrusted to you.**
> **How trustworthy are you?**

WE RESPOND

Integrity is like losing weight: simple, but not easy. Make a list of things in your life that fit together with your commitment to bear the name of Christ. List the things that do not fit, and think of steps you can take to bring your life in line.

TWENTY-SIXTH SUNDAY IN ORDINARY TIME

FIRST READING » AMOS 6:1a, 4-7

Woe to you who think you live on easy street in Zion,
who think Mount Samaria is the good life.

Woe to those who live in luxury
and expect everyone else to serve them!
Woe to those who live only for today,
indifferent to the fate of others!
Woe to the playboys, the playgirls,
who think life is a party held just for them!
Woe to those addicted to feeling good—life without pain!
those obsessed with looking good—life without wrinkles!
They could not care less
about their country going to ruin.

But here's what's really coming:
a forced march into exile.
They'll leave the country whining,
a rag-tag bunch of good-for-nothings.

When reading prophets like Amos, my social worker friend Mary reminds me, it feels good not to own a couch. Mary and I worked together at a homeless shelter years ago, and the commitment she made in the sight of human misery stuck with her. She vowed then never to buy a couch. People need beds, chairs, tables, Mary reckoned. Couches are luxuries. She never wants to get too comfortable, while others still live in want.

Of course, the couch is just a symbol for Mary. Very fine Christians own couches. I've met struggling families who ONLY have a couch, which doubles as their communal bed. I worked with a young man taking night classes to be a nurse. He told me he'd never had a bed or even a couch to sleep on in his life. As a child in a poor family, he slept on the floor near the radiator. Now that he has his own apartment, he still sleeps on the floor. "Habit," he says, shrugging. How comfortable should we be with the poverty of others?

What can you do about poverty, and what do you do?

SECOND READING » 1 TIMOTHY 6:11-16

But you, Timothy, man of God: Run for your life from all this. Pursue a righteous life—a life of wonder, faith, love, steadiness, courtesy. Run hard and fast in the faith. Seize the eternal life, the life you were called to, the life you so fervently embraced in the presence of so many witnesses.

I'm charging you before the life-giving God and before Christ, who took his stand before Pontius Pilate and didn't give an inch: Keep this command to the letter, and don't slack off. Our Master, Jesus Christ, is on his way. He'll show up right on time, his arrival guaranteed by the Blessed and Undisputed Ruler, High King, High God. He's the only one death can't touch, his light so bright no one can get close. He's never been seen by human eyes—human eyes can't take him in! Honor to him, and eternal rule! Oh, yes!

Children of God, when faced with decisions, choose the course that brings a blessing. Man of God, show devotion to God and to family. Woman of God, hold onto faith even when your soul is crushed under its burdens. People of God, love one another, and love the stranger and the enemy. Lover of God, be patient with those who most need your forbearance. Chosen of God, reveal your strength in acts of gentle kindness, and be a caress on the face of the earth.

The virtues extolled to Timothy, a new shepherd serving the Christian community, are meant for all of us. Think of what it would be like to live in a community which practices these things! Then recognize the difference between *that* community, and the one we know now, is you and me.

How many of the virtues in Timothy's list do you practice?
Which one is hardest for you?

GOSPEL » LUKE 16:19-31

"There once was a rich man, expensively dressed in the latest fashions, wasting his days in conspicuous consumption. A poor man named Lazarus, covered with sores, had been dumped on his doorstep. All he lived for was to get a meal from scraps off the rich man's table. His best friends were the dogs who came and licked his sores.

"Then he died, this poor man, and was taken up by the angels to the lap of Abraham. The rich man also died and was buried. In hell and in torment, he looked up and saw Abraham in the distance and Lazarus in his lap. He called out, 'Father Abraham, mercy! Have mercy! Send Lazarus to dip his finger in water to cool my tongue. I'm in agony in this fire.'

"But Abraham said, 'Child, remember that in your lifetime you got the good things and Lazarus the bad things. It's not like that here. Here he's consoled and you're tormented. Besides, in all these matters there is a huge chasm set between us so that no one can go from us to you even if he wanted to, nor can anyone cross over from you to us.'

"The rich man said, 'Then let me ask you, Father: Send him to the house of my father where I have five brothers, so he can tell them the score and warn them so they won't end up here in this place of torment.'

"Abraham answered, 'They have Moses and the Prophets to tell them the score. Let them listen to them.'

"'I know, Father Abraham,' he said, 'but they're not listening. If someone came back to them from the dead, they would change their ways.'

"Abraham replied, 'If they won't listen to Moses and the Prophets, they're not going to be convinced by someone who rises from the dead.'"

When you're given the choice between couches of ivory and the bosom of Abraham, choose wisely! Abraham cultivated a very special relationship with God, and he would be a very good friend to have. But many of us have cultivated a much closer communion with our couches. We like our creature comforts. Abraham can wait!

The rich man probably felt that way. At least he was content to live well, consume conspicuously, and ignore the misery of Lazarus at his door. If only the rich man had realized that the way to Abraham's bosom was in forging a relationship with Lazarus! Instead he allowed Lazarus to fend for himself. We might note carefully that this was *all* the rich man did, by the way. He didn't hurt Lazarus; chase him off; and he wasn't directly the cause for his poverty or his sores. The dude simply ignored another man's suffering. We don't have to make the same mistake.

> What's the greatest sacrifice you ever made for someone in need?
> What's the greatest sacrifice that was ever made for you?

WE RESPOND

Let's get off our couches and get moving! Unclutter your life of futile things. Give to someone who has less. Help someone nearby who needs you. Listen more. Talk about yourself less. Make room for others in the world in how you use worldly resources.

TWENTY-SEVENTH SUNDAY IN ORDINARY TIME

FIRST READING » HABAKKUK 1:2-3; 2:2-4

GOD, *how long do I have to cry out for help*
before you listen?
How many times do I have to yell, "Help! Murder! Police!"
before you come to the rescue?
Why do you force me to look at evil,
stare trouble in the face day after day?
Anarchy and violence break out,
quarrels and fights all over the place.

And then GOD *answered: "Write this.*
Write what you see.
Write it out in big block letters
so that it can be read on the run.
This vision-message is a witness
pointing to what's coming.
It aches for the coming—it can hardly wait!
And it doesn't lie.
If it seems slow in coming, wait.
It's on its way. It will come right on time.

"Look at that man, bloated by self-importance—
full of himself but soul-empty.
But the person in right standing before GOD
through loyal and steady believing
is fully alive, really alive."

What good are the bad times in our lives?

Three really awful things happen to the Israelites in biblical history. Each defines the community's relationship with God. The first is their enslavement in Egypt. After deliverance from Pharaoh, Israel learns their God is a God who saves. The second bad time comes in 587 B.C., as Jerusalem falls to Babylon and the nation goes into exile. When the community returns home, they know their God is a God of second chances. The third crisis is in the year 70 A.D., when Rome destroys the Jerusalem Temple. Once their center of worship is gone, the people learn God can be worshipped in spirit and truth.

The era of Habakkuk is just before the Babylonian crisis. The prophet challenges God to explain the approaching catastrophe. The first two chapters are a poignant dialogue between the prophet and the Lord. The third chapter, however, is a pledge of confidence in the God who remembers compassion. Trusting in God wasn't easy in Habakkuk's generation—nor is it for us when the walls come tumbling down. Yet we too are offered this chance to "be alive, really alive."

Draw a timeline of your life.
Indicate the crises from which you've been delivered.
What did you learn from each?

SECOND READING » 2 TIMOTHY 1:6-8, 13-14

And the special gift of ministry you received when I laid hands on you and prayed—keep that ablaze! God doesn't want us to be shy with his gifts, but bold and loving and sensible.

So don't be embarrassed to speak up for our Master or for me, his prisoner. Take your share of suffering for the Message along with the rest of us. We can only keep on going, after all, by the power of God.

So keep at your work, this faith and love rooted in Christ, exactly as I set it out for you. It's as sound as the day you first heard it from me. Guard this precious thing placed in your custody by the Holy Spirit who works in us.

Friends can be our best teachers along the way of faith. Timothy learned a lot from Paul during Paul's second missionary tour. Timothy became a companion of the great apostle through many cities in the service of the gospel. In this letter, written in a rare separation during Paul's imprisonment, Paul encourages his friend not to falter. The Spirit they share gives them what they need to be "bold and loving and sensible."

I have a friend who teaches me what those words mean. She's an Anglican priest now, but I remember when she was a struggling young woman asking some pretty hard questions of God. Recently divorced, bruised in spirit, she needed a place to put her passion. Not content to wait for God to show up with answers to her questions someday, she embarked on a ten-year quest to learn the heart of God. After a decade of prayer, tears, and searching, she emerged as a modern mystic, as surprised to embrace the call to priesthood as anyone. Her letters to me over the years have helped me to find what is strong, loving, and wise in me. Holy friends double our ability to attend to God's voice.

Name the holy friends in your life.
How do they teach you about God's Spirit at work in you?

GOSPEL » LUKE 17:5-10

The apostles came up and said to the Master, "Give us more faith."

But the Master said, "You don't need more faith. There is no 'more' or 'less' in faith. If you have a bare kernel of faith, say the size of a poppy seed, you could say to this sycamore tree, 'Go jump in the lake,' and it would do it.

"Suppose one of you has a servant who comes in from plowing the field or tending the sheep. Would you take his coat, set the table, and say, 'Sit down and

eat'? Wouldn't you be more likely to say, 'Prepare dinner; change your clothes and wait table for me until I've finished my coffee; then go to the kitchen and have your supper'? Does the servant get special thanks for doing what's expected of him? It's the same with you. When you've done everything expected of you, be matter-of-fact and say, 'The work is done. What we were told to do, we did.'"

We like Jesus when he tells us we're guaranteed a seat at the banquet of God's kingdom. But we're troubled by the Jesus who tells us to wait on tables for now. Being defined as a mere obedient servant seems a little cold, but it's a useful corrective to the notion that God owes us something special for all our hard work being the good guys. God is not, after all, our employer. God isn't obliged to put a little extra in the envelope when we put in overtime. God owes us nothing. It is we who are indebted for everything.

The disciples are obsessed with proportions nonetheless. They think "more faith" will make them more faithful! Jesus reminds them that God makes a lot with a little, as when the world was created from chaos, or humanity formed out of clay. A smattering of faith is enough—when it's used. But if we don't listen to God? All the faith and good works we can stockpile will be pitifully inadequate.

> Think of the five biggest things you've ever done for God.
> Compare them with the five biggest things God has done for you.
> Does the story of the useless servant make more sense now?

WE RESPOND

Ask God today to speak to you: in Scripture, in the day's events, through other people. Listen for what God says to you today. Write down the words of God that come to you, and pray over them tonight.

TWENTY-EIGHTH SUNDAY IN ORDINARY TIME

FIRST READING » 2 KINGS 5:14-17

Naaman went down and immersed himself in the Jordan seven times, following the orders of the Holy Man. His skin was healed; it was like the skin of a little baby. He was as good as new.

He then went back to the Holy Man, he and his entourage, stood before him, and said, "I now know beyond a shadow of a doubt that there is no God anywhere on earth other than the God of Israel. In gratitude let me give you a gift."

"As GOD lives," Elisha replied, "the God whom I serve, I'll take nothing from you." Naaman tried his best to get him to take something, but he wouldn't do it.

"If you won't take anything," said Naaman, "let me ask you for something: Give me a load of dirt, as much as a team of donkeys can carry, because I'm never again going to worship any god other than GOD."

Naaman came from a foreign land, dragging his leprosy with him. He was hoping for a cure from the Holy Man of Israel, and he almost didn't get one (see earlier verses 9-13). The problem was that Naaman took his leprosy very seriously. He wanted a divine intervention as profound as his disease. When the prophet told him to wash it away, Naaman was insulted. His pride almost cost him the cure he was seeking.

Some of us drag our wounds around for years, taking them very seriously. We've been hurt so deeply; perhaps it adds gravity to our pain to think it is incurable. The suggestion that there could be a simple solution—say, forgiving my mother for being who she was; stop making my husband responsible for my happiness; letting go of the past and moving ahead—may seem offensive. If God offers us the opportunity to be made whole on such terms, we may prefer the dignity of our wounds.

At the last minute, Naaman swallows his pride and goes for the cure. The result is newborn baby flesh and a new God in the bargain. The God of his leprous days is gone. From now on, Naaman will worship the God of the cure.

> **Which wounds have been long in healing in your life?**
> **How does a healing affect your relationship with God?**

SECOND READING » 2 TIMOTHY 2:8-13

Fix this picture firmly in your mind: Jesus, descended from the line of David, raised from the dead. It's what you've heard from me all along. It's what I'm sitting in jail for right now—but God's Word isn't in jail! That's why I stick it out here—so that everyone God calls will get in on the salvation of Christ in all its glory. This is a sure thing:

If we die with him, we'll live with him;
If we stick it out with him, we'll rule with him;
If we turn our backs on him, he'll turn his back on us;
If we give up on him, he does not give up—
  for there's no way he can be false to himself.

From prison, Paul shouts the gospel that makes him more free than the guards who hold him. Casting our lot with Christ, to the death, means we will know the fruits of his resurrection. Paul was very close to a literal understanding of that theology, as his life was on the line for preaching the message that made him an outlaw.

Proclaiming the gospel is still treasonous in this world, though in a subtler way. It's unlikely that many of us will go to prison for our faith (though some are arrested for civil disobedience out of religious conviction). The softer treason to which we're called is nothing less than the rejection of a social system that denies responsibility for the poor; views the elderly as irrelevant; questions the value of the dying; ignores the humanity of the unborn; imagines the state has the right to take lives; sees war as okay so long as we're "right"; puts the environment secondary to the economy; or treats migrant workers badly for local profit. Maybe there ought to be more Christians in jail than out of it.

How far are you willing to go
with the "treasonous" message of the gospel?

GOSPEL » LUKE 17:11-19

It happened that as he made his way toward Jerusalem, he crossed over the border between Samaria and Galilee. As he entered a village, ten men, all lepers, met him. They kept their distance but raised their voices, calling out, "Jesus, Master, have mercy on us!"

Taking a good look at them, he said, "Go, show yourselves to the priests."

They went, and while still on their way, became clean. One of them, when he realized that he was healed, turned around and came back, shouting his gratitude, glorifying God. He kneeled at Jesus' feet, so grateful. He couldn't thank him enough—and he was a Samaritan.

Jesus said, "Were not ten healed? Where are the nine? Can none be found to come back and give glory to God except this outsider?" Then he said to him, "Get up. On your way. Your faith has healed and saved you."

Luke loves this kind of story. Jesus straddles the border between Samaria and Galilee when he heals some folks. This means we don't know how many in this leper band were Jews, how many foreigners. But we do know only one Samaritan shows gratitude. Luke celebrates the unlikely hero: foreigners, sinners, women, the poor. A Samaritan leper inhabited the near bottom of the social barrel to the crowds around Jesus. (The only person lower would be a poor Samaritan female leper!)

It's intriguing to note these ten traveled together as lepers: the distance between Jew and Samaritan dissolved by their common affliction. Once healed, would these ten even speak to each other on the street across the chasm of ethnic identity? That's why Jesus commends the faith—the *faith*—of the Samaritan. Because faith in Jesus' eyes isn't about group identity or religious systems. It's about knowing divine grace when you receive it. The Samaritan, who will be despised by all tomorrow, walks away free with salvation in his pocket. The other nine, cleansed of leprosy, will still wear their chains.

How many people do you recognize outside of your religious system who obviously enjoy a state of grace?

WE RESPOND

Many of us are still burdened by chains of fear, unforgiveness, indecision, or bitterness. Pray for the release of one of these chains that bind your heart or the heart of someone close to you.

If we die with him, we'll live with him;
If we stick it out with him, we'll rule with him.

TWENTY-NINTH SUNDAY IN ORDINARY TIME
.... Raise Up Holy Hands

FIRST READING » EXODUS 17:8-13

Amalek came and fought Israel at Rephidim. Moses ordered Joshua: "Select some men for us and go out and fight Amalek. Tomorrow I will take my stand on top of the hill holding God's staff."

Joshua did what Moses ordered in order to fight Amalek. And Moses, Aaron, and Hur went to the top of the hill. It turned out that whenever Moses raised his hands, Israel was winning, but whenever he lowered his hands, Amalek was winning. But Moses' hands got tired. So they got a stone and set it under him. He sat on it and Aaron and Hur held up his hands, one on each side. So his hands remained steady until the sun went down. Joshua defeated Amalek and its army in battle.

One of the required classes for a Divinity degree concerns the curious matter of "celebrational style": learning to preside at Mass and other liturgies. I remember practicing the *orans* position, which is the posture of a priest during the Eucharistic Prayer. It is an ancient prayer posture, demonstrated by Moses during the war against Amalek: arms raised, hands open. (Moses is holding the staff of God at the same time, which makes it really tricky.) The orans posture indicates praise and also openness to God's will. It's an invitation for God to act. Try it for a moment. Take a deep breath and open your arms, your hands, your heart. It's a vulnerable and liberating pose.

It's also a pose hard to maintain for long. If you hold your arms up for the length of the Eucharistic Prayer, even, you'll be surprised how tiring it is. Imagine raising them from dawn until dusk! No wonder Moses needed a little help from his friends.

Persistence in prayer, no matter what the posture, is rewarded by God. We could use some hardy prayer warriors like Moses in the church. Looking for work?

> **How often do you pray?**
> **How would you describe your prayer?**
> **What keeps you from prayer?**

SECOND READING » 2 TIMOTHY 3:14 – 4:2

But don't let it faze you. Stick with what you learned and believed, sure of the integrity of your teachers—why, you took in the sacred Scriptures with your mother's milk! There's nothing like the written Word of God for showing you the way to salvation through faith in Christ Jesus. Every part of Scripture is God-breathed and useful one way or another—showing us truth, exposing our rebellion, correcting our mistakes, training us to live God's way. Through the Word we are put together and shaped up for the tasks God has for us.

I can't impress this on you too strongly. God is looking over your shoulder.

Christ himself is the Judge, with the final say on everyone, living and dead.
He is about to break into the open with his rule, so proclaim the Message with
intensity; keep on your watch. Challenge, warn, and urge your people. Don't ever
quit. Just keep it simple.

Many of us make quite good Christians—when it's convenient. But what about
when it's inconvenient to practice our faith? Ah, there's the rub.

I used to teach preaching at a local seminary. It was convenient to be Christian
there. I wore a cross around my neck, talked about Jesus, and everyone agreed with
me. How pleasant! I also met folks at a local joint for burritos and beer, and in that
context I sometimes found my faith looking for cover. As my pals lamented their
disappointments, I didn't want to appear too "religious." I held my tongue as they
blamed the usual suspects for their problems instead of owning the truth. I wanted
to tell them what I truly believe, about how Jesus can free us from cycles of destruction and failure. But I was embarrassed to speak, afraid I'd be excluded from the
group if I "preached" at the taqueria what I proclaimed at the seminary.

Paul reminds us we can't turn church membership on and off. When it's inconvenient to talk faith is probably the most crucial time to do so. Dare we buy the next
pitcher, and say what we know?

Where are you least comfortable talking about your faith?

GOSPEL » LUKE 18:1-8

Jesus told them a story showing that it was necessary for them to pray
consistently and never quit. He said, "There was once a judge in some city who
never gave God a thought and cared nothing for people. A widow in that city
kept after him: 'My rights are being violated. Protect me!'

"He never gave her the time of day. But after this went on and on he said
to himself, 'I care nothing what God thinks, even less what people think. But
because this widow won't quit badgering me, I'd better do something and see
that she gets justice—otherwise I'm going to end up beaten black and blue by her
pounding.'"

Then the Master said, "Do you hear what that judge, corrupt as he is, is
saying? So what makes you think God won't step in and work justice for his
chosen people, who continue to cry out for help? Won't he stick up for them?
I assure you, he will. He will not drag his feet. But how much of that kind of
persistent faith will the Son of Man find on the earth when he returns?"

**Jesus must have been feeling mischievous when he told the story of the persistent
widow.** He offers a funny comparison: God is at least as likely to respond to our
prayers as a corrupt judge will cave in under a widow's badgering. Maybe Jesus had
days like that, when someone got on his nerves so much he just gave them what
they wanted. We've all bought a magazine or candy bar at the door just to make the
salesperson go away.

The point of the story isn't God's experience, of course, but ours. Whether God is worn down by eons of listening to prayers remains to be seen. Our task is to keep up the prayers—harder than it sounds to those who don't pray much. Fidelity in prayer is as hard as working at any love relationship. In some seasons the effort will feel greater than the desire. Persistent prayer is more effective than the one-off method, just as daily efforts to build loving relationships are more meaningful than a lone card on Valentine's Day.

> Do you know anyone who is prays well?
> What keeps them faithful?
> What helps you to pray?

WE RESPOND

If you're new to prayer, ask someone you trust to recommend a good book for beginners. If you're starting again, consider finding a prayer partner to keep you faithful. If you're a persistent pray-er, keep the rest of us in your prayers!

Proclaim the Message with intensity; keep on your watch. Challenge, warn, and urge your people. Don't ever quit. Just keep it simple.

THIRTIETH SUNDAY IN ORDINARY TIME

FIRST READING » SIRACH 35:12-14, 16-18

The Lord is the God of justice. The poor who've been wronged shouldn't complain when the prayers of the rich-but-wronged are also heard. On the other hand, the rich shouldn't think poorly of the wails of an orphan or the cries of a widow. Their prayers of grief rise all the way to the heavens.

The prayers of those who adore God will be warmly welcomed; their humble prayers will reach the clouds. Their prayers must arrive before they can be acted upon, but they won't be discarded before they're reviewed. The Most High will take the proper action, if any is needed; he'll get to it as soon as possible.

I came to prayer through the Scriptures. I had grown up in a small town with many Catholic churches. They offered a variety of religious devotions to choose from and as a teenager I sampled them all. I knew prayer was important, so I hit every parish and crashed every mission. But still I felt frustrated as a young adult, not really finding a kind of prayer that engaged me fully. Then I started reading the Bible, which changed everything.

I began by praying the psalms in the Liturgy of the Hours. Then I determined to read the Bible cover to cover, and began to find the "pocket prayers" in every book. I tried to memorize one verse every morning, repeating it throughout the day. For this passage from Sirach, I might select the line: "The Most High will take the proper action, *if any is needed*." I'd spend the day reflecting on how often I jump the gun, acting or speaking when silence would serve better. You can learn a lot of Scripture in a year—or one month—one verse at a time. Prayers begin to speak out of your experiences before you know it.

How do the Scriptures influence your prayer?

SECOND READING » 2 TIMOTHY 4:6-8, 16-18

You take over. I'm about to die, my life an offering on God's altar. This is the only race worth running. I've run hard right to the finish, believed all the way. All that's left now is the shouting—God's applause! Depend on it, he's an honest judge. He'll do right not only by me, but by everyone eager for his coming.

At my preliminary hearing no one stood by me. They all ran like scared rabbits. But it doesn't matter—the Master stood by me and helped me spread the Message loud and clear to those who had never heard it. I was snatched from the jaws of the lion! God's looking after me, keeping me safe in the kingdom of heaven. All praise to him, praise forever! Oh, yes!

Paul anticipates his own death with its grim reality and joyful promise. Though abandoned by supporters in court, he knows the Lord he's served long and faithfully hasn't forgotten him. This image repeated in his letters has become the mantra that sustains him: I've fought the good fight, I've finished the race, I've kept the faith. If we can all say that in the end, we have no reason to fear.

Paul chooses not to hold a grudge against those who deserted him. Rendered here as "But it doesn't matter," other translations read: "May it not be held against them!" Now that is a superior prayer. We could all slip that into our pocket for the next time someone causes us offense. Just think of the light heart you'd take to bed with you, having blessed away potential enemies, surrendering grudges you might have carried home for storage otherwise. Paul concludes with a doxology: a standard recognition of God's glory. Seeing God's glory in the hour of crisis is no casual move. To a veteran pray-er like Paul, it comes with the territory.

> **For whom might you have prayed today:**
> **"May it not be held against them!"?**
> **If you didn't pray for them, what did you do?**

GOSPEL » LUKE 18:9-14

He told his next story to some who were complacently pleased with themselves over their moral performance and looked down their noses at the common people: "Two men went up to the Temple to pray, one a Pharisee, the other a tax man. The Pharisee posed and prayed like this: 'Oh, God, I thank you that I am not like other people—robbers, crooks, adulterers, or, heaven forbid, like this tax man. I fast twice a week and tithe on all my income.'

"Meanwhile the tax man, slumped in the shadows, his face in his hands, not daring to look up, said, 'God, give mercy. Forgive me, a sinner.'"

Jesus commented, "This tax man, not the other, went home made right with God. If you walk around with your nose in the air, you're going to end up flat on your face, but if you're content to be simply yourself, you will become more than yourself."

The Jesus Prayer has its origins in this parable. The text of the prayer is simple: "Lord Jesus Christ, have mercy on me, a sinner." Although prayed since the sixth century, the modern technique associated with this prayer—controlled breathing and mantra-like repetitions—probably didn't come into use until the fourteenth century. Like any prayer, the point isn't to perfect the technique but to find the right spirit.

The tax collector in the parable had the right spirit, even if he couldn't imagine the technique that history would form around his prayer. He simply bowed his head, acknowledged his sins, and counted on God's mercy. The Pharisee, who had more style and undoubtedly greater technique, gave himself over to self-celebration, reporting his good deeds in the event God might have missed them. In the process, he missed the heart of prayer, which is humility.

The lesson on prayer is simple. Pray however you want, but be sure of two things: that you DO pray, and that your heart is invested in your prayer.

How do pride and humility figure in your experience of prayer?

WE RESPOND

Pocket a Scripture for the week. You may want to take a line from this week's readings, or any other Scripture that attracts you. Pray it often, and note how it affects your relationships, responses, or decisions.

I've run hard right to the finish,
believed all the way.
All that's left now is the shouting—
God's applause!
Depend on it, he's an honest judge.

THIRTY-FIRST SUNDAY IN ORDINARY TIME
.... New Ideas for Halloween

FIRST READING » WISDOM 11:22 – 12:2

Like a speck of dust on a scale—that's how the whole world weighs in before you—like a drop of morning dew. But have mercy on us all. You can do that; pay no attention to our sins—we're already doing the penance. You look upon created things with delight; you dislike nothing you've created. Honestly, if you dislike something you shouldn't have created it in the first place.

How could the china keep from chipping if you hadn't made it unbreakable in the first place?

Likewise, how could something not called into existence by you last forever?

Spare us, O Lord; we come from your collection; we wear your label; we bear your mark.

In all created beings, O Lord, you find a spark of your own immortal spirit. To those who wander from the straight and narrow, you provide mid-course correction. To those who sin against you, you give a sharp warning plus a hopeful word; you want everyone to leave the wicked life behind and believe in you.

Tired of dressing up like a witch or a recent president for Halloween? How about having a theme party and inviting all your friends to come as someone or something in the Scriptures for the day? (Please note: Unless all your friends belong to churches which use the common lectionary—Catholics, Episcopalians, Lutherans, and a few others—they may not use the same readings. Best to email the selections ahead.) The second caveat is that this is not a serious suggestion. (Although if your parish decides to host such a party, I want to see the pictures.)

Take today's passages, for example. The first reading has only one living character in it—the Lord—but you can be creative. How about going to the party as The Sins God Chooses to Overlook? You and six friends could go as the Seven Deadlies. Come on, it would be fun.

> **How would you design costumes for the seven deadly sins?**
> **Can you name them? How many of them are particularly "fatal" for you?**

SECOND READING » 2 THESSALONIANS 1:11 – 2:2

Because we know that this extraordinary day is just ahead, we pray for you all the time—pray that our God will make you fit for what he's called you to be, pray that he'll fill your good ideas and acts of faith with his own energy so that it all amounts to something. If your life honors the name of Jesus, he will honor you. Grace is behind and through all of this, our God giving himself freely, the Master, Jesus Christ, giving himself freely.

Now, friends, read these next words carefully. Slow down and don't go jumping to conclusions regarding the day when our Master, Jesus Christ, will come back and we assemble to welcome him. Don't let anyone shake you up or get you excited over some breathless report or rumored letter from me that the day of the Master's arrival has come and gone.

Saint Paul doesn't make Halloween costume planning any easier. For characters, we have Paul himself, his Thessalonian "friends," God, and Jesus Christ to consider. It might be historically interesting to go as a Thessalonian, but you'd have to do some research into what citizens of Greece wore in the first century. You would betray a lot about your own theology if you were to create a costume persona of God.

Kids might enjoy considering how to dress up as "Grace" to counteract the adults trying to model "The Sins" in the first reading. (Adults do a good job of modeling sins to children in any event, and Jesus did say the kids would show us the way to the Kingdom.) Me, I'd give serious thought to how to pose as "The Day of the Master's Arrival." A little something Apocalyptic would be just the thing for Halloween!

> **Make a list of how you see grace operating in our modern world.
> How do you participate in its good purposes?**

GOSPEL » LUKE 19:1-10

Then Jesus entered and walked through Jericho. There was a man there, his name Zacchaeus, the head tax man and quite rich. He wanted desperately to see Jesus, but the crowd was in his way—he was a short man and couldn't see over the crowd. So he ran on ahead and climbed up in a sycamore tree so he could see Jesus when he came by.

When Jesus got to the tree, he looked up and said, "Zacchaeus, hurry down. Today is my day to be a guest in your home."

Zacchaeus scrambled out of the tree, hardly believing his good luck, delighted to take Jesus home with him. Everyone who saw the incident was indignant and grumped, "What business does he have getting cozy with this crook?"

Zacchaeus just stood there, a little stunned. He stammered apologetically, "Master, I give away half my income to the poor—and if I'm caught cheating, I pay four times the damages."

Jesus said, "Today is salvation day in this home! Here he is: Zacchaeus, son of Abraham! For the Son of Man came to find and restore the lost."

As usual, the gospel is peopled with more characters than the other readings, giving us lots to think about for masquerade purposes. You get a second chance to consider Jesus—though here he is the historical person and not the post-resurrection "Christ" that Paul references in his letter. Would there be a difference between the two costumes of Jesus and Christ, in your design plan? And how about "the Son of Man," a particular title for Jesus, the meaning of which even scholars are divided about? If you had three people in costume as Jesus—the Christ, the man, and the Son of Man—how would you distinguish them, if at all?

If that's too much theology to handle at a Halloween party, you might take the easy way out and come as Zacchaeus. (Only short people should consider Zacchaeus, since that's his outstanding characteristic.) Nature lovers might take a shot at portraying the sycamore tree. Endless possibilities!

**How many titles for Jesus can you name,
and what does each reveal about who he is?**

WE RESPOND

Okay, most folks will not have a Halloween party on biblical themes. But using religious imagination to reflect on Scripture is a time-honored tradition. Each Sunday, identify with a member of the biblical cast. Consider what you learn through this identification.

*In all created beings, O Lord,
you find a spark of your own immortal spirit.*

THIRTY-SECOND SUNDAY IN ORDINARY TIME

FIRST READING » 2 MACCABEES 7:1-2, 9-14

A Jewish mother and her seven sons were apprehended by thugs sent by Antiochus IV, know by his fans as Godlike, which he certainly was not. After refusing to eat pork, which was against the Law, the boys were bullied and whipped to try to force them to even touch it.

One of the young men, the eldest of them, spoke up. "Why are you beating us? Why do you care whether we eat pork or not? One thing we'll tell you; we'd rather die than break the dietary rules that were given to us by our ancestors."

His last words were: "You wretched excuse for a king! You can snuff the life out of us now, but not in eternity; the king of the world will raise us up."

They then made sport with the third young man. When it came time for them to do their blade work, he stretched out his hands and stuck out his tongue, but not before he said a few last words.

"These I have from heaven, but I love God's word more than my hands and tongue; besides he'll give them back to me in the future."

The king was impressed by the young man's resilience, but he was also annoyed that he thought death by torture was no great deal.

After the third came the fourth. He too had some last words.

"Being put to death by human beings is nothing; to be raised up by God, that's something to look forward to. You kill me, but you have nothing to look forward to."

Do you believe in eternal life? Before you say yes, answer another question: How ready are you to die today? Sometimes our answers to these two questions are in conflict. We often live in the ambiguity of the Arab proverb: *Trust in God, but tie your camel.*

Many people believe in resurrection but aren't prepared to bet their lives on it. The allure of life's projects is compelling. Whatever lies beyond death, however attractive, is too mysterious to produce the kind of longing our present circumstances hold for us. God's companionship may be a wonderful thing—but so is human relationship. The heavenly choir may be full of angels, but the delight of hearing your favorite song on the radio is also a moment of near-perfect pleasure.

The seven brothers in Maccabees undergo a hideous scourge and martyrdom for their faith. It's a bit grisly for a Sunday morning, but the illustration of complete surrender is unforgettable. Since our lives will certainly be required of each of us someday, we too will have to "disdain" this world for the sake of the next. How nearly does our profession of faith match our reality?

To what do you "tie your camel" in this world?
What would it take to trust in God more?

SECOND READING » 2 THESSALONIANS 2:16 – 3:5

May Jesus himself and God our Father, who reached out in love and surprised you with gifts of unending help and confidence, put a fresh heart in you, invigorate your work, enliven your speech.

One more thing, friends: Pray for us. Pray that the Master's Word will simply take off and race through the country to a groundswell of response, just as it did among you. And pray that we'll be rescued from these scoundrels who are trying to do us in. I'm finding that not all "believers" are believers. But the Master never lets us down. He'll stick by you and protect you from evil.

Because of the Master, we have great confidence in you. We know you're doing everything we told you and will continue doing it. May the Master take you by the hand and lead you along the path of God's love and Christ's endurance.

Paul's ministry was dogged by people he termed scoundrels and evildoers. We all know a lot of "morally undeclared" folks; we ourselves may feel a fair amount of moral ambivalence. But evil, true evil, is rare. Thank God! Still, it's important to recognize the genuine spirit of evil when we encounter it. One of evil's greatest victories, as *The Screwtape Letters* reminded us, is that most people don't believe it exists.

Evil is different from ambivalence in being absolutely deliberate. Evil knows better and chooses worse. It's not chosen in the passion of the moment, but considers its path in cool hours of clarity. Evil gains at the expense of good and doesn't care who gets hurt. It's not the addict seeking drugs, but the millionaire financing the drug invasion. Evil is generally removed from the scene of its crimes. The result of evil is found in every ghetto, while evil lives uptown. Evil wears a good suit and goes to church. Evil knows when to smile for the camera. We must pray, as Paul says, to be protected from every evil. But we must also unmask evil so the weak will not be fooled by it.

> **What forms of evil are evident in our culture?**
> **How do they affect your community locally?**

GOSPEL » LUKE 20:27-38

Some Sadducees came up. This is the Jewish party that denies any possibility of resurrection. They asked, "Teacher, Moses wrote us that if a man dies and leaves a wife but no child, his brother is obligated to take the widow to wife and get her with child. Well, there once were seven brothers. The first took a wife. He died childless. The second married her and died, then the third, and eventually all seven had their turn, but no child. After all that, the wife died. That wife, now—in the resurrection whose wife is she? All seven married her."

Jesus said, "Marriage is a major preoccupation here, but not there. Those who are included in the resurrection of the dead will no longer be concerned with marriage nor, of course, with death. They will have better things to think about, if you can believe it. All ecstasies and intimacies then will be with God. Even Moses exclaimed about resurrection at the burning bush, saying, 'God: God of Abraham, God of Isaac, God of Jacob!' God isn't the God of dead men, but of the living. To him all are alive."

God doesn't rule over the dead but is Lord of the living. So the question remains: Are we dead or alive? Moses once posed two alternatives at the edge of the promised land: "I place before you Life and Death, Blessing and Curse. Choose life so that you and your children will live" (Deuteronomy 30:19). Life means embracing the freedom of the children of God. Death is mere existence governed by the shadowy values of a passing world. Most of us aren't as free as we could be. We're chained to the expectations of a society we claim has no hold over us. We're not yet children of the age to come.

But we can move in that direction. We can stop defining ourselves in terms of material success or failure, physical attraction, popularity and possessions. We can start living by beatitude values, sharing more in common with saints and angels than the faces smiling out of every billboard and commercial. Like the Sadducees in the gospel, we may try to impose upon God the petty systems we hold dear. But God lives by different rules and they outlast ours.

> **How alive are you?**
> **What aspects of your current life**
> **are "dead" to the age to come?**

WE RESPOND

Time to be roused to new life! Examine one aspect of your behavior that's been dead to God's rule. Shake off the chains of this age and follow your Lord.

THIRTY-THIRD SUNDAY IN ORDINARY TIME

.... The Day of Fire

FIRST READING » MALACHI 3:19-20

"Count on it: The day is coming, raging like a forest fire. All the arrogant people who do evil things will be burned up like stove wood, burned to a crisp, nothing left but scorched earth and ash—a black day. But for you, sunrise! The sun of righteousness will dawn on those who honor my name, healing radiating from its wings." GOD-of-the-Angel-Armies says so.

The Book of Malachi contains this prophecy, which was considered so frightening the scribes who copied it refused to let it end at its natural conclusion with verse 24. Instead, they repeat verse 23, to offer the reader a bit of hope. Even so, the terror of the message is hard to escape. "The day" that's coming, known as the *Dies Irae* or day of God's wrath, has permeated our sense of what God's presence is like. When God comes, popular religion would have us believe, it's gonna be hell.

Even when we muse on the Second Coming humorously, the tone is negative: "Jesus is coming...everybody look busy!" The truth is, we know we aren't who we should be, and we aren't doing what we should be doing. So we project the negative assessment onto God, in proportion to our guilt at our own behavior. What's most terrible, perhaps, is not God's presence in the end but our own exposure. God is love. So we profess. What will it be like to stand in the presence of absolute love with our small, jealous hearts?

> If Jesus were coming today, what would you do to "look busy"?
> What keeps you from doing that anyway?

SECOND READING » 2 THESSALONIANS 3:7-12

We showed you how to pull your weight when we were with you, so get on with it. We didn't sit around on our hands expecting others to take care of us. In fact, we worked our fingers to the bone, up half the night moonlighting so you wouldn't be burdened with taking care of us. And it wasn't because we didn't have a right to your support; we did. We simply wanted to provide an example of diligence, hoping it would prove contagious.

Don't you remember the rule we had when we lived with you? "If you don't work, you don't eat." And now we're getting reports that a bunch of lazy good-for-nothings are taking advantage of you. This must not be tolerated. We command them to get to work immediately—no excuses, no arguments—and earn their own keep.

Paul must have felt like an eternal parent, scolding his communities in person and by mail. No matter how carefully he instructed them, the moment his back was turned, human nature reasserted itself. No one said being an apostle would be easy.

If the problem wasn't heresy, it was sexual misconduct. If it wasn't sex, it was greed. If it wasn't greed, it was partying before idols. If not idols, it was lack of charity. Here, it happens to be laziness. Maybe Paul experienced some of his time in prison as a respite from his missions!

Church hasn't changed much in 2,000 years. The same old human nature still opposes the gospel being preached. Sin is a very uncreative condition. There haven't been advances in sin beyond the big deadly ones identified in the earliest centuries by Evagrius Ponticus in the fourth century. What does advance is the decision each of us makes to break the cycle and adopt fidelity. That's not only creative, it's compelling.

How does sin keep you trapped in uncreativity?

GOSPEL » LUKE 21:5-19

One day people were standing around talking about the Temple, remarking how beautiful it was, the splendor of its stonework and memorial gifts. Jesus said, "All this you're admiring so much—the time is coming when every stone in that building will end up in a heap of rubble."

They asked him, "Teacher, when is this going to happen? What clue will we get that it's about to take place?"

He said, "Watch out for the doomsday deceivers. Many leaders are going to show up with forged identities claiming, 'I'm the One,' or, 'The end is near.' Don't fall for any of that. When you hear of wars and uprisings, keep your head and don't panic. This is routine history and no sign of the end."

He went on, "Nation will fight nation and ruler fight ruler, over and over. Huge earthquakes will occur in various places. There will be famines. You'll think at times that the very sky is falling.

"But before any of this happens, they'll arrest you, hunt you down, and drag you to court and jail. It will go from bad to worse, dog-eat-dog, everyone at your throat because you carry my name. You'll end up on the witness stand, called to testify. Make up your mind right now not to worry about it. I'll give you the words and wisdom that will reduce all your accusers to stammers and stutters.

"You'll even be turned in by parents, brothers, relatives, and friends. Some of you will be killed. There's no telling who will hate you because of me. Even so, every detail of your body and soul—even the hairs of your head!—is in my care; nothing of you will be lost. Staying with it—that's what is required. Stay with it to the end. You won't be sorry; you'll be saved."

The end of another church year is near. We can tell because the readings are winding down to the end of the world. It's a cheerful note to end on, if you're a true believer. What could be better than the fulfillment of all of God's promises?

On the other hand, the end-times means the destruction of creation as we know it and a certain amount of real persecution and suffering. There's betrayal and hatred and the chance to plead your case in a court of lies—none of which we look forward to. On the third hand (if we're permitted a third hand), all of those conditions exist right now. We can pretend they're not there and turn a blind eye. But end-time suffering is happening in real time.

Goodness and justice are always on trial. Creation is ever endangered and suffering is no stranger. The old world is on the verge of slipping away. The new creation aches to be born. The end of the world is more familiar than we imagine, and the reign of God closer than we dream.

What part of you pledges allegiance to the old world?
Which part aches to be reborn?

WE RESPOND

Give your testimony in favor of the new creation of God's love. Put your time, money, presence, and signature behind a campaign of justice. Let the new creation be born in you.

The sun of righteousness
will dawn on those who honor my name,
healing radiating from its wings.

THE FEAST OF CHRIST THE KING

FIRST READING » 2 SAMUEL 5:1-3

All the tribes of Israel approached David in Hebron and said, "Look at us—your own flesh and blood! In time past when Saul was our king, you're the one who really ran the country. Even then GOD said to you, 'You will shepherd my people Israel and you'll be the prince.'"

All the leaders of Israel met with King David at Hebron, and the king made a treaty with them in the presence of GOD. And so they anointed David king over Israel.

The anointing of David as king over Israel has such a lovely unanimity about it. ALL the tribes come and assert his kingship. David has a longer memory, however. He's been anointed king before (1 Samuel 16). Will this anointing be more effective than the last one?

The problem with kingship, as every ruler learns, is that it endures as long as the people support it, and people are notoriously fickle. In our present restless culture, even elected officials get recalled. Celebrities get fifteen minutes of our attention before we turn to someone or something else to enthrall us. The world is too big, life too crowded, for any one person to command much authority. The rulers of this world are doomed to irrelevance soon enough.

Jesus declared a kingdom not of this world, and his reign survives the test of time. Without a fortress, army, or economy, he has followers in every age. Anointed by God, Jesus didn't wait for the popular vote to assume authority. And from the cross, Jesus exercised more authority than anyone who ever occupied a throne.

> **Name three people who currently enjoy a certain authority or attention in our world. What gives them power? How does it compare to the power of Christ?**

SECOND READING » COLOSSIANS 1:12-20

Give thanks to the Father who makes us strong enough to take part in everything bright and beautiful that he has for us.

God rescued us from dead-end alleys and dark dungeons. He's set us up in the kingdom of the Son he loves so much, the Son who got us out of the pit we were in, got rid of the sins we were doomed to keep repeating.

We look at this Son and see the God who cannot be seen. We look at this Son and see God's original purpose in everything created. For everything, absolutely everything, above and below, visible and invisible, rank after rank after rank of angels—everything got started in him and finds its purpose in him. He was there before any of it came into existence and holds it all together right up to this moment. And when it comes to the church, he organizes and holds it together, like a head does a body.

He was supreme in the beginning and—leading the resurrection parade— he is supreme in the end. From beginning to end he's there, towering far above everything, everyone. So spacious is he, so roomy, that everything of God finds its proper place in him without crowding. Not only that, but all the broken and dislocated pieces of the universe—people and things, animals and atoms—get properly fixed and fit together in vibrant harmonies, all because of his death, his blood that poured down from the Cross.

Who or what exerts power over your life? Parents? Teachers? Employers? Time? Money? Fear? The past?

Who or what do you exercise power over? Children? A spouse? Employees? Parishioners? Your health? Your lifestyle? Your future?

The question of power is an important and often subterranean concern in our lives. Most of what controls us is not the fluctuation of outward circumstances but the hidden forces within us. Your parents may be deceased or your marriage long over. But that doesn't mean that the power to make you laugh or cry doesn't still reside in those camps.

As Christians, we proclaim the primacy of Jesus. Jesus is Lord. Jesus is first. Jesus is my savior, he is Christ the King. But Lordship or Kingship is only a title if Jesus has no real power over the way we live our lives. Does Jesus even figure in the top-ten list of your concerns when you struggle to make life decisions? The feast of Christ the King can only have meaning if Jesus is the deciding factor in your choices.

Is Christ your king? Make your case.

GOSPEL » LUKE 23:35-43

The people stood there staring at Jesus, and the ringleaders made faces, taunting, "He saved others. Let's see him save himself! The Messiah of God—ha! The Chosen—ha!"

The soldiers also came up and poked fun at him, making a game of it. They toasted him with sour wine: "So you're King of the Jews! Save yourself!"

Printed over him was a sign: THIS IS THE KING OF THE JEWS.

One of the criminals hanging alongside cursed him: "Some Messiah you are! Save yourself! Save us!"

But the other one made him shut up: "Have you no fear of God? You're getting the same as him. We deserve this, but not him—he did nothing to deserve this."

Then he said, "Jesus, remember me when you enter your kingdom."

He said, "Don't worry, I will. Today you will join me in paradise."

Some king! Poor, dishonored, naked, mocked, Jesus dies while villains howl with glee. What kind of king is this, defenseless and alone? The criminal next to him lays down the challenge: If you ARE a king, save yourself! Save us! And Jesus, authorized to save the whole world, reaches out to rescue one last soul, the humble fellow who admits his sin.

That's the kind of king Jesus is: one who champions the sinner who turns to him. Jesus never shows much interest in building a kingdom of righteousness, or shepherding strong and pious souls into his reign. Jesus spends his final hour on the lookout for small sad people who make mistakes and know who they are—and who he is.

This is how Christ chooses to spend his time to the end of time, as we understand it: building a kingdom of contrite hearts. If we don't allow ourselves to be built into that kingdom, we'll certainly be incorporated into another.

What goes into the assemblage of a contrite heart?

WE RESPOND

Honor Christ the King by honoring the least of his people, the poor and the powerless. Lift up the lowly with your voice, your friendship, your concern.

For everything, absolutely everything,
above and below, visible and invisible,
rank after rank after rank of angels—
everything got started in him
and finds its purpose in him.

OTHER FEASTS, SOLEMNITIES AND HOLY DAYS

PRESENTATION OF THE LORD (FEBRUARY 2)

.... The Child of Promise

FIRST READING » MALACHI 3:1-4

"Look! I'm sending my messenger on ahead to clear the way for me. Suddenly, out of the blue, the Leader you've been looking for will enter his Temple—yes, the Messenger of the Covenant, the one you've been waiting for. Look! He's on his way!" A Message from the mouth of GOD-of-the-Angel-Armies.

But who will be able to stand up to that coming? Who can survive his appearance?

He'll be like white-hot fire from the smelter's furnace. He'll be like the strongest lye soap at the laundry. He'll take his place as a refiner of silver, as a cleanser of dirty clothes. He'll scrub the Levite priests clean, refine them like gold and silver, until they're fit for GOD, fit to present offerings of righteousness. Then, and only then, will Judah and Jerusalem be fit and pleasing to GOD, as they used to be in the years long ago.

About a decade ago, I sent my sister some money. She was experiencing a tough time financially and I wasn't, so it was a simple choice to make. I sent a check as a surprise gift with no strings attached. After the usual rounds of thank-you and you're-welcome, we both promptly forgot about it.

I didn't think about it again until this past winter, when I was having an unusually tough time making ends meet. And suddenly, out of the blue comes this check from my sister, returning the money I'd sent her ten years ago with a considerably generous helping of what she called "interest." The amount she sent, God help me, was precisely the amount I needed to cover a stack of bills sitting on my desk. She didn't know this. I hadn't told her. But there it was.

Divine rescue, as it's described in Scripture, is routinely the out-of-the-blue variety. You can't plan ahead for it, so it's best to always be prepared for it. Sometimes it's soft as a dove and sometimes as strong as lye. But it always gets the job done.

> **What do you do annually, weekly, daily, to prepare for the out-of-the-blue appearance of God's messengers?**

SECOND READING » HEBREWS 2:14-18

Since the children are made of flesh and blood, it's logical that the Savior took on flesh and blood in order to rescue them by his death. By embracing death, taking it into himself, he destroyed the Devil's hold on death and freed all who cower through life, scared to death of death.

It's obvious, of course, that he didn't go to all this trouble for angels. It was for people like us, children of Abraham. That's why he had to enter into every detail of human life. Then, when he came before God as high priest to get rid of the people's sins, he would have already experienced it all himself—all the pain, all the testing—and would be able to help where help was needed.

Some of us grew up in a theological environment that viewed the Trinity as a sort of God-Blob. We didn't distinguish very much between Father, Son, and Holy Spirit, including the whole God-Blob in a swift Sign of the Cross that covered all the divine bases. While it's true that Trinity is a mystery that isn't meant to be solved at all, much less defined in a paragraph, there are ways to get it wrong in our understanding. One wrong way to approach the reality of God is that Jesus and God are precisely the same, period. This "high Christology," as it's called, leaves no room for the humanity of Jesus and, in fact, negates the Incarnation.

The Letter to the Hebrews carefully takes the opposite tactic in detailing the very real humanity of Jesus, flesh and blood, suffering and temptation. The writer of Hebrews suggests that the solution to our mortal peril had to be truly mortal too. That God took such a radical step to save us must never be reabsorbed into a Divinity Blob as if it were only a mirage.

> **How does the real humanity of Jesus make the encounter
> you have with the Eucharist more vital and accessible?**

GOSPEL » LUKE 2:22-40

Then when the days stipulated by Moses for purification were complete, they took him up to Jerusalem to offer him to God as commanded in God's Law: "Every male who opens the womb shall be a holy offering to God," and also to sacrifice the "pair of doves or two young pigeons" prescribed in God's Law.

In Jerusalem at the time, there was a man, Simeon by name, a good man, a man who lived in the prayerful expectancy of help for Israel. And the Holy Spirit was on him. The Holy Spirit had shown him that he would see the Messiah of God before he died. Led by the Spirit, he entered the Temple. As the parents of the child Jesus brought him in to carry out the rituals of the Law, Simeon took him into his arms and blessed God:

> *God, you can now release your servant;*
> *release me in peace as you promised.*
> *With my own eyes I've seen your salvation;*
> *it's now out in the open for everyone to see:*
> *A God-revealing light to the non-Jewish nations,*
> *and of glory for your people Israel.*

Jesus' father and mother were speechless with surprise at these words. Simeon went on to bless them, and said to Mary his mother,

> *This child marks both the failure and*
> *the recovery of many in Israel,*
> *A figure misunderstood and contradicted—*
> *the pain of a sword-thrust through you—*
> *But the rejection will force honesty,*
> *as God reveals who they really are.*

Anna the prophetess was also there, a daughter of Phanuel from the tribe of Asher. She was by now a very old woman. She had been married seven years and a widow for eighty-four. She never left the Temple area, worshiping night and day with her fastings and prayers. At the very time Simeon was praying, she showed up, broke into an anthem of praise to God, and talked about the child to all who were waiting expectantly for the freeing of Jerusalem.

When they finished everything required by God in the Law, they returned to Galilee and their own town, Nazareth. There the child grew strong in body and wise in spirit. And the grace of God was on him.

Two prophets were hanging around the Temple on the day that the parents of Jesus brought him for the ritual presentation of a new son. One prophet was a good man, Spirit-led, who'd been waiting for the child of promise all of his life. The other was an old woman, widow and mystic, who'd spent a lifetime at prayer expecting her nation's liberator. On the day Mary and Joseph carried their son into the Temple, both of these holy people knew that heaven had answered their fondest hopes for Israel and beyond.

We too have hopes for our country. We hope to solve the tragedy of our racial divide, and to make good on our promises to the native peoples of this land. We hope to fix our immigration policy, bridge the education gap between communities, foster better health for our citizens, safeguard our natural environment, live in peace with the global community. What is needed to make those goals our reality?

> **What are your fondest hopes for our country in this generation?**
> **How do you support those directions with your efforts?**

WE RESPOND

Make or renew a commitment to pray for your country and its leaders. Commit your resources to local and national concerns. Vote knowledgeably and responsibly.

BIRTH OF JOHN THE BAPTIST (JUNE 24)

.... The Polished Arrow

FIRST READING » ISAIAH 49:1-6

Listen, far-flung islands,
  pay attention, faraway people:
GOD put me to work from the day I was born.
  The moment I entered the world he named me.
He gave me speech that would cut and penetrate.
  He kept his hand on me to protect me.
He made me his straight arrow
  and hid me in his quiver.
 He said to me, "You're my dear servant,
  Israel, through whom I'll shine."

But I said, "I've worked for nothing.
  I've nothing to show for a life of hard work.
Nevertheless, I'll let GOD have the last word.
  I'll let him pronounce his verdict."

"And now," GOD says,
  this God who took me in hand
  from the moment of birth to be his servant,
To bring Jacob back home to him,
  to set a reunion for Israel—
What an honor for me in GOD's eyes!
  That God should be my strength!
He says, "But that's not a big enough job for my servant—
  just to recover the tribes of Jacob,
  merely to round up the strays of Israel.
I'm setting you up as a light for the nations
  so that my salvation becomes global."

You're my dear servant, God says. You are Israel. "Who, me?" We can imagine the person addressed being a little uneasy at this calling, flattering though it may be. "I am to represent your chosen people? I am to be a light for the nations?" Whatever else it may mean to receive this commission, you can bet there are no paid vacations.

Yet the servant is ready to become the sword-like speaker on God's behalf, the sleek arrow at God's beck and call. Though the hours will be long and the work seemingly "for nothing," the servant trusts that being on God's payroll is the best job security in this world and then some.

How about you and me? Are we willing to labor long and hard, not making much of a dent in the world's poverty, its violence, lies, and injustice? Are we willing to accept an assignment on God's payroll, though the apparent benefits (in this world) are not exactly competitive? Will we allow ourselves to be sharpened for God's service, carefully polished for the day and hour of God's desire to make use of us?

Look at the images in this passage. Are you the penetrating speaker, the straight arrow, the babe summoned from the womb, or a light before all in your present circumstance?

SECOND READING » ACTS OF THE APOSTLES 13:22-26

"Up to the time of Samuel the prophet, God provided judges to lead them. But then they asked for a king, and God gave them Saul, son of Kish, out of the tribe of Benjamin. After Saul had ruled forty years, God removed him from office and put King David in his place, with this commendation: 'I've searched the land and found this David, son of Jesse. He's a man whose heart beats to my heart, a man who will do what I tell him.'

"From out of David's descendants God produced a Savior for Israel, Jesus, exactly as he promised—but only after John had thoroughly alerted the people to his arrival by preparing them for a total life-change. As John was finishing up his work, he said, 'Did you think I was the One? No, I'm not the One. But the One you've been waiting for all these years is just around the corner, about to appear. And I'm about to disappear.'

"Dear brothers and sisters, children of Abraham, and friends of God, this message of salvation has been precisely targeted to you."

I wonder if there were moments, in those dark desert nights when John the Baptist curled up alone, if he was tempted to use his celebrity for his own ends. Such moments come to most leaders, preachers, teachers, and public servants who come to celebrity. They have to decide whether to lay down their fame for the sake of those whom they serve, or take it up and use its tremendous power for personal gain.

The papers report to us every day about those who take the latter course and falter along its dangerous slopes. Sex scandals, embezzlements, power plays, and people going off the deep end altogether are the usual results of the human ego left unchecked. It's an intoxicating mix: a swelling ego and the power to feed it insatiably. Whatever John's midnight temptations might have been, he wrestled them down by morning. And he continued to serve as the faithful signpost of the one who is "just around the corner," who would be the real story. John remained merely the storyteller.

Are you the storyteller of God's divine story, or are you the only story your listeners hear?

GOSPEL » LUKE 1:57-66, 80

When Elizabeth was full-term in her pregnancy, she bore a son. Her neighbors and relatives, seeing that God had overwhelmed her with mercy, celebrated with her.

On the eighth day, they came to circumcise the child and were calling him Zachariah after his father. But his mother intervened: "No. He is to be called John."

"But," they said, "no one in your family is named that." They used sign language to ask Zachariah what he wanted him named.

Asking for a tablet, Zachariah wrote, "His name is to be John." That took everyone by surprise. Surprise followed surprise—Zachariah's mouth was now open, his tongue loose, and he was talking, praising God!

A deep, reverential fear settled over the neighborhood, and in all that Judean hill country people talked about nothing else. Everyone who heard about it took it to heart, wondering, "What will become of this child? Clearly, God has his hand in this."

The child grew up, healthy and spirited. He lived out in the desert until the day he made his prophetic debut in Israel.

Nobody ever expected more from a helpless baby than was expected of John, son of Zachariah and Elizabeth. Yet despite the fact that his father was a priest and had good connections, we hear nothing about John enjoying a fine education among the scribes in Jerusalem. Instead, we hear the peculiar news that he lived in the desert until his public ministry began.

What happened here? Perhaps Zachariah and Elizabeth, quite old at the time of John's birth, simply died during his childhood. John may have been free to roam wild. Or perhaps Zachariah had connections with the religious desert sect at Qumran, the ancient keepers of what would one day be known as the Dead Sea Scrolls. John may have been shipped off to Qumran as a sort of holy boarding school among the Essene monks there.

Whoever had a hand in his education, John emerged from the desert at the appointed hour, ready to be the voice crying in the wilderness that the world urgently needed. He came out breathing fire and preaching thunder. No man born of a woman would be greater than John. And yet he had the humility to realize he was the least member of the kingdom he proclaimed.

> **John the Baptist was not timid about denouncing corruption in his day wherever he saw it. Which of our contemporary institutions might he rail against today?**

WE RESPOND

Take some of the power currently available to you—a seat on a committee, a surplus of money, a role of responsibility you exercise over someone—and put it at the service of God's reign, as John did. Be the signpost of the One who is to come.

SAINTS PETER AND PAUL, APOSTLES (JUNE 29)

.... Twins, Not Identical

FIRST READING » ACTS OF THE APOSTLES 12:1-11

King Herod got it into his head to go after some of the church members. He murdered James, John's brother. When he saw how much it raised his popularity ratings with the Jews, he arrested Peter—all this during Passover Week, mind you—and had him thrown in jail, putting four squads of four soldiers each to guard him. He was planning a public lynching after Passover.

All the time that Peter was under heavy guard in the jailhouse, the church prayed for him most strenuously.

Then the time came for Herod to bring him out for the kill. That night, even though shackled to two soldiers, one on either side, Peter slept like a baby. And there were guards at the door keeping their eyes on the place. Herod was taking no chances!

Suddenly there was an angel at his side and light flooding the room. The angel shook Peter and got him up: "Hurry!" The handcuffs fell off his wrists. The angel said, "Get dressed. Put on your shoes." Peter did it. Then, "Grab your coat and let's get out of here." Peter followed him, but didn't believe it was really an angel—he thought he was dreaming.

Past the first guard and then the second, they came to the iron gate that led into the city. It swung open before them on its own, and they were out on the street, free as the breeze. At the first intersection the angel left him, going his own way.

Have you ever followed an angel through a dark alley to freedom after being miraculously released from prison? If you think a little harder, you probably have. Peter himself is described as being unsure if this experience is real or a dream sequence. Celestial freedom is offered to us in every knotty bind we face, though we may not always recognize or accept it. The God of the Bible is routinely presented as the God of liberty, who breaks the chains of slaves and leads captives to freedom. Such freedom may be dependent on accepting a few conditions compatible with liberation. First we may have to tell the truth about ourselves; confess our sin; accept the blame; take the risk; surrender the security; agree to the commission; depart on the journey. Finally, of course, we do have to follow the angel's lead! That can take us down some very surprising paths.

> **When have we been held captive**
> **to some situation, habit, or pattern?**
> **How did we manage to escape**

SECOND READING » 2 TIMOTHY 4:6-8, 17-18

You take over. I'm about to die, my life an offering on God's altar. This is the only race worth running. I've run hard right to the finish, believed all the way. All that's left now is the shouting—God's applause! Depend on it, he's an honest judge. He'll do right not only by me, but by everyone eager for his coming.

The Master stood by me and helped me spread the Message loud and clear to those who had never heard it. I was snatched from the jaws of the lion! God's looking after me, keeping me safe in the kingdom of heaven. All praise to him, praise forever! Oh, yes!

Some say Paul wrote these words from a prison cell. Others suspect a Christian leader from the next generation found himself in Paul's shoes and adopted his name to communicate the similarity of his circumstance. Sooner or later we might all find ourselves twinned with Peter or Paul in the need for divine rescue from great distress. Daniel was hardly the last hero of God to face the open mouth of a hungry beast. All the saints find themselves cornered by the lion in their generations—as so do we in ours. Will we too compete well, finish the race, and keep the faith?

Some of us may not view ourselves as Christian-hero material. We've not made a habit of following angels or expecting help from higher powers. Yet, as heirs to the church of Peter and Paul, we inherit their faith—and the source of their hope.

Do you expect help from celestial sources? Why or why not?

GOSPEL » MATTHEW 16:13-19

When Jesus arrived in the villages of Caesarea Philippi, he asked his disciples, "What are people saying about who the Son of Man is?"

They replied, "Some think he is John the Baptizer, some say Elijah, some Jeremiah or one of the other prophets."

He pressed them, "And how about you? Who do you say I am?"

Simon Peter said, "You're the Christ, the Messiah, the Son of the living God."

Jesus came back, "God bless you, Simon, son of Jonah! You didn't get that answer out of books or from teachers. My Father in heaven, God himself, let you in on this secret of who I really am. And now I'm going to tell you who you are, really are. You are Peter, a rock. This is the rock on which I will put together my church, a church so expansive with energy that not even the gates of hell will be able to keep it out.

"And that's not all. You will have complete and free access to God's kingdom, keys to open any and every door: no more barriers between heaven and earth, earth and heaven. A yes on earth is yes in heaven. A no on earth is no in heaven."

Peter got a lot of things wrong during his apprenticeship as a disciple. But he got one thing incredibly right, and for that the Chair of Peter remains the seat of authority in the church for all time. Anyone who's ever been in school knows that one right answer in three years isn't normally enough to earn an "A." Peter's prize comes for knowing the answer to the most vital question, in light of which all other errors are insignificant. Peter, it seems, knows who Jesus is, who he REALLY is.

The rest of the disciples most likely understood Jesus to be something: a great teacher, a wonder worker, an up-and-coming rabbi, maybe even the next leader of Israel. But until the end of the ages, the Chair of Peter will be occupied by someone who testifies that Jesus is the Divine Son of the Living God, before whom all earthly authorities must bow.

Which example inspires you particularly: that of Peter's life or Paul's? How do you seek to emulate their path of discipleship?

WE RESPOND

Imitate Peter: Make a firm confession of faith in Jesus as you presently understand your relationship with him. Imitate Paul: Be prepared to go anywhere, to do anything, to bring good news to those who need it.

"You will have complete and free access to God's kingdom, keys to open any and every door: no more barriers between heaven and earth, earth and heaven."

THE TRANSFIGURATION (AUGUST 6)

....Seeing With Kingdom Eyes

FIRST READING » DANIEL 7:9-10, 13-14

"As I was watching all this,

"Thrones were set in place
and The Old One sat down.
His robes were white as snow,
his hair was white like wool.
His throne was flaming with fire,
its wheels blazing.
A river of fire
poured out of the throne.
Thousands upon thousands served him,
tens of thousands attended him.
The courtroom was called to order,
and the books were opened.

"My dream continued.

"I saw a human form, a son of man,
arriving in a whirl of clouds.
He came to The Old One
and was presented to him.
He was given power to rule—all the glory of royalty.
Everyone—race, color, and creed—had to serve him.
His rule would be forever, never ending.
His kingly rule would never be replaced."

Prophets get to see amazing things. Both Daniel and Isaiah report visions of the throne of God. Ezekiel could see the restoration of longed-for Jerusalem all the way from Babylonian captivity. Jeremiah could read the divine will in a blossoming branch, a smashed pot, even a soiled loincloth. If we spent as much as they did seeking God's will and contemplating God's word, what might you and I perceive? What possibilities would we discover hiding in plain view in our trouble-ridden generation?

Maybe we'd find the way out of racism, or seeing the world beyond war. God knows the road that leads to justice and the path to making all children safe, healthy, literate, and loved. Our vision is partial because we're blinded by so many things: self-involvement, long-rehearsed biases, stale thinking. To see prophetically includes thinking creatively and glimpsing the possibilities everyone else is overlooking. Pray for the grace to see through kingdom eyes.

What conditions foster mystical sight?
What sort of environment assists you in glimpsing the sacred view?

SECOND READING » 2 PETER 1:16-19

We weren't, you know, just wishing on a star when we laid the facts out before you regarding the powerful return of our Master, Jesus Christ. We were there for the preview! We saw it with our own eyes: Jesus resplendent with light from God the Father as the voice of Majestic Glory spoke: "This is my Son, marked by my love, focus of all my delight." We were there on the holy mountain with him. We heard the voice out of heaven with our very own ears.

We couldn't be more sure of what we saw and heard—God's glory, God's voice. The prophetic Word was confirmed to us. You'll do well to keep focusing on it. It's the one light you have in a dark time as you wait for daybreak and the rising of the Morning Star in your hearts.

A light in a dark time. It might have been the one friend who was there for you—even if you did nothing to merit such fidelity. It could have been the love of a parent beyond all reason, when you were especially difficult to love. The light may have been a therapist's confidence in your recovery, when you swam in a sea of doubt about your chances. A kindly nurse at the hospital, the unexpected repentance or forgiveness of a spouse, a stranger's affirming cheerfulness, a child's innate sympathy—so many lights are given to us when the way seems incredibly dark and unsurvivable.

The light we follow may seem so far from where we stand, yet we walk toward it, guided as if by a star to a more hopeful future. Sometimes that light reveals itself to be just what it is: simple faith in the God who seeks the lost and saves the damned. If you can't see the light anywhere around you with your eyes open, close your eyes and ask for the inner light to shine its radiance and encouragement right where you are.

How have you experienced light in the dark chapters of your life?

GOSPEL » LUKE 9:28b-36

About eight days after saying this, he climbed the mountain to pray, taking Peter, John, and James along. While he was in prayer, the appearance of his face changed and his clothes became blinding white. At once two men were there talking with him. They turned out to be Moses and Elijah—and what a glorious appearance they made! They talked over his exodus, the one Jesus was about to complete in Jerusalem.

Meanwhile, Peter and those with him were slumped over in sleep. When they came to, rubbing their eyes, they saw Jesus in his glory and the two men standing with him. When Moses and Elijah had left, Peter said to Jesus, "Master, this is a great moment! Let's build three memorials: one for you, one for Moses, and one for Elijah." He blurted this out without thinking.

While he was babbling on like this, a light-radiant cloud enveloped them. As they found themselves buried in the cloud, they became deeply aware of God. Then there was a voice out of the cloud: "This is my Son, the Chosen! Listen to him."

When the sound of the voice died away, they saw Jesus there alone. They were speechless. And they continued speechless, said not one thing to anyone during those days of what they had seen.

Jesus was always there, and always Lord. He was always "consubstantial with the Father," the very essence of divinity for those with eyes to see. But his closest friends didn't see it, which means they didn't really know him. They knew Jesus was a really great teacher, a surprisingly talented healer. They knew he was very, very special when it came to being out of wine at a wedding, or needing emergency lunch for 5,000 people. But somehow they missed the "consubstantial with the Father" part—until the day Jesus shone like the sun and a voice from heaven claimed him.

We often miss the manifestations of Christ-presence in our midst. We eat the bread and take the wine and miss the divinity. We see love on the faces of family members and forget the source of all love. We hear the crying need of the world's poor and suffering and don't see the crucified Lord. We view the beauty of the natural world and are blind to the Creator. How easy it is to make the same mistake as those other friends of Jesus.

Have you seen Jesus today?
Where was he, and what did he look like?

WE RESPOND

Spend one day conscious of your continual proximity to the sacred. Look for Jesus, expect the encounter, and acknowledge him every time he shows up.

ASSUMPTION OF THE BLESSED VIRGIN MARY (AUGUST 15)

.... Sing a Song of Grace

FIRST READING » REVELATION 11:19a; 12:1-6a, 10ab

The doors of God's Temple in Heaven flew open, and the Ark of his Covenant was clearly seen.

A great Sign appeared in Heaven: a Woman dressed all in sunlight, standing on the moon, and crowned with Twelve Stars. She was giving birth to a Child and cried out in the pain of childbirth.

And then another Sign alongside the first: a huge and fiery Dragon! It had seven heads and ten horns, a crown on each of the seven heads. With one flick of its tail it knocked a third of the Stars from the sky and dumped them on earth. The Dragon crouched before the Woman in childbirth, poised to eat up the Child when it came.

The Woman gave birth to a Son who will shepherd all nations with an iron rod. Her Son was seized and placed safely before God on his Throne. The Woman herself escaped to the desert to a place of safety prepared by God.

Then I heard a strong voice out of Heaven saying,

> *Salvation and power are established!*
> *Kingdom of our God, authority of his Messiah!*

Where do you look for signs of God's enduring love for you? Ancient Israel looked to its glorious Temple and legendary Ark of the Covenant. After both were lost the nation came to view itself as "the People of the Book": joined to God in fidelity to the divine will expressed in sacred texts. The Jewish people today remain favored with "a permanent vocation" as God's people, our bishops remind us in their *Guidelines for Catholic-Jewish Relations*. Faithful attendance to the beauty of God's word in teaching, prophecy, and wisdom guarantees the Jewish community that God's promises to them can never be revoked. Pope John Paul II called Judaism the elder brother to Christianity, which means believers of both traditions share a family bond before God. "God's love endures forever" isn't just a pretty phrase. There's plenty of grace to go around for those who place their hope in God.

Today we call a Jewish girl, Mary, an ark of God's grace.
How might you also bear God's grace into the world by your choices today?

SECOND READING » 1 CORINTHIANS 15:20-27

But the truth is that Christ has been raised up, the first in a long legacy of those who are going to leave the cemeteries.

There is a nice symmetry in this: Death initially came by a man, and resurrection from death came by a man. Everybody dies in Adam; everybody comes alive in Christ. But we have to wait our turn: Christ is first, then those with him at his Coming, the grand consummation when, after crushing the opposition, he hands over his kingdom to God the Father. He won't let up until the last enemy is down—and the very last enemy is death! As the psalmist said, "He laid them low, one and all; he walked all over them."

Consider the tabernacle in your local church. Catholics believe the consecrated Body of Christ resides in that hallowed space. In similar fashion, ancient Israelites believed God chose to manifest the Holy Presence upon the Ark of the Covenant. Forget what you saw in "Raiders of the Lost Ark" about some overwhelming source of power hidden *inside* the box. The Ark was not a divine storage crate. It was designed as a throne for God here on earth. When God's glory settled in among the Israelites, the Ark was God's chair. The power that created the universe, the authority over life and death itself—*this* God preferred to take a seat in close proximity to mortals. And if this sounds far-fetched, consider something more: When God's glory overshadowed Mary of Nazareth, God took proximity with us to a whole new level.

> **How close do you want to be to God?**
> **What can you do to welcome that nearness?**

GOSPEL » LUKE 1:39-56

Mary didn't waste a minute. She got up and traveled to a town in Judah in the hill country, straight to Zachariah's house, and greeted Elizabeth. When Elizabeth heard Mary's greeting, the baby in her womb leaped. She was filled with the Holy Spirit, and sang out exuberantly,

> *You're so blessed among women,*
> *   and the babe in your womb, also blessed!*
> *And why am I so blessed that*
> *   the mother of my Lord visits me?*
> *The moment the sound of your*
> *   greeting entered my ears,*
> *The babe in my womb*
> *   skipped like a lamb for sheer joy.*
> *Blessed woman, who believed what God said,*
> *   believed every word would come true!*

And Mary said,

> *I'm bursting with God-news;*
> *   I'm dancing the song of my Savior God.*
> *God took one good look at me, and look what happened—*
> *   I'm the most fortunate woman on earth!*
> *What God has done for me will never be forgotten,*
> *   the God whose very name is holy, set apart from all others.*

His mercy flows in wave after wave
  on those who are in awe before him.
He bared his arm and showed his strength,
  scattered the bluffing braggarts.
He knocked tyrants off their high horses,
  pulled victims out of the mud.
The starving poor sat down to a banquet;
  the callous rich were left out in the cold.
He embraced his chosen child, Israel;
  he remembered and piled on the mercies, piled them high.
It's exactly what he promised,
  beginning with Abraham and right up to now.

Mary stayed with Elizabeth for three months and then went back to her own home.

Do you sing in the shower? Or whistle while you work? Do you belt out a song barreling along on the freeway? Or do you catch yourself humming throughout the day? I stood at the bus stop last week while a young man, very plugged in to his iPod, hip-hopped his way through some devilishly complicated lyrics, prancing around the whole time quite unaware of the rest of us. I think young Mary was similarly plugged in to God's rhythms when Elizabeth acknowledged that her young kinswoman was, indeed, full of grace and blessing, not to mention a child. Mary's response was to burst out singing. Part of what she sang echoes another surprising mother's song of long ago. (See 1 Samuel 2.) Part of the song was all her own. Sometimes you just can't help yourself. When God's song is in you, you have to sing it.

Imagine this is Karaoke Sunday.
Which songs of grace would you gladly get up and sing?

WE RESPOND

Angels belong to choirs in heaven, we're told. Holy women like Miriam and Deborah, Hannah and Mary, sing in Scripture. Consider how sacred songs might feature in your prayer life.

EXALTATION OF THE HOLY CROSS (SEPTEMBER 14)

.... There's Power in the Symbol

FIRST READING » NUMBERS 21:4b-9

The people became irritable and cross as they traveled. They spoke out against God and Moses: "Why did you drag us out of Egypt to die in this godforsaken country? No decent food; no water—we can't stomach this stuff any longer."

So GOD sent poisonous snakes among the people; they bit them and many in Israel died. The people came to Moses and said, "We sinned when we spoke out against GOD and you. Pray to GOD; ask him to take these snakes from us."

Moses prayed for the people.

GOD said to Moses, "Make a snake and put it on a flagpole: Whoever is bitten and looks at it will live."

So Moses made a snake of fiery copper and put it on top of a flagpole. Anyone bitten by a snake who then looked at the copper snake lived.

Here's a biblical trivia question: Whatever happened to the copper flagpole snake Moses used to cure the Israelites? If I had a serpent that could cure people from poisonous episodes, I wouldn't junk it in the wilderness! Evidently the Israelites felt the same way. The pole snake shows up again after the settlement of Israel in the land of Canaan. In 2 Kings 18, we learn the snake has since garnered a name, *Nehushtan*, and is kept in the Temple in Jerusalem. People burn incense to it, and it's become an object of worship. Because of this tendency, idol-hating King Hezekiah has it destroyed.

So Nehushtan is gone. But the snake as symbol of healing remains. The Greeks imagined Hermes, the divine messenger who could bring healing from the gods, with two snakes on a winged pole known as the caduceus. Asclepius the healer was also known by the sign of a poled serpent. Our modern medical logo owes something to all three of these stories. Symbols are notoriously hard to kill. Think of the peace sign, or the heart shape, which continue to engage our imaginations.

Which modern symbols hold particular meaning for you?

SECOND READING » PHILIPPIANS 2:6-11

He had equal status with God but didn't think so much of himself that he had to cling to the advantages of that status no matter what. Not at all. When the time came, he set aside the privileges of deity and took on the status of a slave, became human! *Having become human, he stayed human. It was an incredibly humbling process. He didn't claim special privileges. Instead, he lived a selfless, obedient life and then died a selfless, obedient death—and the worst kind of death at that: a crucifixion.*

Because of that obedience, God lifted him high and honored him far beyond anyone or anything, ever, so that all created beings in heaven and on earth—

even those long ago dead and buried—will bow in worship before this Jesus Christ, and call out in praise that he is the Master of all, to the glorious honor of God the Father.

For Christians, no symbol speaks as powerfully and directly as the cross. Two simple intersecting lines evoke two thousand years of theology! The cross sign predates Christianity and has various meanings in other religions like that of the Native Americans, who regard it as the unification of the four directions and four great elements. We can assign more meanings to this symbol: the unification of heaven and earth in the vertical line, and the unity of the whole human race in the horizontal bar. So many powerful ideas find their intersection in the cross: life and death, despair and hope, endings and beginnings, humiliation and glory, flesh and spirit, humanity and divinity.

When we make the sign of the cross over ourselves, we embrace all of these meanings. We pledge ourselves to the redemption of all that's lost, to the healing of suffering, to the exchange of values from what this world covets and what the next exalts. The cross looks like failure. It's God's great victory. This is why we keep the cross before us always.

Which aspects of the cross hold special meaning for you?

GOSPEL » JOHN 3:13-17

"No one has ever gone up into the presence of God except the One who came down from that Presence, the Son of Man. In the same way that Moses lifted the serpent in the desert so people could have something to see and then believe, it is necessary for the Son of Man to be lifted up—and everyone who looks up to him, trusting and expectant, will gain a real life, eternal life.

"This is how much God loved the world: He gave his Son, his one and only Son. And this is why: so that no one need be destroyed; by believing in him, anyone can have a whole and lasting life. God didn't go to all the trouble of sending his Son merely to point an accusing finger, telling the world how bad it was. He came to help, to put the world right again."

Some folks view religion as a giant pointing stick which calls attention to the world's great sinfulness. Others see it as a tool for pulling themselves upward to a higher state of moral perfection or personal enlightenment. The evangelist John says the central purpose of the gospel is to tell everyone that God doesn't hate us. God loves us. God doesn't seek to destroy us for our faults but to rescue us by divine mercy. Not every Christian we know has signed on to this message. But there it is.

It's easy to be a believer when you embrace God's love first and fundamentally. It's harder to be one if you view Christianity in a piecemeal way: dead man on a cross, love your enemies, feed the world's hungry, give away your possessions. If we don't adopt the core principle of absolute divine love, the rest of our religion sounds like a lot of hard work and dark times in exchange for dubious pie in eternity. I'm a fan of pie. But it would be a stretch to rearrange my whole life now in anticipation of a slice in the afterlife.

God desires the world's rescue.
How does this affect your plans for the day?

WE RESPOND

Look around your home or office for symbols: religious signs, logos, flags. Reflect on how these symbols communicate who you are or hope to be.

"God didn't go to all the trouble
of sending his Son merely to point
an accusing finger,
telling the world how bad it was.
He came to help, to put the world right again."

ALL SAINTS (NOVEMBER I)

.... You Are God's Child Now

FIRST READING » REVELATION 7:2-4, 9-14

I, John, saw another Angel rising from where the sun rose, carrying the seal of the Living God. He thundered to the Four Angels assigned the task of hurting earth and sea, "Don't hurt the earth! Don't hurt the sea! Don't so much as hurt a tree until I've sealed the servants of our God on their foreheads!"

I heard the count of those who were sealed: 144,000! They were sealed out of every Tribe of Israel.

I looked again. I saw a huge crowd, too huge to count. Everyone was there— all nations and tribes, all races and languages. And they were standing, dressed in white robes and waving palm branches, standing before the Throne and the Lamb and heartily singing:

Salvation to our God on his Throne!
Salvation to the Lamb!

All who were standing around the Throne—Angels, Elders, Animals—fell on their faces before the Throne and worshiped God, singing:

Oh, Yes!
The blessing and glory and wisdom and thanksgiving,
The honor and power and strength,
To our God forever and ever and ever!
Oh, Yes!

Just then one of the Elders addressed me: "Who are these dressed in white robes, and where did they come from?" Taken aback, I said, "O Sir, I have no idea—but you must know."

Then he told me, "These are those who come from the great tribulation, and they've washed their robes, scrubbed them clean in the blood of the Lamb."

Church tradition often dresses us in white garments. Babies are presented for Baptism in their satiny christening gowns. Shiny seven-year-olds dress in pure white for First Communion. Brides prepare for a life of love in oceans of white. The newly baptized at the Easter Vigil stand before us in white robes, and priests and their assistants wear white albs at every celebration of Eucharist. A white pall dignifies the casket of every believer at a funeral. All are reminders of the purity of our first faith, and the final stand we take with the white-robed saints of John's vision.

In between Baptism and death, of course, there's plenty of time to do some sinning. We get that white robe pretty dirty in the normal course of our lives; thanks be to God there's enough Lamb's blood to wash them all clean again. Being God's children never implies that we're perfect, which is good for us. As the psalmist for this feast says, we're the people who long to see God's face—not the folks worthy to do so.

SECOND READING » 1 JOHN 3:1-3

What marvelous love the Father has extended to us! Just look at it—we're called children of God! That's who we really are. But that's also why the world doesn't recognize us or take us seriously, because it has no idea who he is or what he's up to.

But friends, that's exactly who we are: children of God. And that's only the beginning. Who knows how we'll end up! What we know is that when Christ is openly revealed, we'll see him—and in seeing him, become like him. All of us who look forward to his Coming stay ready, with the glistening purity of Jesus' life as a model for our own.

The tenderness and passion in John's letter reminds us that religion isn't just about what we believe in our heads but also about the nature of our hearts. Are we children of God or offspring of the secular mindset? Do we pursue the way of holiness or self-promotion? Is my life fundamentally about me or something much more wonderful?

The saints are the folks who "get it." They arrive at the point of recognition that a life lived primarily for the self is a dead end, a sorry thing. Saints aren't perfect people, but they are awake to divine reality. Seeking the ways of God becomes more important than anything else they could be doing with their lives. They let the dead bury the dead. They walk away from ordinary values and become extraordinary people. The shift in perspective, a small thing at first, becomes all-consuming in the long run. The saints change just their hearts, and everything changes from there. Are we children of God or of the world? How we answer that question could be the start of an amazing transformation.

> **What is at the center of your passion?**
> **How does that assist or obstruct your faith?**

GOSPEL » MATTHEW 5:1-12

When Jesus saw his ministry drawing huge crowds, he climbed a hillside. Those who were apprenticed to him, the committed, climbed with him. Arriving at a quiet place, he sat down and taught his climbing companions. This is what he said:

"You're blessed when you're at the end of your rope. With less of you there is more of God and his rule.

"You're blessed when you feel you've lost what is most dear to you. Only then can you be embraced by the One most dear to you.

"You're blessed when you're content with just who you are—no more, no less. That's the moment you find yourselves proud owners of everything that can't be bought.

"You're blessed when you've worked up a good appetite for God. He's food and drink in the best meal you'll ever eat.

"You're blessed when you care. At the moment of being 'carefull,' you find yourselves cared for.

"You're blessed when you get your inside world—your mind and heart—put right. Then you can see God in the outside world.

"You're blessed when you can show people how to cooperate instead of compete or fight. That's when you discover who you really are, and your place in God's family.

"You're blessed when your commitment to God provokes persecution. The persecution drives you even deeper into God's kingdom.

"Not only that—count yourselves blessed every time people put you down or throw you out or speak lies about you to discredit me. What it means is that the truth is too close for comfort and they are uncomfortable. You can be glad when that happens—give a cheer, even!—for though they don't like it, I do! And all heaven applauds. And know that you are in good company. My prophets and witnesses have always gotten into this kind of trouble."

Those whom God blesses have a lot in common with those whom the world ordinarily curses. Think about it: what would a worldly beatitude look like?

Blest are they who make lots of money, for they shall live well.
Blest are they who learn how to manipulate others, for they shall have their way.
Blest are they who have hardened hearts, for they shall never feel regret.
Blest are they who grasp power, for they shall be in charge.
Blest are the beautiful people—so long as they stay beautiful.

God makes a curious selection in blessing the world's underdogs. It's all part of the Kingdom reversal that even a child (especially a child) can appreciate. In a world that tolerates and promotes so much injustice, we hunger for a realm where the bully is banished and the kid with the broken glasses is the hero. Every fairytale and Disney movie ends up on the same page with the teachings of Jesus: Evil is defeated and goodness wins. The Kingdom isn't a tough sell; it matches our desire for justice missing from the world. If we opt to live guided by God's beatitudes instead of the world's, someday they'll call us saints.

Which divine beatitude blesses your life right now?
How are you blessed by worldly values?
Which set of beatitudes exercises more power over your life at this time?

WE RESPOND

Compose some beatitudes for your family, neighborhood, or community. Who gets blessed? Meditate on it this week.

ALL SOULS (NOVEMBER 2)

FIRST READING » WISDOM 3:1-9

As for the souls of the just, they're in the hands of God; the torment of death never lays a finger on them. In the eyes of the not-so-just, the just seem to have died and gone to hell; but such affliction as they may have suffered was merely their exit fee from this world to the next. Their departure was misinterpreted as their demise; in reality they're at peace. Yes, the just suffer as much as the unjust during the death process; but their passing is full of hope and the promise of immortality.

Such punishments as the just incur are few, but their rewards are great. God puts them to the test, and they always pass with flying colors. Like gold ore in the furnace the Lord refines them; like burnt offering from the sacrificial fire he receives them.

When it's Final Awards Day, you'll be able to pick them out; they're the sparks dancing about in the harvest after death, the final, burn-the-stubble bonfire. They'll govern the nations and lord it over nationalities; their Lord will reign forever.

Those who put their faith in the Lord will understand truth; those who are faithful will enjoy eternal rest. He showers grace and mercy on those who are committed to him. From time to time he even drops by for a personal chat with them.

This year our family buried its matriarch. Another elder, her sister, quickly took her place as the new generational ceiling of our line. As with most families, the funeral brought together many who rarely gather in the same room. Yet despite the years and the distances, we prayed together in the church, held onto each other at the gravesite, then shared a meal that lasted for hours as we told stories of love, loss, gratitude, and hope.

It's natural on such occasions to look around the table at the long and winding branches of your family tree and wonder: Who's next? Around which of us will we gather again, pray and hold hands, eat and tell stories? Whoever that may be, it's good to belong to a family of faith that encourages us even in the valley of the shadow of death. When it's my turn, I know that the warm circle of church will pray for me and hold my loved ones fast.

How has your faith enabled you in times of loss?

SECOND READING » ROMANS 5:5-11

In alert expectancy such as this, we're never left feeling shortchanged. Quite the contrary—we can't round up enough containers to hold everything God generously pours into our lives through the Holy Spirit!

Christ arrives right on time to make this happen. He didn't, and doesn't, wait for us to get ready. He presented himself for this sacrificial death when we were far too weak and rebellious to do anything to get ourselves ready. And even if we hadn't been so weak, we wouldn't have known what to do anyway. We can understand someone dying for a person worth dying for, and we can understand how someone good and noble could inspire us to selfless sacrifice. But God put his love on the line for us by offering his Son in sacrificial death while we were of no use whatever to him.

Now that we are set right with God by means of this sacrificial death, the consummate blood sacrifice, there is no longer a question of being at odds with God in any way. If, when we were at our worst, we were put on friendly terms with God by the sacrificial death of his Son, now that we're at our best, just think of how our lives will expand and deepen by means of his resurrection life! Now that we have actually received this amazing friendship with God, we are no longer content to simply say it in plodding prose. We sing and shout our praises to God through Jesus, the Messiah!

Once every year, the liturgical calendar invites us to talk frankly about death. On All Souls Day, we remember those whom we've lost to this world. Depending on our mileage, that list can be short or lengthy. For some of us, the list of names is so long we have to trust that God remembers the ones we forget now and then. In reciting the litany of names, we testify to our faith that these people are not lost to life in ultimate ways, nor are they lost to God. They stand now with the cloud of witnesses in the company of the saints.

And what if some of our loved ones traveled really rough roads, leaving a lot of unfinished business and unmended fences? In the economy of grace, we understand prayer to be our most valuable currency. In praying for the dead, we help them do what may have been left undone.

How do you remember the dead?
How do you partner with them
in what has been done, and what is yet to do?

GOSPEL » JOHN 6:37-40

"Every person the Father gives me eventually comes running to me. And once that person is with me, I hold on and don't let go. I came down from heaven not to follow my own whim but to accomplish the will of the One who sent me.

"This, in a nutshell, is that will: that everything handed over to me by the Father be completed—not a single detail missed—and at the wrap-up of time I have everything and everyone put together, upright and whole. This is what my Father wants: that anyone who sees the Son and trusts who he is and what he does and then aligns with him will enter real life, eternal life. My part is to put them on their feet alive and whole at the completion of time."

My young nephew grabbed up my suitcase from the guestroom as I was leaving after a family visit. The bag was half as big as he was, but he wanted to be helpful. We started at the top of the stairs together, but when I was nearly to the bottom, I realized he was no longer beside me. Looking back, I saw the little boy with the oversized bag only a few steps from the top, wearing an expression that was deeply pained.

My love for that small boy propelled me back up those stairs. Of course I had to help him: Who wouldn't? I traded my small purse for the bag that threatened to crush him. And we made it down those stairs together. In the same way, you and I assist those whom we love who have gone before us in death with burdens they can't carry alone. In the work of prayer, the strong assist the weak. And we all arrive together. This is how love operates.

> **Consider your family tree, your friends, your community, both living and deceased. Where is your prayer needed?**

WE RESPOND

Make every Friday a special day to remember to pray for the dead. Keep a written list, or create a shrine of names to keep vigil for until we're all together again.

If, when we were at our worst,
we were put on friendly terms with God
by the sacrificial death of his Son,
now that we're at our best,
just think of how our lives
will expand and deepen
by means of his resurrection life!

DEDICATION OF THE LATERAN BASILICA (NOVEMBER 9)

....Sacred Places for Holy People

FIRST READING » EZEKIEL 47:1-2, 8-9, 12

Now he brought me back to the entrance to the Temple. I saw water pouring out from under the Temple porch to the east (the Temple faced east). The water poured from the south side of the Temple, south of the altar. He then took me out through the north gate and led me around the outside to the gate complex on the east. The water was gushing from under the south front of the Temple.

He told me, "This water flows east, descends to the Arabah and then into the sea, the sea of stagnant waters. When it empties into those waters, the sea will become fresh. Wherever the river flows, life will flourish—great schools of fish—because the river is turning the salt sea into fresh water. Where the river flows, life abounds.

"But the river itself, on both banks, will grow fruit trees of all kinds. Their leaves won't wither, the fruit won't fail. Every month they'll bear fresh fruit because the river from the Sanctuary flows to them. Their fruit will be for food and their leaves for healing."

We call churches houses of God and places of prayer. But other grounds are considered consecrated: cemeteries, oratories, shrines, and retreat centers. Still other places may whisper to us *sotto voce* that they are holy ground: an ancestral home, a solitary hilltop, a lakeside cabin, a park bench where you first pronounced your love. What makes a place holy may not be the shape of the building or the beauty of the landscape. It's the encounter with the sacred that touches a plot of ground and makes it blessed. If we're paying attention, holy places multiply rather than diminish. That rushing stream over there, this busy city street, our neighbor's porch, a best friend's kitchen table: All of these and more may be places of sacred encounter with the binding force of divine love.

Have you visited a holy place today?
What makes a place sacred for you?

SECOND READING » 1 CORINTHIANS 3:9c-11, 16-17

You are God's house. Using the gift God gave me as a good architect, I designed blueprints; Apollos is putting up the walls. Let each carpenter who comes on the job take care to build on the foundation! Remember, there is only one foundation, the one already laid: Jesus Christ.

You realize, don't you, that you are the temple of God, and God himself is present in you? No one will get by with vandalizing God's temple, you can be sure of that. God's temple is sacred—and you, remember, are *the temple.*

Today we celebrate the Lateran Basilica, a feast which invites two questions. The first is: What's a basilica? The term means "king's hall," and originated in the time of the Roman Empire to designate offices of official business. Christianity adopted the phrase in honor of Christ, king of kings, sometimes literally taking over secular office buildings. Basilicas are now historically significant churches, models of liturgy, and places of pilgrimage.

The second question is: What's so special about the Lateran Basilica? One of four major basilicas in Rome, the Lateran is the pope's cathedral, or seat of his episcopacy as Bishop of Rome. Donated to the church by Constantine in the fourth century, it's withstood earthquakes, fires, and barbarian invasion. The Lateran has become the symbol of the church itself, tested in every age yet continually renewed and restored.

> **Which church buildings have been places**
> **of pilgrimage on your journey in faith?**

GOSPEL » JOHN 2:13-22

When the Passover Feast, celebrated each spring by the Jews, was about to take place, Jesus traveled up to Jerusalem. He found the Temple teeming with people selling cattle and sheep and doves. The loan sharks were also there in full strength.

Jesus put together a whip out of strips of leather and chased them out of the Temple, stampeding the sheep and cattle, upending the tables of the loan sharks, spilling coins left and right. He told the dove merchants, "Get your things out of here! Stop turning my Father's house into a shopping mall!" That's when his disciples remembered the Scripture, "Zeal for your house consumes me."

But the Jews were upset. They asked, "What credentials can you present to justify this?" Jesus answered, "Tear down this Temple and in three days I'll put it back together."

They were indignant: "It took forty-six years to build this Temple, and you're going to rebuild it in three days?" But Jesus was talking about his body as the Temple. Later, after he was raised from the dead, his disciples remembered he had said this. They then put two and two together and believed both what was written in Scripture and what Jesus had said.

One last question on this feast of sacred places: What's a temple? The term implies a sacred precinct, the most famous of which was the Temple of Jerusalem built to honor the God of Israel. Biblically, it was understood to be more than a house of worship: It was more like God's temporal address. The community around Jesus were shocked to hear him speak of the Temple's destruction: historically, the Temple had been ruined once at the time of the Babylonian invasion in 587 B.C. and took the life out of the nation. It would be destroyed again, and permanently, in the year 70 A.D.

Jesus of course was referring to himself as the residence of divine indwelling. Saint Paul coined the phrase "temple of the Holy Spirit" as a description of all believers. God's Spirit of holiness lives in us as authentically as it does in consecrated places and sacramental signs. The sacred encounter happens wherever we are.

Being God's temple is an honor, a surprise, a responsibility, and a challenge. Which reality is most present to you now?

WE RESPOND

Wherever you reside is holy. Reflect on the elements that designate a site as holy: sacred objects, behaviors, atmospheres, rituals. Adopt elements that might make your home a sacred place.

You realize, don't you,
that you are the temple of God,
and God himself is present in you?

THE IMMACULATE CONCEPTION
OF THE BLESSED VIRGIN MARY (DECEMBER 8)

....Nothing's Impossible

FIRST READING » GENESIS 3:9-15, 20

GOD *called to the Man: "Where are you?"*

He said, "I heard you in the garden and I was afraid because I was naked. And I hid."

GOD *said, "Who told you you were naked? Did you eat from that tree I told you not to eat from?"*

The Man said, "The Woman you gave me as a companion, she gave me fruit from the tree, and, yes, I ate it."

GOD *said to the Woman, "What is this that you've done?"*

"The serpent seduced me," she said, "and I ate."

GOD *told the serpent:*

> *"Because you've done this, you're cursed,*
> > *cursed beyond all cattle and wild animals,*
> *Cursed to slink on your belly*
> > *and eat dirt all your life.*
> *I'm declaring war between you and the Woman,*
> > *between your offspring and hers.*
> *He'll wound your head,*
> > *you'll wound his heel."*

The Man, known as Adam, named his wife Eve because she was the mother of all the living.

When we read the Genesis story of how sin and death came to inhabit our history, we can't overlook the resignation of the original storyteller, not to mention those who repeated this narrative through many generations. This account was fashioned to explain why life is as it is: messy, problematic, and ultimately tragic in its brevity. The first people are a disappointment to God and to each other. An incurable wound opens between humans and their Maker, between the Man and the Woman, and between humanity and the natural order. Things could hardly get worse than that. The unwritten bottom line is evident: "And there's nothing you can do about any of this. What's done is done."

Except it's not. This immutable state of affairs is no match for the mercy of a God who fully intends to save us. The "incurable" wound, isn't. Rescue is already in the works. The soon-to-be-written happy ending is just a Testament away.

> How do you experience the "original wound" in your relationship
> with God, others, the world around you?
> Where do you discover the healing that's available?

SECOND READING » EPHESIANS 1:3-6, 11-12

How blessed is God! And what a blessing he is! He's the Father of our Master, Jesus Christ, and takes us to the high places of blessing in him. Long before he laid down earth's foundations, he had us in mind, had settled on us as the focus of his love, to be made whole and holy by his love. Long, long ago he decided to adopt us into his family through Jesus Christ. (What pleasure he took in planning this!) He wanted us to enter into the celebration of his lavish gift-giving by the hand of his beloved Son.

It's in Christ that we find out who we are and what we are living for. Long before we first heard of Christ and got our hopes up, he had his eye on us, had designs on us for glorious living, part of the overall purpose he is working out in everything and everyone.

In lovely hours we learn to cherish, we know ourselves to be the focus of someone's devotion. You may have had a doting parent or a grandparent who claimed you as a favorite. A teacher, coach, or scout master may have taken a special interest in your potential. A pastor or mentor on the job may have spied something good in you that you didn't suspect in yourself, and dedicated themselves to nurturing that spark. A soul mate or best friend may remind you every time their eyes light up as you walk in the room that you are the source of great happiness to another human being.

God feels that way about us. Doesn't that take your breath away? Right now you are the focus of God's benevolent and devoted attention. You are the light in God's eyes. God is excited about what you might become. God desires your total fulfillment. God can't bear to see you fail, and can't wait to see you succeed. God is rooting for you, every step of the way, all the days of your life. God is on your side!

Think of the person or people who love you best. Is it easy or hard to imagine God feeling that way about you?

GOSPEL » LUKE 1:26-38

In the sixth month of Elizabeth's pregnancy, God sent the angel Gabriel to the Galilean village of Nazareth to a virgin engaged to be married to a man descended from David. His name was Joseph, and the virgin's name, Mary. Upon entering, Gabriel greeted her:

Good morning!
You're beautiful with God's beauty,
Beautiful inside and out!
God be with you.

She was thoroughly shaken, wondering what was behind a greeting like that. But the angel assured her, "Mary, you have nothing to fear. God has a surprise for you: You will become pregnant and give birth to a son and call his name Jesus.

He will be great,
    be called 'Son of the Highest.'
The Lord God will give him
    the throne of his father David;
He will rule Jacob's house forever—
    no end, ever, to his kingdom."

Mary said to the angel, "But how? I've never slept with a man."
The angel answered,

The Holy Spirit will come upon you,
    the power of the Highest hover over you;
Therefore, the child you bring to birth
    will be called Holy, Son of God.

"And did you know that your cousin Elizabeth conceived a son, old as she is?
Everyone called her barren, and here she is six months pregnant! Nothing, you
see, is impossible with God."
And Mary said,

Yes, I see it all now:
    I'm the Lord's maid, ready to serve.
Let it be with me
    just as you say.

Then the angel left her.

**If you want to divide up the world into Two Kinds of People, this would be a handy
way to do it.** One kind of person has the word Impossible on the contact list of his
or her active vocabulary. And the other kind of person believes that Gabriel knows
what he's talking about: that with God, nothing is impossible.

I spent most of my life in the first camp. Everything seemed impossible because
of how I grew up. People who come from small coal towns like mine are often told
to expect little and prepare for less. I was told early on not to be a dreamer, not to
anticipate happiness, not to set my sights too high. The first three vocations I identified in myself, I was told, were flat-out impossible. One of them was being a writer. It
took me thirty years to come back around to reclaiming that sense of myself. Once I
knew that it was possible to do something impossible like become a writer, I began
to reexamine other discarded dreams.

Mary is "blessed among women" and "full of grace" precisely because she believed an angel that told her nothing is impossible. If Impossible is in your speed-
dialed vocabulary, maybe it's time to delete it.

> **When has an impossible thing been proven to be real and accessible?**
> **How does our willingness to hope make room for grace to operate?**

WE RESPOND

Become a practitioner of the possible. Refuse to give in to resignation, doubt, and despair. Be the one that others turn to when they need a little hope.

Long before we first heard of Christ
and got our hopes up, he had his eye on us,
had designs on us for glorious living,
part of the overall purpose
he is working out in everything and everyone.

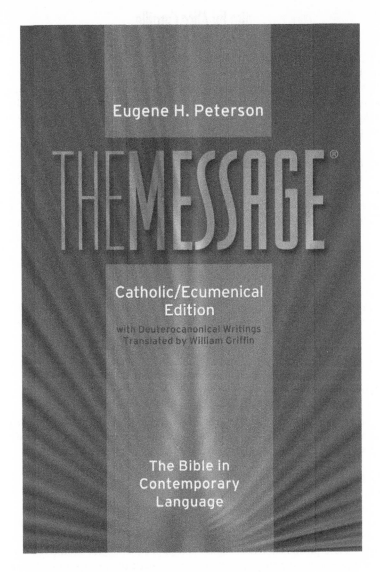

Eugene H. Peterson

THEMESSAGE®

Catholic/Ecumenical Edition

with Deuterocanonical Writings
Translated by William Griffin

The Bible in
Contemporary
Language

Paperback, 978-0-87946-494-3, $29.95
Hardcover, 978-0-87946-495-0, $37.95
Ebook, $9.95

AVAILABLE FROM ACTA PUBLICATIONS
actapublications.com • 800-397-2282

Also by Alice Camille

ISAIAH AND THE KINGDOM OF PEACE
An Illustrated Autobiography for Adults
This unique and stunning "autobiography of the biblical prophet Isaiah" captures the intensity, the mysticism, the prophetic faith and wisdom, and the vision of a "kingdom of peace" for those of us living in the twenty-first century. (96 pages, 11 x 14" four color paperback, $19.95)

ANIMALS OF THE BIBLE FROM A TO Z
In this brand-new children's picture book, beautiful artwork from debut artist Sarah Evelyn Showalter depicts 26 animals from the Bible—one for each letter of the alphabet. In the back of the book are chapter-and-verse citations for each letter, where Alice Camille provides "Pages for Grownups" so that parents, grandparents, and teachers can explain the significance of each animal. (64 pages, hardcover, $16.95)

INVITATION TO CATHOLICISM
Beliefs + Teachings + Practices
Everyone from inquirers and catechumens to lifelong Catholics will welcome the easy-to-understand, logical explanations found in this clear, concise overview of Catholic beliefs and church teachings. Discussion questions and activities at the end of each chapter make this book ideal for RCIA and adult study groups. (234 pages, paperback, $9.95)

INVITATION TO THE OLD AND NEW TESTAMENTS
A Catholic Approach to the Scriptures
Here are separate award-winning volumes written in language that is both inviting and accessible that help Catholics and others understand the intent and relevance of the Bible for life today. (two 104-page paperbacks, $9.95 each)

THE FORGIVENESS BOOK
A Catholic Approach
with Paul Boudreau
Catholics obviously don't have a corner on the forgiveness market. But Catholicism does have a specific approach to forgiveness that is time-tested, comprehensive, and proven effective. This book explores that approach through stories, observation, and the experience garnered from the two authors' lifelong dedication to ministry, scripture study, and religious formation. (112 pages, paperback, $10.95)

THE ROSARY
Mysteries of Joy, Light, Sorrow and Glory
The Rosary contains a series of reflections that explain each mystery and offer practical applications to modern-day life. Camille provides readers with a renewed appreciation of the rosary as a path to love and peace in the new millennium. (112 pages, paperback, $6.95)

Available from booksellers or from ACTA Publications
800-397-2282 • www.actapublications.com